Marking Thought and Talk in New Testament Greek

Marking Thought and Talk in New Testament Greek

New Light from Linguistics on the Particles ἵνα and ὅτι

Margaret G. Sim

Foreword by Larry W. Hurtado

☙PICKWICK *Publications* · Eugene, Oregon

MARKING THOUGHT AND TALK IN NEW TESTAMENT GREEK
New Light from Linguistics on the Particles ἵνα and ὅτι

Copyright © 2010 Margaret G. Sim. All rights reserved. Except for brief quotations in critical publications or reviews, no part of this book may be reproduced in any manner without prior written permission from the publisher. Write: Permissions, Wipf and Stock Publishers, 199 W. 8th Ave., Suite 3, Eugene, OR 97401.

Pickwick Publications
A Division of Wipf and Stock Publishers
199 W. 8th Ave., Suite 3
Eugene, OR 97401

www.wipfandstock.com

ISBN 13: 978-1-61097-089-1

Cataloging-in-Publication data:

Sim, Margaret G..

Marking thought and talk in New Testament Greek : new light from linguistics on the particles ἵνα and ὅτι / Margaret G. Sim.

xvi + 224 p. ; 23 cm. Includes bibliographical references and indexes.

ISBN 13: 978-1-61097-089-1

1. Greek language, Biblical—particles. 2. Bible. N.T.—Language, style. I. Title.

PA847 S37 2010

Manufactured in the U.S.A

Contents

Foreword by Larry W. Hurtado — xiii

Acknowledgements — xv

Abbreviations — xvii

Chapter 1 Introduction — 1
1.1 Background to Study — 1
1.2 Problem to be Addressed — 2
1.3 Review of Scholarly Opinion — 4
   1.3.1 Classical Greek - Grammars — 4
   1.3.2 Koine Greek — 5
      1.3.2.1 TRADITIONAL GRAMMARS — 6
      1.3.2.2 PARTICULAR PROPOSALS FOR THE USE OF ἵνα — 11
      1.3.2.3 ANALYSIS PRESENTED BY GREEK GRAMMARIANS — 13
1.4 Corpus — 15
1.5 Theoretical Basis for Book — 15
1.6 Arrangement of Chapters — 17
1.7 Summary — 20

Chapter 2 Theoretical Basis for Study — 21
2.1 Introduction — 21
2.2 Relevance Theory — 22
   2.2.1 General Background — 22
   2.2.2 Delineation of Theory — 24
      2.2.2.1 INFERENCES — 25
      2.2.2.2 HOW INFERENCES ARE SAID TO BE DRAWN — 27
      2.2.2.3 CONDITIONS FOR SUCCESSFUL COMMUNICATION — 28
      2.2.2.4 UNDERDETERMINACY — 29
         2.2.2.4.1 SHARED CONTEXTUAL ASSUMPTIONS — 30
         2.2.2.4.2 UNDERDETERMINACY IN PARTICIPLES — 31
         2.2.2.4.3 UNDERDETERMINACY IN PARTICLES — 32
      2.2.2.5 METAREPRESENTATION — 32

2.2.2.6 PROCEDURAL MARKERS		37
2.2.2.7 OSTENSIVE BEHAVIOUR		39
2.3 Purpose or Intention in Koine		40
2.4 Summary		41

Chapter 3 Independent Clauses Introduced by ἵνα — 43
3.1 Introduction — 43
3.2. Use of ἵνα to Give an Answer to Question — 46
3.3 Question and Answer by the Same Speaker — 48
   3.3.1 Examples from Polybius and Epictetus — 49
   3.3.2 New Testament Examples — 51
3.4. Expressing Desire and Intention — 54
   3.4.1 Johannine Examples — 54
   3.4.2 Examples from Orators and Rhetoricians — 57
      3.4.2.1 DEMOSTHENES — 58
      3.4.2.2 DIONYSIUS OF HALICARNASSUS — 58
   3.4.3 Examples from Septuagint and Non-Literary Papyri — 59
      3.4.3.1 SEPTUAGINT — 59
      3.4.3.2 EXAMPLES FROM PAPYRI — 59
   3.4.4 Examples from the Epistles — 61
3.5 Introducing a Quotation from the Old Testament — 64
3.6 Indicating Speaker's Interpretation — 68
3.7 Reporting the Thoughts or Speech of Others — 71
3.8 Summary — 73

Chapter 4 Requests, Commands, Prayers Introduced by ἵνα — 75
4.1 Introduction — 75
4.2 Authorial Choice — 77
Table 1 — 79
4.3 Synoptic Examples in Indirect Commands — 81
   4.3.1 Healing of Jairus' Daughter — 81
      4.3.1.1 MATTHEW 9:18 — 82
      4.3.1.2 MARK 5:23 — 82
      4.3.1.3 LUKE 8:41, 42 — 83
      4.3.1.4 CONCLUSION — 84
   4.3.2 The Healing of a Boy with a Demon — 85
      4.3.2.1 MATTHEW 17:15, 16 — 85

4.3.2.2 MARK 9:17, 18	86
4.3.2.3 LUKE 9:38, 40	87
4.3.2.4 CONCLUSION	88
4.3.3 The Healing of the Demon Possessed Man	88
4.3.3.1 MATTHEW 8:34	89
4.3.3.2 MARK 5:17	89
4.3.3.3 LUKE 8:37	90
4.3.3.4 CONCLUSION	91
4.3.4 Authorial Choice in Same Context	91
4.4 Examples from Literary Koine	92
4.4.1 Examples from Dionysius of Halicarnassus	93
4.4.2 Examples from Polybius	94
4.4.3 Examples from Epictetus	95
4.5 Summary	97

Chapter 5 Noun Clauses Introduced by ἵνα — 99

5.1 Introduction	99
5.2 Review of Metarepresentation	100
5.3 Explication of a Noun, Adjective or Demonstrative	102
5.3.1 Adjectives in Stative Clauses	103
5.3.1.1 NEW TESTAMENT EXAMPLES	103
5.3.1.2 EXAMPLES FROM THE DISCOURSES OF EPICTETUS	105
5.3.2 Nouns and Demonstratives in Stative Clauses	107
5.3.3 Nouns in Non-Stative Clauses Complemented by ἵνα Clauses	110
5.3.3.1 NEW TESTAMENT EXAMPLES	110
5.3.3.2 EXAMPLES FROM DIONYSIUS OF HALICARNASSUS	111
5.4 Noun Clauses with Impersonal Verbs	112
5.5 Noun Clauses which Function as Object of Main Verb	115
5.5.1 Examples from the New Testament	116
5.5.2 Examples from Epictetus	119
5.6 Prophetic Utterance Introduced by ἵνα	121
5.7 Summary	123

Chapter 6 Purpose Clauses Introduced by ἵνα — 126

6.1 Introduction	126
6.2 Purpose as Indicating Intention, and Beyond	127

6.2.1 The Role of Context in Interpreting ἵνα	129
6.2.2 Purpose Attributed	132
6.2.2.1 AUTHOR'S ACKNOWLEDGED ATTRIBUTION OF INTENT	133
6.2.2.2 REPRESENTATION OF INTENTION OF SUBJECT	134
6.2.2.3 PURPOSE FROM OBSERVABLE BEHAVIOUR	136
6.2.2.4 INTERPRETATION OF BEHAVIOUR PATTERNS	137
6.2.2.5 ATTRIBUTION OF INTENTION WITHOUT EVIDENCE	140
6.3 Other Ways of Expressing Purpose	142
6.4 Disputed Purpose Clauses	144
6.5 Summary	148

Chapter 7 Investigating ὅτι — 150

7.1 Introduction	150
7.2 Classical Greek	150
7.2.1 Direct Speech	150
7.2.2 Indirect Speech	151
7.2.3 Causal Clauses	152
7.3 Koine Greek	153
7.3.1 Direct Speech	153
7.3.2 Indirect Speech	156
7.3.2.1 EXAMPLES FROM EPICTETUS AND POLYBIUS	157
7.3.2.2 EXAMPLES FROM THE NEW TESTAMENT	160
7.3.3 Causal Clauses	163
7.3.3.1 EXAMPLES FROM EPICTETUS AND POLYBIUS	163
7.3.3.2 EXAMPLES FROM NEW TESTAMENT	166
7.4 Summary	172

Chapter 8 Diachronic Use of ἵνα — 174

8.1 Introduction	174
8.2 Classical Greek 500-300 BCE	175
Table 2	177
8.3 Hellenistic Greek 300-150 BCE	178
8.4 Graeco-Roman 150 BCE to 300 CE	181
8.4.1 Separation of Registers	181
8.4.1.1 HIGH LEVEL OF LANGUAGE: DIONYSIUS AND LUKE-ACTS	182
8.4.1.2 MORE COLLOQUIAL: EPICTETUS AND PAUL	184

8.4.2 Trends in Hellenistic Becoming More Marked ... 186
8.4.3 General Linguistic Changes ... 187
    8.4.3.1 PHONETIC CHANGES ... 187
    8.4.3.2 SYNTACTIC CHANGES ... 188
8.4.4 Language of the New Testament ... 189
Table 3 ... 191
8.4.5 Explanations Advanced for Use of ἵνα in New Testament ... 191
8.5 Modern Greek ... 192
8.6 Summary ... 194

Chapter 9 Conclusion ... 196
9.1 Introduction ... 196
9.2 A Relevance Theoretic Approach to ἵνα ... 197
  9.2.1 A Lexical Meaning for ἵνα? ... 197
  9.2.2 Taxonomic Approach to ἵνα ... 199
  9.2.3 The Combination of ἵνα and a Subjunctive Verb ... 200
  9.2.4 Diachronic Change in the Use and Frequency of ἵνα ... 202
  9.2.5 Interpretation of ἵνα Clauses ... 203
9.3 Implications of Hypothesis ... 203
  9.3.1 Implications for Interpretation ... 204
    9.3.1.1 THE COMBINATION OF ἵνα AND πληρῶ ... 204
    9.3.1.2 'IMPERATIVAL' ἵνα ... 206
    9.3.1.3 ὥρα WITH A FOLLOWING ἵνα CLAUSE ... 207
    9.3.1.4 CAUSAL ἵνα ... 208
    9.3.1.5 ἵνα INTRODUCING 'RESULT' CLAUSES ... 210
  9.3.2 Implications for Teaching New Testament Greek ... 212
9.4 Concluding Comments and Future Research ... 213

Bibliography ... 215

Scripture and Ancient Sources Index ... 221

Author Index ... 225

Foreword

It was my personal pleasure to serve as one of Margaret Sim's supervisors in the research lying behind this volume. (My colleague in Linguistics, Dr. Ronnie Cann, co-supervised the study.) I confess that when she first proposed investigating the function of the familiar Greek word ἵνα, I wondered what there was to discover. But Margaret's finished thesis proposal convinced me that she definitely had something to offer, and potentially something that could be of significance for exegesis of the New Testament and other Koine Greek texts. The finished thesis, revised here for publication, confirmed this, and I commend her study to anyone seriously interested in fathoming the subtleties of these Greek texts. To put her results in simplest terms, her study requires us to revise the lexical entries for this term, and, accordingly, to revise our understanding of quite a number of sentences in which the term is used in Koine texts. She contends, persuasively to my mind, that ἵνα should be understood to function more to signal that something is to be taken as the intention or aspiration of a given speaker or writer, rather than as a "word" to be translated simply as "in order that". This difference, though subtle in some instances, is important, and in some other cases makes a noteworthy difference in how we understand some sentences. Dr. Sim's study provides ample examples of this.

In addition to the specifics of her findings about the function of ἵνα, this study is a model of clarity, good sense, and thoroughness in the approach taken. By empirical analysis involving comparison with other texts, she tests, and shows dubious, some widely-touted notions, such as the oft-repeated claim that the frequency of ἵνα in the Gospel of John likely reflects the influence of underlying Aramaic syntax. Her selection of evidence, the care with which she handles it, the linguistic sophistication (so lightly worn) that she brings to the analysis, and her measured but effective argumentation all are admirable and exemplary. Indeed, this study would make good reading for those contemplating future PhD studies, as a model of careful and solid work.

I commend this study to all those involved in exegesis of the New Testament and other Koine texts. I urge also that future editions of lexica take account of Dr. Sim's findings. This is one of those studies whose results comprise genuine progress in scholarship. Its deceptively modest scope should not deter readers. For anyone who delights in solid research, careful analysis, cogent reasoning, and findings that must be reckoned with in the field, this study is highly recommended.

L. W. Hurtado
New College
University of Edinburgh

Acknowledgements

The author would like to acknowledge the encouragement and support of many academic mentors, colleagues and students both in UK and in Nairobi. They are too many to be named individually but they have provided a strong support base for the research and teaching which preceded the original thesis and now this book. My own husband, family and friends have been a constant delight in reiterating the belief that this study was possible! Finally I would like to express my deep appreciation of Anthony Cross and Robin Parry who have been extraordinarily encouraging as this text was prepared for publication.

Margaret Sim
Glasgow,
September 2010

Abbreviations

AB	Anchor Bible.
ATR	A. T. Robertson, *A Grammar of the Greek New Testament* Nashville: Broadman Press, 1934 4th edition.
AV	Authorised Version = KJV.
BAGD	W. Bauer, W. F. Arndt, F. W. Gingrich and F. W. Danker. *A Greek- English Lexicon of the New Testament and other Early Christian Literature.* 2nd ed. Chicago, 1979.
BDF	F. Blass, A. Debrunner, and R. W. Funk, *A Greek Grammar of the New Testament and Other Early Christian Literature.* Chicago, 1961.
BNTC	Black's New Testament Commentary.
CUP	Cambridge University Press.
JSNT	*Journal for the Study of the New Testament.*
JSOT	*Journal for the Study of the Old Testament.*
JTS	*Journal of Theological Studies.*
KJV	King James Version = AV
LCL	Loeb Classical Library.
LXX	Septuagint.
MG	W. F. Moulton and A. S. Geden *Concordance to the Greek New Testament* 6th edition, Edinburgh, 2002.
MGreek	Modern Greek.
MM	J. H. Moulton, and G. Milligan *The Vocabulary of the Greek New Testament.* London, 1930. Reprint, Peabody, Mass., 1997.
NA	*Novum Testamentum Graece* Nestle-Aland, 27th edition.
NEB	New English Bible.
NIGTC	New International Greek Testament Commentary.
NIV	New International Version.
NRSV	New Revised Standard Version.
NT	New Testament.
OT	Old Testament.
OUP	Oxford University Press.
RSV	Revised Standard Version.

UBS	*The Greek New Testament.* United Bible Societies, 4^(th) edition.
WBC	Word Bible Commentary.

CHAPTER 1

Introduction

The rationale for this book is dissatisfaction with the treatment of particles in Koine Greek, and in particular with the lack of a reasonable theoretical framework by which their use might be described. This may seem to be esoteric and irrelevant for biblical studies, focusing as it does on small parts of the Greek language, but I argue that the conclusions reached have serious implications for exegesis and translation, leading the way to a clearer understanding of the position of Koine in the history of Greek as well as the way in which it functioned in the first century CE. The particular particle which is the focus of this study is ἵνα, but ὅτι, whose development parallels ἵνα in the Koine, is also dealt with in one chapter.

1.1 Background to Study

The background to this study is the change in use of particles in Koine Greek and in particular the increase in the frequency and variation in the use of the particle ἵνα. From being used exclusively as a particle which introduced purpose clauses in Classical Greek, it came to be used to introduce both dependent and independent clauses, as well as a wide range of the former. Its frequency especially in the writers of the New Testament and Epictetus is surprising. It occurs 663 times in the New Testament, but only 63 times in the first five books of the *Histories* of Polybius. Particles are often said to be a reliable indicator of language change in general and grammatical change in particular.[1] This is especially true of the change in both use and frequency not only of ἵνα but also of ὅτι.[2] Although this change was gradual and may be seen incipiently even in Aristotle and Demosthenes, the pace of that change gained momentum in the centuries after the conquest of Alexander and the concomitant spread of the Greek language geographically. This change marks a new direction for the ancient language, but probably reflects the situation in the spoken rather than the literary language even before Koine became widespread. This is a question of register which will be dealt with in Chapter 8.

---

[1] *ATR*, p. 1144 '...the particles mark the history of the effort to relate words with each other, clause with clause, sentence with sentence, paragraph with paragraph'.

[2] The significance in the increase of these two particles is the development of the subordinate clauses which they introduce in place of the previously dominant infinitival construction.

Grammarians differ as to which words are particles,[3] but I use the word in its wider sense, since 'conjunction', although usually an adequate term to describe ἵνα, does not fit every context.[4] In recent years, many scholars have focused on the intersentential particles in the Koine, both inferential[5] and conjunctive,[6] but very little study has been carried out specifically, as far as I am aware, on those particles which relate clauses, introduce subordination and seem to direct much of the logical argument of the sentence.[7]

In the Koine, ἵνα followed by a clause in the subjunctive mood seems to be increasing the scope of its operations in the works of certain authors such as Polybius, Dionysius, Epictetus[8] and the writers of the New Testament, while ὅπως is steadily retreating. Further, ἵνα may introduce clauses which would be described in traditional grammar as purpose, result, cause,[9] indirect command, imperatival, nominal. This increase is frequently at the expense of the infinitive, but there are many verbs which may have their arguments explicated either by a ἵνα clause or by the infinitive. It is often assumed that the choice between these two constructions is based on authorial style, but I argue that while this may be true to a certain extent, it deals neither with the reason for that particular style[10] nor with the inferences which the writer, perhaps not completely consciously, expects a reader to draw from such a choice.

1.2 Problem to be Addressed

The question raised in this book is: what inference does the use of ἵνα with the subjunctive invite the reader to draw in her[11] interpretation of the clause it introduces and its relationship to the rest of the sentence? This question arises because it seems to be a general assumption, based on an earlier stage of the

---

[3] *ATR* is inclusive in his treatment of this subject, but Denniston (1953) limits his study to those particles which connect clauses and sentences, leaving aside subordinating conjunctions.

[4] Chapter 3 deals with the independent use of this particle, which therefore cannot be conjunctive.

[5] R. Blass (1993), Levinsohn (1999) and (2000).

[6] S. Black (2002), Poythress (1984), Winedt (2000).

[7] Jannaris (1897), Mandilaras (1976) and Caragounis (2004) have examined these in much wider grammars of the language from a historical perspective. Levinsohn (2003) has an unpublished paper on ὅτι which is discussed in 7.2.1.

[8] Epictetus did not write but his lectures were recorded by Arrian as *Discourses*.

[9] I am not convinced of this category, but it will be dealt with at 9.3.1.4.

[10] I will show that 'style' is based on authorial choice which in turn is guided by relevance. The author intends the reader to draw inferences from the construction chosen.

[11] The masculine pronoun 'he' is used in this book to refer to a speaker or writer, while the female pronoun 'she' is used for the hearer or reader. This, or the reverse usage, has become a convention in the literature of relevance theory. Note further points at footnote 80.

Introduction

language, that the 'meaning', or dictionary entry for ἵνα is 'in order that'. A study of the NT texts alone, however, shows that for Luke and John this is true for only 40% and 62% of such uses[12] respectively. The remaining instances show a wide range of clause types, in terms of traditional grammar, as noted above, together with contexts in which a telic interpretation of this particle is simply impossible.[13]

Consider the following example (1) from 1 John 1:9:

Example (1) [14] ἐὰν ὁμολογῶμεν τὰς ἁμαρτίας ἡμῶν, πιστός ἐστιν καὶ δίκαιος, ἵνα ἀφῇ ἡμῖν τὰς ἁμαρτίας καὶ καθαρίσῃ ἡμᾶς ἀπὸ πάσης ἀδικίας.
If we confess our sins, he (God) is faithful and just that he should forgive our sins and cleanse us from all wrongdoing.

The content of the clause introduced by ἵνα 'that he should forgive our sins…' cannot be the purpose of the righteous and faithful nature of God. It is rather the reverse: the author is claiming that the faithfulness and righteous nature of God is the basis on which such forgiveness might be predicated.[15]

A further example (2) from Luke 1:43 also shows the difficulty of insisting on a telic interpretation for a clause introduced by this particle:

Example (2) καὶ πόθεν μοι τοῦτο ἵνα ἔλθῃ ἡ μήτηρ τοῦ κυρίου μου πρὸς ἐμέ;
So what is this to me/ why did this happen to me that the mother of my lord should come to me?

Again, the clause introduced by ἵνα may explain the preceding τοῦτο or may introduce a prophetic insight,[16] but it cannot indicate a relationship of purpose with the preceding clause. I do not deny that this particle may introduce a purpose clause, but it does not follow from this that the particle itself has a lexical meaning of 'in order that'. If the clause it introduces is telic, then the reader has been able to infer this from the context. Consider Example (3):[17]

Example (3) ἔδοξε κἀμοὶ …καθεξῆς σοι γράψαι, κράτιστε Θεόφιλε, ἵνα ἐπιγνῷς περὶ ὧν κατηχήθης λόγων τὴν ἀσφάλειαν.
It seemed good to me also…to write for you in an orderly fashion, excellent

---

[12] This figure is arrived at by counting all instances of ἵνα which might be analysed as indicating purpose. This might not be the only or even the most relevant analysis.
[13] Consider John 5:7; 12:7.
[14] Since this study involves two disciplines: biblical studies and linguistics, the usual linguistic practice of introducing examples by bracketed numbers has been modified. The word 'example' prefaces each bracketed number, in order that there may be no confusion with the numbering of biblical text.
[15] This example is dealt with in detail at 6.2.1.
[16] This analysis is dealt with at 5.3 and 5.4.
[17] Luke 1:3-4, which is also dealt with at 6.1 Example (1).

Theophilus, in order that you might know the certainty of the accounts you have heard.

It is the context in the above example which alerts the reader to expect the ἵνα clause to give the purpose of the 'writing'. The desired outcome of this writing is that the reader, Theophilus, should be assured concerning reports which he has heard. We do not infer this from the particle ἵνα alone, but from the context also.

We cannot claim that one clause is in a relationship of purpose to the other *solely* on the basis of the lexical meaning of ἵνα and in defiance of the context. In other words, we cannot insist that someone did something in order to achieve a certain purpose if the *context*, and not merely the introductory particle, does not support this. I argue that ἵνα does not have a fixed meaning of 'in order that', but rather that its function is to alert the reader to expect a thought, desire or intention of the speaker, and the fact that the verb of that clause is in the subjunctive mood signals that this represents a potential rather than an actual state of affairs. [18]

1.3 Review of Scholarly Opinion

Since particles such as ἵνα have been dealt with traditionally as part of a wider grammatical framework, my review will outline briefly the views of the standard grammatical works of Blass Debrunner, J.H. Moulton, C.F.D. Moule, A.T. Robertson and Winer, together with the historical approaches of Horrocks, Jannaris and Mandilaras, the latter two in addition contributing their intuitive knowledge of their own language. Caragounis' comprehensive volume on the development of Greek in relation to the NT[19] is also relevant to this topic and its significance will also be noted at this point.

Since wider scholarly comment on ἵνα in the NT relates to its use in particular sentences, this will be adduced throughout the book when each example is discussed. This appears to be the simplest way of dealing with comment which is pertinent, but also disparate. In this section only the contribution of the major grammatical works listed above will be noted.

1.3.1 Classical Greek - Grammars

Grammarians concerned with Classical Greek, such as Goodwin and Smyth, understood the particle ἵνα to be used exclusively to introduce final clauses. This was in contrast to the particle ὅπως which together with a verb in indicative mood, could introduce a wider range of clauses than ἵνα, particularly after verbs of striving, asking or commanding. Consider the following example which has a future tense after ὅπως:

---

[18] This is dealt with under 'Theoretical basis' at 1.3 as well as in Chapter 2.
[19] Caragounis (2004).

Example (4) Χρὴ ὁρᾶν τοὺς Ἀργείους ὅπως σωθήσεται ἡ Πελοπόννησος.
The people of Argos must see that the Peloponnese is saved. (MGS)[20]

These uses of ὅπως were in addition to its function, when accompanied by a subjunctive verb, as a particle introducing final clauses. Goodwin points out that very rarely the particle ἵνα might introduce an object (i.e. noun) clause in Classical Greek, but 'it reappears in the later language, as in the New Testament'.[21] He also gives a useful chart[22] which shows the shift in the use of both these particles, with ἵνα gradually becoming the particle of choice for introducing final clauses, even in the classical language. It was also the case in the classical language that if a purpose was *not* fulfilled, because the action on which it was predicated did not take place, then the clause introduced by ἵνα would have a verb in the indicative mood.[23] This is noted because I shall argue that the function of this particle in Koine is also related to the mood in which its accompanying verb appears.

Of course there were other ways in which purpose might be expressed, such as the infinitive - with or without ὥστε or ὡς - and indeed this construction seems to have been more frequently used than a clause with ἵνα. The future participle was also a potentially telic construction, as was the relative with a future indicative.[24] This fact leads one to ask what the factors were which were involved in the choice of a particular construction. This study does not focus on Classical Greek and so I have not pursued this, but those Greeks who have written grammars of their own language suggest that ἵνα clauses were more popular in spoken language in classical times than they were in the literary register of that period.[25] The subject of register will be dealt with in Chapter 8.

1.3.2 Koine Greek

The limiting of ἵνα to a telic function noted for Classical Greek seems to be the criterion by which the later use in Koine is judged, in spite of the fact that before the time of the NT the use of this particle was extending in that it introduced 'object' clauses after verbs of commanding and striving, much as the particle ὅπως had in an earlier form of the language. This can be clearly seen in the formal documents and inscriptions from the Ptolemaic period[26] as well as the contemporary papyri. In the former ὅπως is used as much as, if not

---

[20] Thucydides 5.27, example given in Goodwin (1965 reprint) §339.
[21] Goodwin §357. He gives several examples from Homer (hence the use of the term 'reappear') but only one example from Demosthenes.
[22] Goodwin p. 398. This is adapted from the work of Dr Philip Weber (no publication date given), and is given in this book at 8.2.
[23] Goodwin §333. Smyth (1920), Example (1) at 8.2.
[24] Goodwin §338.
[25] Jannaris (1897) §05,022, Appendix VI §5. Caragounis (2004) more generally p. 40.
[26] Bradford Welles (1974).

more than ἵνα, but the latter appears after verbs and verbal phrases such as φροντίζω, πρόνοιαν ποιούμενος, παρακαλέω and γράφω. [27]

Polybius and Dionysius of Halicarnassus also use ἵνα after verbs of commanding and striving, as well as to introduce a noun clause.[28] Only one example[29] is given at this point:

> Example (5) καταπαυσάντων δὲ τὸν λόγον, κοινῇ μὲν ἔφη πειρᾶσθαι φροντίζειν ἵνα μηδὲν ἀδίκημα γίνηται ῾Ρωμαίοις ἐξ ᾿Ιλλυριῶν· ἰδίᾳ γε μὴν οὐ νόμιμον εἶναι τοῖς βασιλεῦσι κωλύειν ᾿Ιλλυριοις τὰς κατὰ θάλατταν ὠφελείας.
>
> When they had finished their speech, she said that in the public realm she would try to see to it that the Romans would suffer no wrong from the Illyrians, but in the private realm it was not the custom for the kings to hinder the booty from the sea to the Illyrians/ to stop the Illyrians from gains from the sea. (MGS)

Here the clause introduced by ἵνα explicates what Teuta (she) will attempt to pay attention to (following φροντίζειν). The use of literary features such as accusative and infinitive for indirect speech may be seen here: πειρᾶσθαι, εἶναι as well as the Attic -ττ- for the Koine -σσ-, but together with these there is the use of the particle ἵνα to indicate what the subject (Teuta) would strive for: *there should be no wrong done to the Romans*.

Several perceptive grammarians such as A.T. Robertson and J.H. Moulton, as well as the Greek grammarians Jannaris, Mandilaras and Caragounis appreciated the way in which the language had been developing in that the literary use of the infinitival constructions was giving way to a simpler, more perspicacious grammatical form, not only in the writings of the NT but in writers of literary Koine also.

1.3.2.1 TRADITIONAL GRAMMARS

The position of the most notable grammarians with reference to the use and function of ἵνα can be distinguished as follows:

> 1. those who insist on a telic meaning, based on the classical language, for most of the uses of this particle, and
> 2. those who see the particle as broadening the scope of its use in the language generally and not only in the biblical text.

---

[27] Bradford Welles (1980) p. 19, 34, 119, 163, 180.

[28] Note Examples (16) and (17) at 4.3.2.1 and Examples (18) and (19) at 4.3.2.2 for clauses of indirect command following this particle in Dionysius and Polybius respectively.

[29] Polybius *Histories* Book II.4.8. Although Polybius is regularly quoted to exemplify literary Koine, he wrote in the period which Jannaris describes as 'Hellenistic', that is 208-126 BCE.

The grammarians Burton and Winer take the first position. Although they *note* the different clauses which the particle seems to introduce, they are able to suggest 'purpose' as being behind many of these uses. Their particular concern is the question of an ecbatic use for ἵνα which they view as being appealed to in order to avoid a theological difficulty. 'There is no certain, scarcely a probable, instance in the New Testament of a clause introduced by ἵνα denoting actual result as such.'[30]

Also they view some epexegetic clauses as expressing 'conceived' but not actual result. It has to be said that these grammarians,[31] familiar as they were with the classical language,[32] held certain presuppositions which coloured their analysis of ἵνα. The most salient of these was the conviction that, since 'purpose' was behind the use of this particle, the notion that 'result' might also be included in its meaning was viewed as weakening the sense of the particle to accommodate theological considerations. This seems ironic, since it was a theological presupposition, the 'divine will', which caused Winer at least to refuse all but a telic interpretation for a ἵνα clause. He explained the difficult uses of this particle as having 'divine government'[33] behind them, a position which seems to be supported by *BAGD*,[34] albeit on a slightly different platform of 'Jewish thought'. Moule more reasonably widens this to be a reference to the 'Semitic mind' being 'notoriously unwilling to draw a sharp dividing line between purpose and consequence.'[35] This may be true in terms of a different world view, without necessarily invoking the nebulous concept of 'divine government.'[36] Moule's comments also are related particularly to the vexed question of purpose versus result clauses. His approach fits better in the second group of scholars.

Those clauses introduced by ἵνα which older grammarians describe as 'object clauses',[37] 'complementary and epexegetic clauses' are viewed as

---

[30] Burton (1894) §222. Note comments at 3.1.
[31] In particular Burton (1894) and Winer (1882).
[32] The comparisons made are always with the classical language, while there are no references to papyri evidence in support of language change, unlike the grammar of A.T. Robertson.
[33] Winer p. 573-4.
[34] *BAGD* p. 377-8.
[35] Moule (1982 reprint) p. 142.
[36] In many Afro Asiatic languages today (Hebrew falls within this grouping) there is no distinction made between a particle which introduces a final clause and one which introduces a consecutive clause. I suggest that for these speakers the notions of intended result and actual result do not require to be distinguished. Note that Classical Greek *did* distinguish, by means of mood, those purpose clauses which were not actualised from those which were, but Koine did not.
[37] *ATR* pp. 991-4; Goodwin (1965 reprint) §303A, 304, 339, 340.

'taking the place of the infinitive'.[38] This is true diachronically, but it does not explain the process by which speakers and then writers preferred to use such constructions instead of the infinitive. Again, since the classical language was the criterion against which the NT usage was judged, there was a strong predisposition to view 'purpose' as the primary indication in this particle's use. The wider use of ἵνα in pagan Greek was not considered at all. It is possible that even in the classical language the use of the particle ἵνα may have indicated a thought, desire or intention of the speaker or subject rather than having a fixed dictionary meaning of 'in order that'. Since this is not the focus of this book, I do not offer evidence for this.

The grammarians who take the second view accept that the language was changing and particle use with it. Some, like Turner, see it as a change for the worse, a deterioration deriving from Semitic influence,[39] while others such as Blass,[40] J.H. Moulton, Moule and Robertson accept it as an historical fact, making no value judgement on it. I will briefly summarise the comments of these scholars regarding the use of ἵνα in the NT and the reasons for the extension of its use in comparison to the classical language.

Blass, Debrunner and Funk see certain uses of the infinitive retreating in the face of 'analytical constructions with ἵνα and ὅτι'.[41] They acknowledge that this trend could be seen in 'early Hellenistic' but point out that even in the NT 'the infinitive is still used abundantly by all authors and the choice between the inf. and ἵνα appears to be a matter of preference in each case'.[42] I agree that this is the case, but argue that this is motivated by the communicative desire to make the thought of the speaker or subject clear for the reader. The comments on ἵνα clauses come within the general section on 'Mood' in *BDF*, that is in the units which deal with the infinitive.[43] The section which deals with final clauses[44] is concerned mainly with mood (optative, indicative) and only briefly with the use of ἵνα in place of the Attic ὅπως or ὅπως μή after verbs of striving. By contrast it is in the lengthy section on the infinitive that the varied uses of ἵνα are dealt with. These are described as 'analytical constructions' but no rationale is given for this construction and its prominence, nor for the fact that authors seem to use both constructions even after the same main verb. The use of this particle then is viewed predominantly from the perspective of the

---

[38] *BDF* '..analytical constructions with ἵνα and ὅτι have developed into serious rivals of the infinitive' §388.

[39] Turner (1988 reprint): 'If one cannot claim that its (ἵνα) even greater flexibility of use was entirely due to Semitic influence, one must at least underline the difficulty of finding anywhere but in biblical books such a wide variety in the use of ἵνα, imperatival, causal, consecutive, epexegetical, within so small a space' p. 8-9.

[40] Friedrich Blass, noted in Blass, Debrunner and Funk below.

[41] *BDF* §388.

[42] *BDF* §388; 'early Hellenistic' seems to refer to the period 300-100BCE.

[43] *BDF* §388-394.

[44] *BDF* §369.

Introduction

earlier infinitival use, and the decline of the infinitive in both final and complement clauses.

J.H. Moulton's lucid and open minded discussion of the wider use of ἵνα in his *Prolegomena* is a great contrast to the comments of Turner in volume three of that series. After noting that the reluctance of the earlier commentators to yield to a wider understanding of the particle was 'driven by the supposed demands of grammar' he summarises his own view:

> That ἵνα normally meant "in order that" is beyond question. It is perpetually used in the full final sense in the papyri, having gained greatly on the Attic ὅπως. But it has come to be the ordinary construction in many phrases where a simple infinitive was used in earlier Greek ...the burden of making purpose clear is in all cases thrown on the context.[45]

I would add to his comment that if it is *context* which determines the use of this particle then it cannot be said to have a lexical meaning of 'in order that'. We should instead examine the function of the particle, the syntactic contexts in which it appears as well as the pragmatic inferences which a reader is invited to draw from its use in order to determine its role in post Classical Greek. Moulton does discuss the demise of the infinitive in later Greek together with the regional variations in this process. He is open minded about the flexibility of this particle but does not discuss reasons for this change and for the increase in its use.

C.F.D. Moule is likewise very open in his examination of this particle: 'Biblical Greek must not be laid upon the Procrustean bed of Classical grammar.'[46] He rejects a purely final meaning for ἵνα, citing the 'Semitic mind' as the reason for the lack of clear definition between ecbatic and telic uses. He also notes the Septuagintal translation of Genesis 22:14 which cannot surely be a telic use of this particle:

> Example (6) καὶ ἐκάλεσεν Αβρααμ τὸ ὄνομα τοῦ τόπου ἐκείνου Κύριος εἶδεν, ἵνα εἴπωσιν σήμερον Ἐν τῷ ὄρει κύριος ὤφθη.
> So Abraham called the name of that place 'The Lord saw' so that they say today 'In the mountain the Lord was seen.'

He approves of Cadoux's suggestion, noted below, of an imperatival sense for ἵνα, although disagreeing with some of the latter's examples on the ground that they are deontic rather than imperatival. Still other examples he sees as 'denoting content'.[47] This description seems to refer to clauses which follow

---

[45] Moulton (1998 reprint) p. 206 and 207.
[46] Moule (1982 reprint) p. 142.
[47] Cadoux (1941) pp. 144-5.

such verbs as εὐχαριστῶ[48] and συνίστημι.[49] I will argue that his analysis may be extended to see the function of this particle as giving procedural instructions to the reader to expect an expression of the wish, command, intention or understanding of the author or speaker.

A.T. Robertson has references to the extension in the use of ἵνα together with the retreat of the infinitive in Koine throughout his comprehensive grammar of 1454 pages. He sees this as part of a natural process of language change:

> The infinitive as a whole disappears before ὅτι and ἵνα (modern Greek νά)...It was always a matter of discretion with a Greek writer whether in certain clauses he would use the infinitive or an object-clause (ὅτι, ὅπως, ἵνα).[50]

Robertson has been described as having a grasp of developments in Greek which is 'masterly, not to say magisterial.'[51] I would concur with that assessment since my own understanding of the particle is based on authorial choice which attempts to make salient the thought and attitude of a speaker. If it is acknowledged that a writer makes a choice, then the basis on which such a choice is made has to be considered. My argument is that this basis is relevance. I do not claim that this was a conscious process of selection, although with writers such as Dionysius and Polybius it may have been.

Again, because of the breadth of his treatment of the topic, I will refer to Robertson's opinion on various texts as they are in focus throughout the book. Here I note only his concluding comments on this particle's use:

> So, then, we conclude that ἵνα has in the N.T. all three uses (final, sub-final,[52] consecutive), and thus runs a close parallel with the infinitive which it finally displaced.[53]

The Greeks themselves, from Apollonius Dyscolos to Jannaris, Mandilaras and Caragounis,[54] see the advancement of ἵνα as a natural part of language development and reject the notion of Semitic influence. This is the position which I will defend in this book: that ἵνα had extended its role in Hellenistic[55]

---

[48] Ephesians 1:16-17.
[49] Romans 16:1, 2.
[50] *ATR* p. 371.
[51] Horsley (1989) p. 59.
[52] *ATR* uses the term 'sub-final' for imperatival, indirect command, noun clauses, in short every use of the particle which is neither ecbatic nor telic.
[53] *ATR* p. 999.
[54] See under 2.2.3.
[55] As noted in Chapter 8, I use the term Hellenistic to refer to the period 300 to 150BCE, thus distinguishing it from the more general term 'Koine' which I use to describe the language from 150 BCE to 300 CE.

Greek, certainly from 300 BCE, to take over some of the functions of the particle ὅπως and to introduce a wide range of clauses, thereby no longer having a fixed lexical meaning of 'in order that'.

1.3.2.2 PARTICULAR PROPOSALS FOR THE USE OF ἵνα

Other scholars have proposed explanations for both the extension in the use of this particle and its frequency, particularly in the Gospel of John. Cadoux[56] suggested that one particular use could be viewed as 'imperatival', a notion which has found favour with many scholars who have followed him, and which may account for some instances of independent clauses which are introduced by ἵνα. Cadoux based his argument on the post classical use of θέλω followed by a ἵνα clause with the subjunctive. He claimed that it then became common to omit the main verb 'so that the ἵνα-clause virtually became as much a main sentence as if the plain imperative had been used'[57] and gave evidence both from the papyri and Epictetus. For the NT he gave 'at least four unmistakeable cases' from Mark 5:23, 2 Corinthians 8:7, Ephesians 5:33 and Galatians 2:9.[58] Later commentators have accepted Cadoux's suggestion fairly uncritically as being a reasonable alternative to ellipsis, but Moule insightfully suggests[59] that 'it would be better in some cases to describe the ἵνα as "denoting content" rather than as imperatival', a point which is particularly relevant not only to clauses which might be classed as 'imperatival' but also to those coming under the description of 'indirect command'.[60] I argue that a ἵνα clause does 'denote content' but that the function of the particle is to alert the reader to expect that content and to read it as indicating speaker or subject attitude.

The term 'imperatival', however, was not clearly defined which led others to contest this description of such clauses. It seems that Cadoux may have been conflating the notions of 'command' and 'necessity', that is: instead of giving a command a speaker may, in the use of a ἵνα clause, have intended to give a representation of what he thought someone 'should' do. This is a weaker communication than a command. Certainly Cadoux's translation of some of the Johannine examples which he used leads one to view them as deontic rather than imperatival.[61] This does not invalidate Cadoux's hypothesis, but it should be expanded to include the notion of what one 'should' do. I argue that by analysing this particle as alerting the reader to expect the thought or attitude of the speaker or subject, I allow for this to encompass both the thought of what

---

[56] Cadoux (1941).
[57] Cadoux p. 166.
[58] These examples are discussed in Chapters 3 and 4.
[59] Moule p. 145.
[60] These examples will be dealt with in Chapter 4.
[61] For example his translation of ἀλλ' ἵνα μαρτυρήσῃ as 'he had to bear witness' John 1:8.

the subject wants someone to do and what he thinks that someone should do. In English we distinguish between the communicatory effect of the following expressions:

a. Do this.
b. Please do this.
c. I want (would like) you to do this.
d. I think you should do this.

At this point, it should be noted that the *meaning* of ἵνα rather than its *function* has been a point of confusion in the discussion. It is more accurate to see any lexical meaning, reflected in the English translation, as being derived from its function in the clause it introduces as well as from its logical relation to the main clause, or even the rest of the sentence. Even modern grammars of NT Greek[62] give a translation of this particle as 'in order that', in spite of the fact that this is only true for 40% of the occurrences in Luke and 62% in John. This is of course still a substantial use, but in the 46 examples of this particle in Luke, only 21 introduce a purpose clause, while the remaining 25 introduce noun clauses or indirect commands as well as independent clauses. It certainly cannot be said to have a meaning of 'in order that' in those cases.[63]

Burney and to a lesser extent Zerwick have suggested that the varied uses of ἵνα, that is in comparison to the classical language, arose as 'mistranslations' of the Aramaic particle *di*.[64] This suggestion, which is proposed particularly for the uses of this particle in the fourth gospel, has to be based on a proposed Aramaic original for the gospels, as well as first language interference on the part of authors or editors who were presumed to be speakers of Aramaic. The Aramaic particle in question introduces clauses with a much wider range of meaning than ἵνα and it might be considered then to be more likely that a less restrictive particle would be used in translation. Colwell[65] and Torrey[66] deal firmly with Burney's arguments and only Zerwick has revived them, and that for a very limited number of texts.

A further point is the use made of the particle by Epictetus in his *Discourses*, as presented by Arrian. In this work, many types of clause may be introduced by ἵνα: noun, independent, indirect command, consecutive, the particle being found with a frequency which approaches that of John's Gospel. There can be no question of Aramaic interference in the case of either Arrian or

---

[62] Duff (2005), Jay (1958), Wallace (1996) is more cautious.

[63] The difficulty for those teaching Greek via the medium of English is that there is no single word which captures the multiple functions of this particle. The particle 'that' fits many contexts, but is not always a particularly natural translation.

[64] Burney (1922).

[65] Colwell (1931).

[66] Torrey (1933).

Introduction 13

Epictetus, nor in the case of Polybius and Dionysius of Halicarnassus who use the particle less frequently but nevertheless in ways which differ from the classical usage. This makes the suggestion of interference either from a Semitic mindset or Aramaic less than credible.

1.3.2.3 ANALYSIS PRESENTED BY GREEK GRAMMARIANS

The diachronic development of ἵνα will be dealt with in Chapter 8, but at this point it should be noted again that all the Greek[67] grammarians, as well as scholars such as Horsley and Horrocks, view the development in use as a natural part of language change. The reason given for this development is the decline and eventual disappearance of the infinitive. The accusative and infinitive, for example, was a literary construction which was oblique and occasionally ambiguous, rather than being as perspicacious as the later language demanded. This leads to the suggestion that infinitival constructions would have been particularly challenging for the many who spoke Greek as a second or third language in the koine period. On this analysis, the clauses introduced by ἵνα, or ὅτι, could be all those which would have been expressed by the infinitive, or accusative and infinitive, in the classical language. While accepting that ἵνα clauses do seem to have been used in the place of infinitival constructions from the Hellenistic period onwards, I argue that an explanation for this shift in language use, in terms of the communicatory effect which it made, has not yet been given.

Jannaris points out the disadvantages for popular speech of the infinitive, in that it did not mark person which led to occasional ambiguity in distinguishing subject and object.

> A Greek, then, who aimed particularly either at precision, or emphasis, or both, was often compelled to resolve the infinitive into a finite mood with the appropriate particle, and thus obtain the desired effect with regard to the precise meaning, person, number, time.[68]

He saw this as the predominant factor which led to the disappearance of the infinitive from the language in post Byzantine times. Apart from carefully crafted literary works, it was also difficult to keep up an infinitival construction after speech verbs. Consider the following example from the book of Acts, which is considered to exemplify good Koine,[69] in which there are mixed

---

[67] That is, grammarians working on their own language: Greek.

[68] Jannaris (1897) p. 569 who uses the term 'analysis' to describe the use of clauses introduced by either ἵνα or ὅτι with the subjunctive or indicative mood respectively.

[69] That is from the perspective of the NT. Note Mealand (1996) for a comparison with Dionysius of Halicarnassus.

constructions after a verb of implied speech:[70]

> Example (7) παρήγγειλεν αὐτοῖς ἀπὸ Ἱεροσολύμων μὴ χωρίζεσθαι ἀλλὰ περιμένειν τὴν ἐπαγγελίαν τοῦ πατρὸς ἣν ἠκούσατέ μου, ὅτι.....
> He instructed them not to leave Jerusalem but to wait for the promise of the father which you heard from me that...

This mixed construction is found in other parts of both Acts and Luke,[71] which suggests that a prolonged passage which encapsulated information using accusative and infinitive was difficult to maintain. The more natural, I infer, often took over.[72]

Jannaris' comments are supported by the use of the Modern Greek particle νά with the subjunctive, and the demise of the infinitive. I concur with this analysis, but argue that it does not go far enough in giving a theoretical basis for such change, given that in the NT and pagan Greek authors or editors used *both* ἵνα clauses *and* infinitival constructions after the same main verbs.

Caragounis[73] then takes the argument a step further. He makes excellent use of pagan materials in composing his arguments for the natural development of ἵνα by Greeks rather than attributing it to either Semitic or illiterate influence. While I appreciate his use of examples from Classical Greek onwards right up to Modern Greek[74] in support of the role of language change in the development of the use of this particle, I shall contest the validity of reading back into the Koine the uses of νά in *MGreek*. *MGreek* usage may *support* an analysis of earlier usage, but it seems to be methodologically unsound, linguistically, to read present day usage into an earlier stage of the language. Rouchota[75] and Horrocks,[76] for example, consider the particle νά in *MGreek* to be a marker of the subjunctive,[77] which means that it may introduce almost *any* clause which has a subjunctive verb. Since this was certainly not the case in Koine, it would seem to be an invalid step to assume that types of νά clauses which are found in *MGreek* may occur *for the same reason* in the earlier language. As with earlier grammarians who saw the changes in their diachronic perspective, Caragounis acknowledges the changing use of ἵνα, ὅπως and ὅτι but does not give a reason for such change which takes account of the use of

---

[70] Acts 1:4. Compare this with the lengthy constructions maintained for example by Polybius in his *Histories* at Book IV.26.4.

[71] Note Acts 25:4-5 and Luke 5:14, as well as *BDF* §470.

[72] That is not to say that the author did not use the construction in shorter passages: see Luke 24:46.

[73] Caragounis (2004).

[74] Hereafter *MGreek*.

[75] Rouchota (1994) p. 1 and 2, also Mackridge (1985) §1.3.2.

[76] Horrocks (1997) p. 76.

[77] In Chapter 8 the question of grammaticalisation of this particle, which has led to its use in Modern Greek, is discussed.

both constructions, that is infinitival and ἵνα clauses.

1.4 Corpus

The data base used for this study has been the gospels of Luke and John, together with the first five books of the *Histories* of Polybius, the first four books of the *Roman Antiquities* of Dionysius of Halicarnassus and Arrian's account of the *Discourses* of Epictetus. The choice of Luke and John was made on the basis of their use of ἵνα, with Luke having the fewest examples (45) and John the most (145) among the gospel writers. Polybius is widely regarded as presenting a good example of literary Koine, while Dionysius as a teacher of rhetoric and a writer on style and composition must be considered as an exponent of 'good' Greek. The *Discourses* of Epictetus were recorded by Arrian, who himself wrote in Attic, while the teachings of Epictetus are clearly Koine. Since these teachings are close to both the style and vocabulary of the NT they have provided valuable insights into the use of ἵνα.

In addition I have taken examples from the other gospel writers, Acts, the Pauline epistles, the Septuagint, inscriptions and letters from the royal correspondence of the Ptolomaic period as well as examples from the non-literary papyri. I examined several books of the *Jewish War* of Josephus, but do not adduce examples from these as evidence since the Semitic influence of these might be said to militate against their value as literary, but non-biblical Greek. Since the wider use of ἵνα in the NT has been explained in the past in terms of interference from Aramaic or the Semitic mindset, I have selected authors who could not be accused of such bias.

1.5 Theoretical Basis for Book

Studies which cross disciplines present particular challenges, but the insights of a discipline external to the one with which the main body of the material is concerned have considerable potential for throwing fresh light on a topic. Biblical studies has benefitted from both social science approaches and also from linguistics. It is from the latter that I propose to draw principles to guide the study of particles in Koine Greek.

The theoretical basis for my analysis of ἵνα is that of Relevance Theory,[78] a cognitive approach to language first proposed by Dan Sperber and Deirdre Wilson.[79] This theory, which will be explained in greater detail in Chapter 2, claims to articulate the principles behind the cognitive processes by which the mind selects the interpretation of an utterance. In other words it attempts to determine the principles by which speakers and writers of a language communicate with one another, both verbally and non-verbally. The argument developed in this book is that by using the particle ἵνα and a verb in the subjunctive mood the writer is not only selecting a particular grammatical form,

---

[78] Hereafter *RT*.
[79] Sperber and Wilson (1986/1995).

but is doing this having in mind the cognitive effects which his readers may expect to receive from such use. This particle leads the reader to expect a particular type of information which might be informally described as a representation of the subject, or speaker's, attitude.

By examining some of the principles of cognition involved in human communication, I hope to offer a unified analysis of this particle which will contribute to a better understanding of the text of the New Testament. Rather than stating that this particle has a fixed dictionary meaning or that it introduces a variety of clause types which could have been infinitival in the earlier language, I argue that its function is to give the reader directions, inviting her to expect a representation of a thought of the speaker or subject. This has led to the expansion of its function in Koine and later in Modern Greek.

This theoretical basis will be examined in more detail, with examples, in Chapter 2, but at this point it is sufficient to note that the theory deals with communication between implied author and reader, and between speaker and hearer. It asserts that humans speak and listen to one another because they believe, instinctively, that what they are communicating has relevance for the reader or hearer. 'Relevance' indicates that what is being communicated gives information which a hearer or reader wants or needs to hear, in that it confirms what she[80] knows already, or causes her to reassess her existing assumptions. Of course a communicator may be mistaken in thinking that what he has to say is relevant, but it is this belief which causes him to make the attempt anyway.

A further prominent claim of *RT* is that language is underdetermined: speakers do not say all that they 'mean' but rely on inference to communicate. Inferencing relies on knowledge which is common to both parties, both contextually and in terms of shared world view. This is known in *RT* as the speaker and hearer's cognitive environment. The parables of the NT rely heavily on such a shared cognitive environment, without which many of them are less than fully understood.[81] Certainly individual words have content, but that content has to be developed by inferences which are drawn from the context as noted above. It is true nevertheless that in spite of a shared cognitive environment a hearer may fail to make the inferences which a speaker intended, or even may make inferences which he did *not* intend.[82] In such cases, the communication may fail. *RT* does, I argue, offer a powerful explanatory model for the success and also the failure of oral and written communication.

---

[80] In this book the speaker or writer is referred to as 'he' and the hearer or reader as 'she'. Blakemore (1987) and R. Blass (1990) use this scheme, while Carston (2002) reverses it. I have selected the former since there is a general assumption that the authors and editors of both the NT books and the pagan Greek literature used were male.

[81] This point is made strongly by Bailey (1976) with reference to the Lucan parables; while there might be many possible readings, complete ignorance of the context will yield less than satisfactory meaning.

[82] Consider John 21:22-23 in which the author claims to show a mistaken inference.

1.6 Arrangement of Chapters

The arrangement of chapters followed in this book is: a discussion of relevance theory, followed by the presentation of various uses of ἵνα in terms of traditional grammar. These have been grouped as independent clauses, indirect commands, noun clauses and purpose clauses. The use of ὅτι is also dealt with, followed by a brief diachronic study of the change in use of ἵνα.

1.6.1 Summary of Chapter 2

This chapter gives a basic introduction to Relevance Theory, focusing on those aspects which are pertinent to the interpretation of ἵνα in Koine Greek. It discusses the principle of relevance on which the theory claims that communication, whether oral or written, is based. Underdeterminacy as a feature of language is then investigated followed by its inevitable concomitant: inferencing. Examples of underdeterminacy and inferencing are given both from modern English and Koine Greek. Procedural markers, which guide a reader in her interpretation, are then introduced as well as the application of this to the present study. Ostensive communication, both verbal and physical, is explained, again with examples from Koine. Finally the concept of metarepresentation which is a crucial part of the analysis presented in this book is demystified and supported by modern examples from English as well as Koine Greek.

1.6.2 Summary of Chapter 3

The discussion of the function of the particle ἵνα begins in this chapter. This is introduced by an investigation of those ἵνα clauses which cannot indicate purpose because they are not preceded, or followed, by a main clause. Since the notion of purpose logically depends on some action which was carried out with a particular end in view, if there is no indication of such action, then the rationale for the clause's identification as telic is not present. Purpose is not the same as intention. Examples from Koine are given, both from the NT and pagan Greek. Scholarly opinion regarding a suitable analysis of these clauses is also adduced, this frequently involving an hypothetical ellipsis of the main clause, although 'imperatival' ἵνα is also dealt with here. In contrast, an analysis of such clauses in terms of the wish, intention or desire of the speaker or author, or the representation of what he thinks *should* be done is presented. The distinction between purpose and intention is discussed, together with the notion of desirable or potential states of affairs.

1.6.3 Summary of Chapter 4

Many ἵνα clauses in the NT follow verbs of praying, asking, commanding or instructing. These verbs, however, are not always followed by this construction. A comparison of parallel passages in the Synoptic Gospels is made to show the inferences which a reader might be expected to draw from the use of a ἵνα clause rather than, for example, direct speech or an infinitival construction.

Although a notion of 'purpose' may be said to lie behind the giving of a command or prayer, this might be better analysed as a 'desirable outcome' since there is no *action* from which 'purpose' could be derived. The subject is rather expressing his will in an utterance which indicates a potential, rather than actual, state of affairs. An *RT* analysis which presents ἵνα as introducing a desirable state of affairs, from the perspective of the subject, is a more satisfactory interpretation of such clauses. Although indirect commands or requests were formerly introduced by the particle ὅπως followed by the indicative mood, or else an infinitival construction, examples of ἵνα clauses following verbs of asking or instructing may be found from the third century BCE onwards. Examples from this period are given, as well as from the NT.

1.6.4 Summary of Chapter 5

Many of the uses of ἵνα in the NT are described as 'noun clauses'. These are frequently epexegetic in that they explicate a noun, adjective or demonstrative in the main clause. Such clauses are particularly frequent in the Gospel of John (x18) but also occur in pagan Greek in the writings of Polybius, Dionysius of Halicarnassus and Epictetus. It is almost impossible to consider these clauses as telic. They did occur in the earlier language, but were rare.[83] Examples of such clauses from the writers mentioned above are given, together with NT examples from the Johannine and Pauline corpus. As with other clause types introduced by this particle, I argue that such noun clauses indicate the thought or wish of the subject, with the particle ἵνα prompting the reader to expect such a representation.

1.6.5 Summary of Chapter 6

The clauses dealt with in this chapter are those which may be considered as truly indicating 'purpose'. They refer to a desired outcome which was the motivation for the action of the main clause. The point is made, however, that many of such clauses refer to attributed purpose, that is: the writer or speaker attributes such a desired outcome as being the motivation for action which he or others have observed. I argue that the writer or speaker is presenting his view of the motivation of another. In many cases we may believe that the subject would refute such an attribution, but humans seem incapable of desisting from attributing such intentions to others, frequently on the basis of very slender evidence. In those cases where the subject is stating his own intention, he is representing his own thought in an utterance and ἵνα, as before, is alerting the reader to read the following clause as such a representation. Again, examples are given from Polybius and Dionysius as well as the NT.

1.6.6 Summary of Chapter 7

It is claimed in earlier chapters that ἵνα is introducing the subject's thought

---

[83] Goodwin (1965 reprint) §357, referencing Demosthenes xvi.28.

concerning a desirable rather than an actual state of affairs, and the use of the subjunctive mood has been said to support such an analysis. A concomitant development in Hellenistic Greek was the great increase in the use of ὅτι with a following indicative verb, rather than the infinitival construction of the classical language. It is of course reasonably likely that the former construction was more frequent in spoken rather than written Greek, even in the fifth century BCE, but it is difficult to find evidence to support this. By the time of Koine ὅτι could be used to introduce direct or indirect speech, as well as causal clauses. Now direct or indirect speech is obviously a representation of the thought of the speaker or another. It reports either directly[84] or by interpretation what someone has said or thought. This particle then gives the reader a signal of such a representation which follows in the clause it introduces.

I argue that in terms of the causal use of this particle someone is also being represented as believing a certain proposition which is presented as a 'state of affairs' by the use of ὅτι with an indicative verb. The speaker might be mistaken or telling lies, but he is presenting as fact a reason for someone's action.[85] Note the difference here between the two particles ἵνα and ὅτι: the former introduces a thought about a state of affairs which is potential and may not in fact be realised, while the latter introduces a clause which claims to be a representation of an actual situation, a real 'state of affairs'. The respective moods used with each particle are claimed to support this analysis.

1.6.7 Summary of Chapter 8

This chapter gives a brief diachronic overview of the relevant developments in the Greek language from the time of Classical Greek through Koine to Modern Greek. The purpose of this is to show that the wider use of ἵνα which is such a prominent feature of NT writings is not a Semitic aberration nor an indication of the supposed semi-literate nature of the language of the NT corpus, but should be seen as a natural development of the language which has continued up to the present day in the use of the particle νά. Greek grammarians themselves do not see this development as alien to the spirit of their language but rather part of the 'genius' of Greek.

Further, the increase in the use of the particle ὅτι (Chapter 7) also fits this pattern which takes into account the general trend in the language from the use of accusative and infinitive to clauses introduced by ἵνα and ὅτι. Explanations are given for this change from linguistic and communicatory perspectives.

---

[84] Said to be 'metalinguistic representation' at footnote 55 of 2.2.2.5. Note examples (8a,b,c) there also.
[85] John 12:5-6 is a good example of this, where the author is rejecting the ostensive reason given by the speaker and giving his own reason for the speaker's utterance, presenting this as an actual state of affairs.

1.6.8 Summary of Chapter 9

The conclusion brings together the evidence for the use of ἵνα with the relevance theoretic approach which claims a unitary analysis for the particle which has been presented in the earlier chapters. It also answers the question: how does this analysis affect the exegesis of biblical text? Several examples of 'difficult' uses of ἵνα are noted here, together with an explanation for such uses in terms of this particle's function as a procedural marker. Such an analysis allows for more than one interpretation of the logical relationship between the dependent clause and the main clause of the sentence, but the reader is guided by the principles of *RT* to take the most relevant of these. In addition, I address the question as to whether or not this conclusion should make any difference to the way in which Koine Greek is taught, and relate the work of earlier scholars to the solution proposed in this book. Finally, suggestions for future work are laid out using *RT* as a basis for such analysis.

1.7 Summary

This book addresses the question of what inferences the implied authors of the New Testament expected their readers and hearers to draw from their use of the particle ἵνα with the subjunctive mood. It refutes the notion that this particle has a fixed meaning in lexical terms, but claims that its function is that of a procedural marker alerting the reader to expect an indication of the speaker or subject's thought, often his desire or intention. It is the responsibility of the reader to draw from the text the most relevant logical relation between the clause introduced by ἵνα and the rest of the sentence. This claim is based on the assumption that a communicator presents information which is relevant to his hearers or readers, and that by using a clause introduced by this particle and in the subjunctive mood, he is inviting the recipients of his communication to draw inferences which would not have been as easily recovered if he had used other grammatical constructions. The use of ἵνα enables the reader or hearer to access the communicative intention of the implied author in a more perspicacious manner than if she was presented with an infinitival construction.

Although the burden of the book is concerned with the use of ἵνα, the use of ὅτι is also relevant here, since it displays a parallel function in signalling a speaker's thought or speech. Its use is therefore noted briefly as confirming the analysis of ἵνα presented in this study.

Throughout the book examples are given not only from the text of the New Testament, but also from the Septuagint and from pagan writers such as Dionysius of Halicarnassus, Polybius and Epictetus, in order to illustrate the wide-ranging nature of the proposed analysis. For the Septuagint and NT examples, I give my own translation into English, but for non biblical material I note the translator after each passage, whether my own (MGS) or that of another (*LCL*:Paton).

CHAPTER 2

Theoretical Basis for Study

2.1 Introduction

Over the past decades, many biblical scholars have used insights from modern linguistic theories to aid them in their analysis of tense-aspect,[1] semantics[2] and authorship of epistolary material.[3] Frequently the scholars have taken an eclectic approach: choosing those aspects of a theory which seemed to be most productive in biblical research, but ignoring those which did not seem pertinent. Further, most biblical scholars seem more comfortable with structuralist theories, which, from the perspective of modern linguistics, are no longer considered to reflect an adequate view of language. In addition to the overt use of linguistic approaches, we should also remember those earlier scholars, such as J.H. Moulton and A.T. Robertson,[4] who dealt with the text in a manner which was truly linguistic albeit without the label of a particular theory. Those scholars tried to understand how Koine Greek *worked* as a language, rather than to apply criteria applicable to the earlier classical language.

> It is the task and duty of the N.T. student to apply the results of linguistic research to the Greek of the N.T. But, strange to say, this has not been adequately done.[5]

Frequently biblical scholars view linguistics with a hermeneutic of suspicion, and not unreasonably since there is little genuine dialogue between the two disciplines and those who analyse the biblical text from a linguistic perspective have frequently ignored the contributions of biblical scholars over decades. Further, it is not always recognised that biblical scholars frequently make linguistic decisions on the text although they do not use linguistic

---

[1] Stanley Porter (1989) who uses Halliday's Systemic Grammar.
[2] Barr (1961); Danove (1993) using Fillmore's Construction Grammar.
[3] Reed (1993) who claims to use Brown & Yule (1983), Grimes (1976), Halliday and Hasan (1980) and Longacre (1983), among others for his understanding of discourse analysis.
[4] Horsley (1989) re Robertson: p. 59 'His grasp of developments in NT philology is masterly, not to say magisterial; and the judiciousness of his assessment of the contribution of various individuals still rings true half a century later'.
[5] *ATR* p. 3 who also quotes Samuel Dickey in *Princeton Theological Review*, Oct., 1903: 'And despite the enormous advances since the days of Winer towards a rational and unitary concept of the N.T. language, we still labour today under the remains of the old conceptions.'

language to explain their conclusions.

The linguistic concept of pragmatics, in particular, has a great deal to offer interpreters, either literary or biblical. The theory which I utilise for this study may be described as pragmatic, being concerned with the way in which speakers and hearers, or writers and readers, communicate with one another. At this point it may be useful to consider two definitions of the term 'pragmatics' which are helpful without being encumbered with linguistic terminology. The first is Geoffrey Leech's concise account of the term as 'the study of meaning in relation to speech situations'.[6] The second by David Crystal is more explicit in expanding what the concept of language in use might be:

> the study of LANGUAGE from the point of view of the users, especially of the choices they make, the CONSTRAINTS they encounter in using language in social interaction, and the effects their use of language has on the other participants in an act of communication[7]

Pragmatics then deals with language in use, which is with the context of utterances. It accounts for the drawing of inferences from shared knowledge such as common cultural assumptions and systems of belief as well as the physical and verbal context of the utterance. It assumes that although individual words may carry some lexical meaning, this is inadequate for successful communication and requires enrichment by the context in which they occur. This may be exemplified briefly by the potentially different translations of the word πράξεις in Acts 19:18. This word has a wide semantic field, but the context, the burning of magical scrolls, invites the reader to select the word 'spells' as the most likely or relevant meaning.[8]

Recently this concept of pragmatics has become an accepted tool for biblical studies.[9] A particular branch of pragmatics is Relevance Theory, and it is with the application of this theory to aspects of Greek grammar that this book is concerned.

2.2 Relevance Theory
2.2.1 General Background

Since in biblical studies context is seen to be an essential component in the analysis of text, pragmatic enrichment of that text by inference is inevitable. This may be described as deriving inferences from social context, historical

---

[6] Leech (1983) p. 6.
[7] Crystal (1999 3rd ed.) p. 271.
[8] So Bruce (1951) p. 359 and Barrett (2002 reprint) p.912. There is much more to be said on this, but that is not the focus of this chapter, the above example being given to illustrate the underdeterminacy of language even at word level.
[9] For example Pattemore's work on Revelation (2004) and Gene Green's application of Relevance Theory to hermeneutics (2002).

reconstruction or literary approaches, but *de facto* what a reader does in order to make text intelligible is to derive from her[10] background knowledge inferences which are not explicitly stated in the text. If such background knowledge is not available, the text will remain obscure. The concept I have described as background knowledge is customarily referred to as encyclopaedic knowledge: 'the entirety of participants' knowledge of the world.'[11] When there is no sharing of such encyclopaedic knowledge then communication may, and usually does, fail.[12]

The use of inference in communication has been the focus of the theory of communication mentioned above: Relevance Theory. Introduced by Dan Sperber and Deirdre Wilson,[13] Relevance Theory,[14] describes the principles behind the cognitive processes by which the mind selects the interpretation of an utterance. In other words, it deals with the way in which speakers of a language understand one another. It accounts for the importance of encyclopaedic knowledge in successful communication and draws attention to the fact that the text or utterance may be public, but the speaker's intention and the hearer's interpretation are not.

RT claims to be a theory of communication, putting forward a hypothesis concerning how speakers use and how hearers process language.[15] Its proponents contrast their approach with older models which view language as a code which associates thoughts with sound. The real problem with such a code model is that it is only one part of the way in which we derive meaning. In fact we communicate with one another all the time by a much more complex but intuitive process, namely by drawing inferences not only from the actual words spoken, but also from the physical context of speaker and hearer as well as from a body of shared knowledge. It is this attention to the inferential process in communication which makes *RT* such a useful model for the interpretation of biblical texts.

Most biblical scholars actually *use* the inferential process in coming to conclusions. John Barclay's article on 'mirror reading' is a case in point. In dealing with Pauline correspondence he shows that readers have to infer the situation and perhaps even the complaints which were being raised by the

---

[10] Recall that in this book the hearer or reader is referred to as 'she'. See Chapter 1 footnote 80.

[11] Levinson (1984) p. 21.

[12] The accusation of John the Baptist against Herod and Herodias has been taken to be based on John's dislike of levirate marriage by readers who do not share knowledge of the fact that his brother Philip was still alive, but who do have the concept of wife inheritance (Matthew 14:3-4; Mark 6:17-18).

[13] Sperber and Wilson (1986, 1995).

[14] Hereafter *RT*.

[15] Although the literature deals more with oral than written communication, it has been applied to written texts by literary critics such as Ian MacKenzie (2002), and students of translation such as Almazan Garcia (2002).

addressees of the letter. This process is described as 'mirror reading', using one side of a conversation to infer the respondent's contribution. He describes inferences on a scale from 'certain' or 'virtually certain' to 'highly unlikely'.[16] Many other scholars also draw inferences but are unaware of a theoretical account which claims to validate such a procedure. Also they seldom articulate the inferences on which their conclusions are based. Since the interpretation of all text involves inferences, the explication of these makes clear the way in which the conclusion is reached. The discipline of outlining the inferences or contextual assumptions on which a conclusion is based is extremely helpful in delineating the strength, or otherwise, of an argument.

RT also has the explanatory power to deal with secondary communication, which is text which was not in the first instance addressed to the readers who later try to interpret it, such as the New Testament. For these reasons, namely its explanatory power in dealing with both pragmatic inferencing and secondary communication, *RT* will be used as the theoretical basis on which to investigate the use of ἵνα in Koine Greek.

2.2.2 Delineation of Theory

The publication of the first edition of *Relevance* in 1986 marked a very different approach to the interpretation of utterances. The authors claimed that the main principle driving successful communication was the principle of relevance, namely that a speaker assumes that a hearer listens to what he has to say because she is interested in it: it has relevance for her.[17] We do not merely throw words at one another; those words relate to situations, contexts in which both speaker and hearer share a common body of knowledge.[18] The principle which drives communication according to Sperber and Wilson is that of relevance. Humans do not make remarks, or even signs, without an assumption that the hearer will increase her knowledge by listening or will be able to reassess some information previously held. This does not necessarily, or even usually, involve a conscious process, but even a superficial consideration of why we communicate with one another involves the belief that the listener will have some interest in what we have to say. This might not necessarily be of benefit to the hearer, but it will be relevant to her. Even those situations in which a speaker wants to obtain information may give some relevance to a hearer. Consider how often we are unwilling to ask a question or for help

---

[16] Barclay (1987) pp. 73-93; in *RT* terms these would be classified as 'strong' and 'weak' implicatures.

[17] Recall that the speaker or writer will be referred to as 'he', and the hearer or reader as 'she'.

[18] If this condition is not fulfilled then communication *may* fail, but the principle of relevance will lead a hearer to persevere until she 'makes sense' of the utterance.

Theoretical Basis

because of the inferences which the hearer will draw from such a request.[19] Sperber and Wilson then allow that words communicate ideas, but that the principle which decides their interpretation in terms of disambiguating pronominal reference and multiple senses is that of relevance.

Certain theoretical constructs are involved in the outworking of this principle such as: inferencing, underdeterminacy, metarepresentation and ostention. If language is underdetermined, then inferences are required to make a communication successful. If utterances are a representation of human thought, then humans must be communicating such representations both of their own thought and that of others. It is reasonable to believe that they may alert a hearer to expect such a representation by giving her procedural instructions, or by making it obvious that they intend to make something clear to her: ostention.

It is necessary to examine these concepts, but it is my intention to keep the terminology as simple as possible, since this study is not primarily addressed to a linguistic audience but is concerned with biblical studies. We shall consider each construct in turn together with the implications it has for the interpretation of text.

2.2.2.1 INFERENCES

In the physical world humans begin to infer as soon as they see another human, before verbal communication has begun.[20] Although this may seem to be situationally distinct from the interpretation of NT text, it does demonstrate the strong role that inference plays in interpreting human behaviour as well as human speech, and in addition, can be seen to be a factor in certain narrative contexts in the NT also.[21] Consider then from the example below the way in which we infer conclusions from observed behaviour, with no word being spoken:

The scene is a kitchen with a pile of unwashed dishes lying beside a sink. Two people enter and one of them removes his jacket and rolls up his sleeves. The other then may respond by saying (1) or even (2):

Example (1) You're going to wash the dishes?
Example (2) Shall I dry?

There was no word spoken from which a conclusion such as (1) could be deduced, but the reasonableness of the statement comes from our ability to infer from the actions of taking off a jacket and rolling up sleeves that some work is going to be done. When the contextual information of a sink and a pile of dirty

---

[19] Consider John 4:27; 21:12 and the author's presentation of the disciples as reluctant to ask a question.
[20] See Carston (2002) p. 43 for elaboration of this point.
[21] See Mark 3:1-2; John 4:27; 11:31; Acts 21:27-29 for inferencing which began from viewing actions or even potential actions.

dishes is added, we can infer a conclusion. Humans seem to do this all the time, both with and without speech. In fact the question asked in (1) might be seen as quite unnecessary, since the answer is obvious, and (2) would be a more relevant, and appreciated, response.

Explaining the success of such communication as Examples (1) and (2) is a problem for older theories, since there is no 'code' which can be translated.[22] Gestures for example work only by inference. Of course cross-culturally these can be misinterpreted: gestures such as winking or giggling are interpreted very differently across cultures, but within a culture, the one gesturing usually assumes that the observer finds his actions relevant because of their shared cultural assumptions. Although words may communicate ideas, it is the principle of relevance which decides their interpretation in terms of disambiguation, assigning of pronomial reference and speaker attitude.[23]

The inferences which a hearer will draw are constrained by relevance. If there are several possible interpretations of an utterance, a hearer will derive the most easily accessible which *RT* defines as the most relevant. Consider the following example:[24]

Example (3) A. I studied Greek for 4 years in Athens.
B. Wow!

The hearer has inferred from the words 'Greek' and 'Athens' that the speaker studied in the capital city of Greece. For her, that is the most easily accessible interpretation, given the use of the words 'Greek' and 'Athens'. In fact the speaker studied in Athens, Georgia. This is *not* an inference which a non-American would find readily accessible, and even for an American, the most *relevant* interpretation would locate the place of study as Greece. The speaker knows that the hearer has recovered the most *relevant* interpretation, indeed he has guided her to it by the use of 'Greek' and 'Athens' with no indication that the 'Athens' in question is in USA. This is called *ostensive* [25] behaviour: the speaker intended the hearer to draw this conclusion, and also to be impressed!

The hearer, however, may have drawn a further inference which led to her being impressed: *The speaker must speak good (Modern) Greek.*[26] This

---

[22] Paul Grice (1989 reprint of earlier articles) recognised this facility of which humans are capable, but scarcely aware, but Sperber and Wilson have developed his ideas into a full theory of communication.

[23] Consider the way in which close friends may use derogatory language in addressing one another, but the recipient takes this as a sign of affection. The speaker's attitude overrides the meaning of the words in isolation.

[24] This interchange was heard during August, 2004 and is used with the speaker's permission.

[25] See 2.2.2.7.

[26] An italic font is used for the inferences a hearer makes but does not necessarily articulate.

Theoretical Basis 27

inference would not have been drawn if the speaker had given more information. The concept of *informativeness* (so Grice) or *manifestness* (*RT*) requires that a speaker gives sufficient information for the hearer to disambiguate, but only as much as is necessary or adequate, in *RT* terms: *relevant*. Example (4), by giving more information, removes the ambiguity from one of the pieces of information, but as a result, creates in the mind of the hearer another one:

> Example (4) A. I studied Greek for 4 years at a seminary in Athens in Georgia.
> B. Modern Greek?

The combination of 'Greek' and 'seminary' will cause the hearer some difficulty. If, however, she understands that a 'seminary' is the usual term for a 'theological college', then she may be able to access a further inference: *He is studying biblical Greek.*

2.2.2.2 HOW INFERENCES ARE SAID TO BE DRAWN

Wilson[27] points out that 'inferential comprehension starts from the recovery of a linguistically encoded sentence meaning, which is typically quite fragmentary and incomplete.' In other words, successful communication is not dependent on a speaker saying everything which he 'means'.[28] He gives a stimulus in the form of certain words, but then contextual information enables the hearer to build up her understanding of the speaker or author's intention. The physical environment and earlier communication between the communicators may account for such contextual information. Further, there will be a body of information which is shared by a wider community: shared contextual assumptions. Both contextual information and shared contextual assumptions aid the speaker in communicating and the hearer in interpreting utterances. Consider a straightforward example from Acts 16:13:

> Example (5) On the Sabbath, we went out of the gate to the river where we thought there was prayer, and sitting down we spoke with the women who had gathered there.

This sentence requires inferences to be made, most of which would be easily drawn by the first readers:

On the Sabbath day Jews met together to pray.
If there was no synagogue in a Gentile town they might meet outside the town.
If there were less than ten Jewish men in a town there would be no

---

[27] Wilson (2000), p. 137.
[28] See 2.2.2.4 for a discussion of underdeterminacy.

synagogue.
If possible Jews choose to site a synagogue near water.[29]
Teachers sat down to teach.

RT claims that a hearer will 'follow the path of least effort'.[30] If such a path leads to a relevant meaning, then the hearer will stop processing. If, however, the search for relevance is not fulfilled, the hearer will move on to a less accessible interpretation, described by Sperber[31] as 'cautious optimism'. Hearers *do* try to make sense of what they hear: this seems to be an intrinsic part of human cognition. They will continue to derive inferences in their attempt to find relevance until the processing effort seems to be greater than the information to be communicated.[32] At this point the hearer stops processing, since the principle of relevance has not been met.

2.2.2.3 CONDITIONS FOR SUCCESSFUL COMMUNICATION
We have considered briefly what Sperber and Wilson contend is the overall principle of communicative success, namely relevance, but this is dependent on a competent and benevolent speaker or writer. We must also take into account the attitude of the speaker: is he being as informative or as truthful as he should or could be? A speaker may tell lies, be deliberately vague or merely be a poor communicator. Sperber[33] addresses this issue by positing three strategies which a hearer will employ in attempting interpretation:

naïve optimism;
cautious optimism;
sophisticated understanding.

Naïve optimism - this is the 'path of least effort' referred to in the section above. The interpretation which is the most relevant to the hearer is the one selected. If this does not produce an utterance which is understandable, then a hearer will move on to *cautious optimism*. In this approach, the hearer believes that the speaker is being truthful, but is perhaps not as competent as he should be in his communicative strategy. The hearer therefore will move on to the next most relevant interpretation.

---

[29] Note Barrett (2002 reprint) p. 781 for a discussion on this issue. The variant manuscripts may give evidence of inferences which were not accepted by all.
[30] Wilson (2000) p. 137.
[31] Sperber (1994) p. 189.
[32] Being extremely condensed, newspaper headlines often fall into this category: a reader makes several attempts at interpretation, changing word classes etc. until she either feels that she has understood or abandons the attempt.
[33] Sperber (1994).

Theoretical Basis 29

Should the hearer suspect, however, that the speaker is *not* being truthful,[34] she will move on to a *sophisticated understanding* of the communication. Some hearers are much more inclined to take this path which treats with suspicion the intentions of the speaker.[35] The hearer knows that the speaker wants her to process the information with naïve optimism, but suspects strongly that he has another agenda. A sophisticated understanding should be able to uncover the speaker's real communicative intention (*he wants me to believe that...*), perhaps by using other relevant contextual or encyclopaedic information, while suspending judgement on its reliability.[36]

Sperber claims that the universal human ability to use such strategies, with the concomitant inferences, is based on the ability to metarepresent what someone is thinking: mindreading, in colloquial terms. We shall consider below what is meant by such a term and the role the process plays in utterance comprehension, but first we must take up the issue which was raised above, namely the fact that a speaker or writer does not say all that he 'means'. In *RT* this is described as *underdeterminacy*.

2.2.2.4 UNDERDETERMINACY
Sperber and Wilson note[37] that a communicator does not require to articulate all his communicative intent:

> all that is required is that the properties of the ostensive stimulus (i.e. the utterance) should set the inferential process on the right track; to do this they need not represent or encode the communicator's informative intention in any detail.

In lay language this statement claims that a speaker does not require to spell out every detail of his potential communication. To do so would make communication overloaded and so be less relevant to the hearer, or even as in Example (6a,b,c) allow her to draw unintended inferences. Example (5) would be overloaded if the inferences noted there had been made overt in the communication. This aspect of *RT* is developed in much more detail by Robyn Carston who points out the extent to which inferencing operates, even before an utterance has been completed.[38] She also points out that underdeterminacy may operate at different levels such as ambiguous words, pronominal reference, or

---

[34] That is 'benevolent' in Sperber's terminology.
[35] There is a strong connection here between the use of a 'hermeneutic of suspicion' in biblical interpretation, and what is termed a strategy of 'sophisticated understanding' in *RT*.
[36] Consider Examples (11) and (17) from Polybius in Chapter 7, and also John 12:6 where the implied author rejects the speech and reasoning of Judas, putting forward instead his own belief about the latter's motives, noted in Example (16), 2.2.2.7.
[37] Sperber and Wilson (1995) p. 254.
[38] Consider also how often we complete a sentence for a speaker if he hesitates. We fill in what seems relevant to us.

missing constituents.[39] A hearer disambiguates, assigns identity to a referent or supplies a constituent by making the necessary inferences. Consider the following minimal, but common, conversational exchange which is substantially underdetermined in terms of both pronominal reference and missing constituents:

Example (6a) Coffee?
Example (6b) No thanks.

Example (6a) requires a substantial amount of inferencing, but this is supplied by the hearer, presumably from the shared context, who gives in (6b) an equally underdetermined, but communicatively acceptable answer. If a speaker were to say everything he meant, supplying all the referents, the utterance would become verbose and cause the reader/hearer too much processing effort. Too much processing effort leads to the hearer abandoning the attempt at understanding. Another potential difficulty about making an utterance such as (6b) more explicit (6c)

Example (6c) No, I do not want any coffee thank you.

is the inferences, unintended by the speaker, which a hearer might make, such as: *She is annoyed with me* or *She thinks I'm stupid*. Saying more than we require will give rise to unintended inferences such as these, or cause the hearer to abandon the attempt to understand because there is a surfeit of information, much of which could have been inferred.

We make many inferences from everything we hear or observe and take huge, but usually logical, leaps from sounds to meaning. Sometimes, of course, these inferences are neither well founded, nor part of the speaker or writer's intended communication, but in spite of this, we do usually succeed in conveying information to one another with much less than full propositions.[40]

2.2.2.4.1 SHARED CONTEXTUAL ASSUMPTIONS
A further area in which we underdetermine is the assumption of a shared body of knowledge. The information which each individual has in a mental store is usually referred to as *encyclopaedic information*. We make statements which are only comprehensible by accessing such encyclopaedic information. To give every piece of conceivably relevant information would, as stated above, make our communication too difficult to process. On the other hand, if such information is not available to the reader, then she will be unable to recover the

---

[39] Carston (2002) p. 28.
[40] Consider biblical material in which there is said to be ellipsis, such as Galatians 2:9, 10 or John 1:8. Because it is secondary communication, modern readers differ about the inferences to be made in these passages.

Theoretical Basis 31

writer's communicative intention. Shared contextual assumptions will include encyclopaedic information available to both parties in communication, indeed they are essential for successful communication, but with NT texts we have to acknowledge that the original readers or hearers shared assumptions and encyclopaedic knowledge with the implied authors which we do not. Consider the following example from John 18:28:

> Example (7) They themselves did not enter the praetorium so that they might not be contaminated but might eat the Passover.

In this example the writer assumes that the whole cultural and religious background of the Jewish people in first century Palestine is available to his readers.[41] The contextual background did not require to be explained because it was assumed. The relevance of the statement that the Jews did not enter the praetorium because they wanted to eat the Passover is assumed by the communicator, but the reader has inferences to draw. Without shared contextual assumptions a reader will be unable to elicit such necessary inferences as:

Roman soldiers were present in the praetorium.
Physical contact with non-Jews made Jews ceremonially unclean.
No Jew who was ceremonially unclean could eat the Passover meal.

Such pragmatic inferencing may be described as 'social context' or 'historical reconstruction', but the logical steps which a reader takes in order to make this text relevant consist in drawing inferences which are not recoverable from the text itself, but from shared contextual assumptions or encyclopaedic knowledge.[42]

2.2.2.4.2 UNDERDETERMINACY IN PARTICIPLES

It is widely recognised in the traditional grammars that participles in Greek (classical or koine) are not morphologically marked to indicate their logical relation to the main verb of a sentence.[43] Only the context can determine what such a logical relationship might be, that is whether or not it is concessive,[44] conditional,[45] causal,[46] or even combinations of these. Temporal and causal

---

[41] The question of secondary communication is relevant here.
[42] The power of *RT* lies in its ability to explicate this communicative process which has always been part of biblical scholarship.
[43] Sim, M.G. (2004).
[44] John 12:37 πεποιηκότος, although he had done; Matthew 7:11 πονηροὶ ὄντες, although you are evil.
[45] Acts 17:25 προσδεόμενός τινος, as if he needed anything.
[46] Luke 7:42 μὴ ἐχόντων αὐτῶν ἀποδοῦναι, because they had no means of repaying.

relations in particular frequently co-occur. Further the temporal relation of such participles to the main verb is regularly derived by inference rather than the tense of the participle. Certainly present participles are usually contemporaneous with the main verb, although examples where this is not strictly chronological may be found.[47] Perfect participles are an exception,[48] but aorist participles are particularly underdetermined, their relationship being potentially contemporaneous with,[49] prior to[50] or even subsequent to[51] the main verb. Biblical scholars recognise this fact, but *RT* deals with it theoretically by describing such participles as 'underdetermined' in terms of temporal reference and logical relationship.

2.2.2.4.3 UNDERDETERMINACY IN PARTICLES

Certain particles may also be analysed as underdetermined. It is more useful to consider what the function of particles such as καί, δέ, γάρ, οὖν and others might be, rather than to insist on a fixed dictionary meaning for each, particularly since different authors invite different inferences from their use. In addition they function at different points in the discourse, linking clauses, or sentences or even paragraphs. This is inferred pragmatically from the way in which they interact with the context, both textually and in terms of background information.[52] Many particles give instructions to the reader to process what follows in a particular way. This aspect of the theory will be utilised in the subsequent treatment of ἵνα, but will be dealt with in more detail at 2.2.2.6.

2.2.2.5 METAREPRESENTATION

In section 2.2.2.3 above, I noted Sperber[53] as claiming that the universal human ability to use interpretive strategies, such as cautious optimism or sophisticated understanding, was based on the ability to metarepresent what someone is thinking. Although humans have this ability and use it constantly, we do not use it consciously.

In describing the way in which speakers communicate with one another, *RT* suggests that every utterance, spoken or written, is a *representation* of the

---

[47] Acts 19:18 ἤρχοντο ἐξομολογούμενοι καὶ ἀναγγέλλοντες they came confessing and telling.

[48] Consider Acts 19:18 where the perfect participle clearly indicates that the believers in focus had become so *before* this incident took place, a fact which is not made clear in most translations.

[49] Matthew 3:15 ἀποκριθεὶς...εἶπεν, he said in reply.

[50] Matthew 2:4 συναγαγών...ἐπυνθάνετο, gathering (them) together he inquired.

[51] Matthew 2:8 πέμψας αὐτοὺς ...εἶπεν, sending them (i.e. before he sent them) he said.

[52] This is not peculiar to *RT*: Denniston (1953) and Rijksbaron (1997) treat particles in the classical language in a similar manner, as does S. Black (2002) for the koine, although none of them use the term 'underdetermined'.

[53] Sperber (1994).

Theoretical Basis

thought of the speaker or writer. It does not attempt to map in detail the mind's conversion of thought into verbal utterance, but is satisfied with stating that an oral or written utterance *represents* a thought of the speaker or writer. As we communicate we regularly represent not only our own thoughts, but the thoughts of others, either by direct or indirect speech, thus claiming to *represent* the utterance of the speaker or writer. Frequently we do this with no conscious thought of the fact of representation. Sperber and Wilson point out[54] that 'direct quotations are the most obvious examples of utterances used to represent not what they describe but what they resemble.'[55]

As well as direct quotations, however, we refer to the beliefs or comments of others regularly, even if this is done tangentially in the form of evidentials.[56] Such representation is said to be *interpretively used*. In addition to reporting the utterances of others, humans also seem to attribute to them thoughts and intentions, thus *interpretively representing* their thought: 'Humans can no more refrain from attributing intentions than they can from batting their eyelids.'[57] Consider the following descriptions and then attributions of 'purpose':

Example (8a) George said, 'I parked there to annoy Mary.'
Example (8b) George said that he parked there to annoy Mary.
Example (8c) George parked there to annoy Mary.

Example (8a) and (8b) represent in direct (8a) and indirect speech (8b) a purpose which George stated. In Example (8b), there is an element of interpretation, in that the quotation is not verbatim, but interprets George's utterance. In both (8a) & (8b), George may not have been telling the truth, or he may have been using irony: for example he may be quoting Mary's understanding of his parking behaviour.[58] The speaker, however, makes no claim about the truth value of George's statement. He merely reports it descriptively (8a) or interpretively (8b). In Example (8c), however, the speaker attributes a purpose to George which does not claim to be based on his utterance, although it may be, but on the speaker's inference from George's action. The speaker's utterance is therefore a second order metarepresentation[59]

---

[54] Sperber and Wilson (1996) p. 228.
[55] Direct quotation has been referred to more recently as *metalinguistic representation*, because of the close resemblance between the original and the quotation. Gutt (2004) unpublished paper, Almazan Garcia (2002).
[56] These may be asides such as 'it seems', 'evidently', 'apparently' etc. but they all presuppose an utterance by a third party. The speaker is not taking responsibility for his own comments, but attributing them to another. See Ifantidou (1994).
[57] Sperber (1994) p. 187.
[58] See Noh (2000) for discussion of the *RT* approach to irony.
[59] The term 'metarepresentation' is used throughout the *RT* literature, but for ease of communication I have simplified this to 'representation'. The reader should understand that this description may indicate several orders of representation, that is: it may indicate

of a thought or intention:

Speaker's thought: *George parked there to annoy Mary.*
George's thought as inferred by the speaker: *If I park there I will annoy Mary.*

Sperber[60] claims that all speakers have such interpretive abilities, although it is also acknowledged that people displaying certain syndromes such as Asperger's or autism may not have developed the ability to access more than second order metarepresentation.[61] It has also been observed that very young children do not metarepresent beyond such level: ironic utterances are usually wasted on young children, as most parents will realise. Nevertheless the understanding of the crucial role which metarepresentation plays in the interpretation of utterances, and of course in communication in general, is a major component of the analysis of ἵνα and other particles which I present in this book.

In addition then to representing our own thoughts and the utterances of others descriptively, we may also represent the thoughts of others interpretively, attributing intention to them which they may or may not acknowledge, as (8c). Further, we may make an utterance about the real world, that is about a state of affairs in the real world, or alternatively we may express our attitude to the real world or to a potential situation, described as a potential state of affairs. Consider the following examples:

Example (9) Peter came to the house today.

This utterance *represents* the speaker's thought, but is a description of an observable situation in the real world: a state of affairs. If, on the other hand, a speaker says:

Example (10) I wanted Peter to come to the house today.

he may be 'describing' in saying 'I wanted', but in the following clause he is not describing an actual 'state of affairs' but *representing* a *desirable* state of affairs.[62] This desirable state of affairs might never happen. The utterance

---

a representation of a representation. Although this simplification may not be acceptable to linguists it has seemed to me to be necessary in presenting this concept to a wider audience.

[60] Sperber p. 187.

[61] This aspect of *RT* is dealt with in much more detail in Wilson (2000), which includes extracts from L.H. Willey's *Pretending to be Normal: Living with Asperger's Syndrome* (London: Jessica Kingsley Publishers, 1999).

[62] In Chapters 3 to 6 it will be seen that in Koine Greek writers frequently chose to mark such representation of a 'desirable' state of affairs by the use of ἵνα with the subjunctive.

indicates the speaker's attitude to a potential state of affairs: Peter's coming to the house. I shall use this distinction in analysing the clauses which are introduced by ἵνα or ὅτι in Koine Greek.

At the heart of metarepresentation, whether first order or beyond, that is representing the thoughts of others, is the concept of the transfer of thought to utterance. The utterance will then be enriched by the recovery of inferences which should lead the hearer or reader to an understanding of the communicative intention of the speaker/writer. Sometimes, in order to make a metarepresentation more salient, procedural markers will be used to highlight the interpretive nature of the utterance. These will be considered in more detail in 2.2.2.6.

According to *RT*, the notion of metarepresentation is foundational for the understanding of figures of speech such as metaphor and irony. It claims to give a more satisfactory account of these tropes than traditional literary analysis. This is based on the notion that when a speaker uses a metaphor he is loosely resembling his thought or that of someone else. The use of an underdetermined or 'loose' expression may give rise to a wider and richer range of inferences for the hearer than a carefully explicit sentence. Consider the following example from Acts 20:29:

Example (11) I know that after my departure fierce wolves will come in to you, not sparing the flock…

The speaker may have been representing his thought: *Men will infiltrate the church and destroy it* but the use of metaphor, known in *RT* as loose resemblance, allows the hearers to draw a much more vivid conclusion and to have a graphic picture of destruction which a literal representation would not have accomplished.[63] Since this aspect of *RT*, the treatment of metaphor, is only tangentially relevant to this study I do not intend to expand this notion, but instead to give more attention to a particular trope that has more significance for my topic, namely irony.

When a speaker metarepresents someone else's utterance and expresses his attitude towards it, that representation is said to be *echoic* in *RT* terms. Consider a very simple example of this:

Example (12) A: 'I'm going to town tomorrow.'
B: 'You're going to town tomorrow?'

Here B is not merely repeating what A has just said, but in repeating is giving rise to her attitude and several weak inferences such as: B is astonished at this information or B is relating this utterance to her own agenda, and plans that A

---

[63] This is explained in much more detail in Noh (2000), but is only referred to here as an introduction to the *RT* account of irony.

do something for her while in town.

Frequently a hearer may echo a previous utterance in order to disagree with it, or express surprise at its content. Consider the following dialogue in John 8:56 from many similar in the same chapter:

> Example (13) 'Abraham your father rejoiced that he should see my day; he both saw it and rejoiced.'
> 'You are not yet fifty and you have seen Abraham?'

The repetition here is not verbatim, but is a loose resemblance of the first utterance. The attitude of the respondents to the first utterance is clear: they echo in order to express incredulity. There are many examples of this in the NT, but this is introduced in order to lead further into the particular echoic use which is irony.

Traditionally the literary analysis of irony[64] has been the articulation of a proposition which the speaker does not mean to be taken literally: in short saying the opposite of what one means. This definition, although popular, is very misleading. In everyday life if someone says the opposite of what is true, although not what they mean, it is regarded as lying. The crucial feature which makes irony work is the hearer's recognition that the speaker does not believe what he is saying and expects the hearer to recognise that also. If the hearer does not recognise this, then communication has failed. *RT* defines irony as 'a type of echoic language by which a speaker tacitly communicates a mocking or, at least, a dissociative attitude to a representation which she attributes to someone other than herself at the time of the utterance'.[65] The difficulty in making irony successful is that its very use is dependent on a lack of overt marking.[66] When we use the word 'ironically' in an utterance it is usually a reference to situational and not verbal irony. Consider the following dialogue from 1Kings 22:15 (*NIV*) in which there is no verbal signal of irony, but the utterance is taken ironically and not literally:

> Example (14) When he arrived, the king asked him, 'Micaiah, shall we go to war against Ramoth Gilead, or shall I refrain?'
> 'Attack and be victorious,' he answered.

---

[64] Only verbal irony is being dealt with here. Biblical scholars frequently treat texts as 'ironic' but it is almost always situational irony which is in focus. A particular example of this is Camery-Hoggatt (1992) who deals with situational irony in Mark although he does not specify this.

[65] Carston (2002) p. 378.

[66] In speech a particular accent or intonation may be used to indicate the representation of another's utterance, but in text this is much more difficult. Consider the comments of MacKenzie (2002) footnote 12 p. 220 *re* Tom Stoppard's suggestion of a typeface for irony.

The king said to him, 'How many times must I make you swear to tell me nothing but the truth in the name of the Lord?'
Then Micaiah answered, 'I saw all Israel scattered on the hills like sheep without a shepherd, and the Lord said, "These people have no master. Let each one go home in peace."'

In this example the king recognises that Micaiah is distancing himself from his utterance. When he challenges the latter to 'speak the truth' Micaiah gives his own opinion or rather the prophecy which he claims to have received. Micaiah's first utterance is an echo of what previous prophets have said to the king. Micaiah then repeats this but the king recognises his dissociative attitude. This example is fairly straightforward, but others in the biblical text may be more controversial, such as Mark 7:27 and Matthew 15:26. The crucial diagnostic for identification of irony is the knowledge that the speaker does not himself believe what he has uttered. If this is not recognised, then communication fails. The contextual effects which the speaker hoped to create by the use of this trope are then not available to the hearer.

2.2.2.6 PROCEDURAL MARKERS

In 2.2.2.5. I argued that procedural markers are sometimes used by a speaker or writer to guide the reader's interpretation of an utterance. Following on the initial publications on *RT*, Diane Blakemore further suggested that certain particles and discourse markers did not so much contribute a concept to the sentence or utterance in which they occurred, but guided the hearer in processing such an utterance. Her initial work[67] was with markers such as *but, after all, also, you see*, but others[68] have followed her in proposing other particles, and in languages other than English, which guide the hearer's understanding either of what has preceded such a marker, or what follows. Carston describes this function as 'reducing the inferential work that the addressee has to do in order to understand the utterance.'[69]

Now this proposal has much to commend it as a description of the way in which many particles operate in Koine Greek. For example, rather than considering οὖν or γάρ as having a fixed lexical content such as 'therefore' 'so' or 'for' 'because' we could more profitably view them as markers which guide the reader in her interpretation.[70] The particle οὖν would then instruct the reader to process that sentence as a conclusion to or deduction from what has gone before. The particle γάρ would then instruct her to process the information in that clause as supporting what has gone before, although not necessarily in the previous sentence. In this way the function of the particle is

---

[67] Blakemore (1987).
[68] R. Blass (1990), Carston (2000) etc.
[69] Carston (2002) p. 162.
[70] See R. Blass (1993).

being addressed, rather than any fixed semantic content being assigned.[71] We have already mentioned[72] the fact that participles in Greek leave their logical relationship with the main verb to be inferred from the context, but sometimes the reader is guided towards this relationship by a procedural marker, such as καίπερ, which directs her to read the relationship as concessive.[73]

In English also there are many discourse particles which almost defy semantic analysis, but which certainly contribute to the way in which a hearer processes an utterance. Consider the particle 'well' either as a sentence initial particle or an exclamation. A hearer is guided to believe that something interesting, different or even contrastive to what has gone before will be forthcoming, but this does not come from our attributing a lexical meaning to this introductory word.[74] An interesting example of a procedural marker to introduce a representation of a speaker's thought in modern colloquial English is the word 'like':

Example (15) 'I'm like: Why is he saying this?'
conservative English gloss: I wondered why he was saying this.

Such a gloss, however, does not do justice to the dramatic effect of the representation introduced by 'like' and this personal ascription 'I'm'. The procedural marker 'like' indicates that the speaker did not actually *say* this, but thought it, the following utterance being a resemblance of his thought. It also indicates his attitude, and in a more dramatic way than the more conservative gloss. In *RT* terms it might be said that the contextual effects derived from the use of this marker and the representation which it introduces are considerably richer also.

It is my argument that the particle ἵνα in Koine Greek guides the reader in processing the subsequent clause as a representation. That is, it leads the reader to infer the speaker's attitude which may indicate his intention or desire.[75] This representation may then be an attributed purpose, an indirect command, a wish or an explication of a previous clause, but the context, including the semantic content of the verb in the main clause, will determine this. If this particle is viewed in this way, then it should no longer be considered as having a fixed semantic meaning of 'in order that', a meaning which does not actually fit 40%

---

[71] Of course the issue of translation is still present, but when the function has been determined a suitable way of indicating that can be found. Frequently in English translations multiple occurrences of γάρ are simply ignored.
[72] See section 2.2.2.4.2.
[73] So Hebrews 5:8; 7:5; 12:17.
[74] See Nicole (2004) for a detailed analysis of this particle.
[75] Rouchota (1994) claims that the subjunctive in Modern Greek indicates speaker attitude and νά 'marks' the subjunctive. I suggest that in Koine Greek this particle might be a procedural marker guiding the reader to interpret the clause following, which has a verb in the subjunctive mood, as expressing the speaker's attitude.

Theoretical Basis 39

of the particle's occurrences in the NT or in Epictetus. In terms of translation, the context will give the necessary clues to this. The particle is guiding the reader, rather than determining the logical connection of clauses. After all, it is the context which reveals those uses of ἵνα for which 'purpose' is a totally inappropriate logical connection.[76]

I argue, then, that in Koine Greek representation is signalled frequently, but not obligatorily, by procedural markers such as ὅτι, ὅπως[77] and ἵνα. A representation interpretively used may refer to an actual or potential state of affairs. If the representation is a statement, indicating a state of affairs in the real world, then ὅτι with the indicative mood will be used. If the representation indicates a *desirable* rather than an actual state of affairs, or an *intention*, whether actual or attributed, then ἵνα or ὅπως with the subjunctive will be the chosen form.

2.2.2.7 OSTENSIVE BEHAVIOUR

A further aspect of communication which *RT* deals with is its deliberate nature: ostension. If communication is ostensive then the speaker intends to communicate certain information to the hearer.[78] In Example (3) above, the speaker intended the hearer to believe that he had studied Greek in Greece, although this was not in fact the case. Body language is a further example of ostensive behaviour, but one which relies on actions and expressions rather than words to effect communication. In Examples (8a,b,c) if George's behaviour was ostensive, then he *intended* Mary to be annoyed. It is also possible, however, that the speaker of Example (8c), believed George's behaviour to be ostensive, but it was *not* so intended. It seems to be a fact of life that humans frequently attribute malicious motives to others on very slim evidence. In such instances the hearer must take responsibility for the inferences she draws.

A biblical example of ostensive communication and the subsequent strategy of 'sophisticated understanding' is given in the following extract from John 12:5-6:

Example (16) 'Why was this perfume not sold for 300 denarii and (the proceeds) given to the poor?' He said this, not because he cared about the poor, but because he was a thief and having charge of the money bag he used to carry off what was put in it.

Here the author presents Judas, the speaker, as intending his hearers to believe that he was concerned about the poor, while the author himself indicates that he

---

[76] See Chapters 3 and 5.
[77] This particle will be dealt with in Chapter 6.
[78] This is in contrast to inferences which a hearer might draw but which are not ostensive because it was not the speaker's intention to communicate such things.

does not believe this to be true. He presents Judas' real intention in criticising the generous act as a desire to keep the money raised by the sale of the ointment for himself. For the author, such ostensive communication failed, because, as he claimed, other information was available which enabled him to effect a strategy of 'sophisticated understanding'.

Similar examples of ostensive communication by physical rather than by verbal means might be seen in the teaching on fasting, also prayer and charitable giving, presented in Matthew 6:16:

> Example (17) μὴ γίνεσθε ὡς οἱ ὑποκριταὶ σκυθρωποί, ἀφανίζουσιν γὰρ τὰ πρόσωπα αὐτῶν ὅπως φανῶσιν τοῖς ἀνθρώποις νηστεύοντες.
> Don't be like the hypocrites with a sad appearance, for they conceal their faces in order that they might appear to people as fasting.

Here an intention is being attributed to certain people to account for their ostensive behaviour. The speaker is claiming that if they had not wanted onlookers to know what they were doing they would have acted differently. These people might have denied that their actions were ostensive, but it was their behaviour which led those watching firstly to recognise that they were fasting and then to infer their behaviour as ostensive.

2.3 Purpose or Intention in Koine

The *attribution* of intention to another is at the heart of much (about 40%[79]) of the use of ἵνα in Greek, not only in the Koine, but in the earlier language where the percentage is much greater. I will show in subsequent chapters[80] that it is such *representation* of *attributed* purpose which marks the authorial selection of ἵνα with the subjunctive rather than an alternative grammatical structure.[81] This particle may of course also be used to introduce a representation of the speaker's own purpose, but it does not introduce a *description* of a state of affairs: it is always a signal of an interpretively used representation.

In the standard grammars of New Testament Greek, it is widely recognised that the role of ἵνα with the subjunctive has expanded considerably since the classical age of Attic Greek.[82] The reason for such expansion is attributed to the decline of the infinitive, and while Greek grammarians such as Jannaris and Mandilaras point out the disadvantages of the infinitive, namely lack of person marking, they do not investigate further than this the very rapid spread of clauses introduced by ἵνα and ὅτι in the NT, Epictetus and the non-literary

---

[79] That is, 40% of ἵνα clauses which introduce a purpose.
[80] See Chapter 6 in particular for a discussion of attributed intention.
[81] Purpose may also be indicated by the infinitive, a preposition with the articular infinitive or a future participle. I discuss in Chapter 6 the choice of a subjunctive clause as making salient the interpretive or attitudinal nature of the representation.
[82] *BDF*§ 388-394; *ATR* pp. 992ff.

Theoretical Basis 41

papyri. It is not only the case that the latter use these particles in contexts where they were almost unknown in the earlier language - Polybius and Dionysius of Halicarnassus do so also - but they exhibit a willingness to use them very frequently:[83] ἵνα x 145 in John's gospel, x 663 in NT as a whole. I intend to show that such an increase in use was a result of the employment of these particles to signal representation. Representation was not *obligatorily* marked in this way, but such particle use did indicate it.[84] It gives a clearer signal to the reader in the following clause, by making explicit the subject, the temporal reference of the utterance and the potential nature of the representation which frequently indicates attitude.

In claiming this, I do not by any means suggest that the particle ἵνα cannot introduce a clause of purpose, merely that the semantic notion of 'purpose' is not a lexical component of that particle. In short, ἵνα does not mean 'in order that' in Koine Greek. It has become a procedural marker rather than a logical conjunction introducing a purpose clause. It is used as a marker to guide the reader in her understanding of the following clause. If this clause indicates the purpose intended by the subject of the main clause, then this will be deduced from the context, including the main verb of the sentence, but at least by the time of Koine an interclausal relationship of purpose is not lexically enshrined in the particle ἵνα. In the NT, there are so many instances of clauses introduced by ἵνα which *cannot* exhibit a telic relationship with the main clause that we must look for a clearer understanding of this particle's function.

The question at the heart of this study is: what inferences did a writer intend his readers to draw by the use of ἵνα with the subjunctive mood? A corollary of this must be: what inferences did a writer intend his readers to draw by the use of ὅτι with the indicative mood?

2.4 Summary

We have examined the possibility of using a theory of communication, Relevance Theory, to investigate the use of the particle ἵνα in Koine Greek. *RT* introduces the concept of inferencing, claiming that this is a major factor involved in the assignation of meaning to an utterance. The reason why inferencing is an essential component in communication is the fact that language is underdetermined at a lexical, grammatical and contextual level. Humans struggle to understand what is said to them, adopting strategies for deriving meaning from an utterance ranging from naïve optimism, through cautious optimism to sophisticated understanding, all employing inference. In

---

[83] The *Discourses* of Epictetus show a much higher use of this particle, much closer to that of the NT.
[84] A topic for future study would be whether or not ἵνα had marked a metarepresentation of intention in classical Greek, when used instead of an infinitival or participial construction. I surmise that this was the case, but this is not the focus of this book.

essence, *RT* claims that it is a factor of human interaction that we both strive to be understood and also to understand what is said to us. We assume that our hearers will listen to us because what we say benefits them in a cognitive sense, and also that as we listen to others we will benefit cognitively. To facilitate this process of understanding a speaker or writer may constrain such inferences by the use of procedural markers, which guide the reader in her interpretation.

It is my argument that in Koine Greek:

- the particle ἵνα is underdetermined in that it does not have a fixed dictionary meaning, but may introduce a representation;
- this representation may indicate purpose, result, intention, desire, indirect command or interpretation of the thought of another, but always a potential rather than actual state of affairs;
- the choice between these will be made by inference from text, context and encyclopaedic knowledge;
- the particle is procedural in that it guides the reader to expect a representation from which she will infer the attitude of the speaker, writer or other participant.

Throughout this book metarepresentation is discussed as 'representation'. There may be several orders of representation, that is it may indicate a representation of a representation, but the language has been simplified because it has seemed to me to be necessary in presenting this essential concept to a wider audience than theoretical linguists. Also 'orders' of representation have been referred to as 'different representations' for the same reason and in order to avoid the conclusion that these may be hierarchically ordered.

CHAPTER 3

Independent Clauses Introduced by ἵνα

3.1 Introduction

In grammar books which deal with Koine Greek, both traditional and more recent, ἵνα is analysed predominantly as a conjunction which introduces a final, that is purpose, clause.[1] Although an extension of this use has been recognised, the general trend has been to see 'goal' evidenced in the clause. A.T. Robertson has been a notable exception. Speaking of the tremendous development in the use of ἵνα, he comments:

> in the Modern Greek vernacular every phase of the subjunctive and the old future ind. can be expressed by νά (ἵνα) and the subj....All in all it is one of the most remarkable developments in the Greek tongue.[2]

Moulton also believed that the extended use of this particle, beyond purpose clauses, was 'deeply rooted in the vernacular.' In this chapter I demonstrate from examples in the NT, papyri, and pagan writers that ἵνα may introduce independent clauses: clauses in which this particle cannot be a subordinating conjunction as it introduces a single clause in a sentence.

In Classical Greek there were various ways in which purpose was indicated: accusative and infinitive, ὡς, ὅπως, ἵνα these last three all introducing a verb in the subjunctive. Of these, ὅπως and ὡς had other functions also, while the accusative and infinitive could also mark indirect speech. The only 'truly final' particle[3] was ἵνα. When this latter particle was used, the purpose indicated was predominantly that of the subject of the main clause, and was attributed to him/her by the author or speaker. In other words, although this particle with the subjunctive marked 'purpose', it was only in first person contexts that the writer himself was stating his *own* purpose. In all others, he was representing his own interpretation or thoughts about the purpose of another. Smyth insightfully comments that certain classical authors regularly used the subjunctive mood rather than the optative after secondary tenses to reflect the

---

[1] *BDF* §369; Burton (1894) §191,197-9, 218 'conceived result'; Green (1907) p. 321 is particularly strong on the notion that 'the final sense' is 'generally discernible'; N. Turner (1988 reprint) pp. 100-105 acknowledges a wider use of the particle, but sees this as evidence of 'Semitic Greek'.
[2] *ATR* p. 982.
[3] Goodwin (1965 reprint) §311; Smyth (1984 reprint) §2193.

actual thought of the grammatical subject. Consider his treatment of the following sentence in Xenophon's *Anabasis*:

Example (1) (τὰ πλοῖα) Ἀβροκόμας....κατέκαυσεν ἵνα μὴ Κῦρος διαβῇ
Abrocomas burned the boats in order that Cyrus might not cross.
Here the thought of Abrocomas was "I will burn the boats that Cyrus might not cross" (ἵνα μὴ διαβῇ) and is given in a kind of quotation.[4]

In essence Smyth is describing a representation of a thought or intention introduced by ἵνα. It is important to keep this in mind in considering the development of the use of ἵνα in Koine.

If the primary function of ἵνα is seen as indicating the purpose of the main verb, then it is essential that a main verb in fact be present so that the reader can access such a function. If the main verb or clause is absent, then there is no syntactic context in which purpose can be expressed in a grammatical sentence. Logically, a purpose clause gives the motivation for an action being taken or an event occurring. That action or event has to be stated if the relationship of purpose is to be effective. A purpose clause differs from a causal clause which gives *factual* information, in that the thought or statement represented by the purpose clause might not be actualised. It gives a potential state of affairs. Classical Greek did make a distinction between purpose clauses which achieved their goal and those which did not by a change of mood, the indicative being used for the latter, and the subjunctive for the former, but both were introduced by ἵνα.[5]

Since intention or motivation is a thought of someone or another, its expression in an utterance by a party other than the 'thinker' is a representation of that thought. Consider the following example from Galatians.[6] When Paul makes a claim as to why certain people wanted the new believers in the Galatian churches to be circumcised, he is representing their motives:

Example (2) ἀλλὰ θέλουσιν ὑμᾶς περιτέμνεσθαι, ἵνα ἐν τῇ ὑμετέρᾳ σαρκὶ καυχήσωνται.
But they want you to be circumcised so that they may boast in your flesh.

That they wanted the Galatian believers to be circumcised seems to have been a fact, together with their persuasion to this end; their motivation for insisting on circumcision on the other hand was not so clear. Paul, by using the subjunctive with ἵνα, is not describing a state of affairs but interpreting the thought of the subjects of the main clause. I have taken this example as a fairly straightforward instance of a 'final clause' which can clearly be seen to

---

[4] Smyth §2197, *Anabasis* 1.4.18.
[5] Goodwin (1965) §316, 333.
[6] Galatians 6:13.

represent the thought someone has about the motivation of another party. It is highly unlikely that those in focus would have accepted this as a representation of their motivation, but Paul is certainly prepared to represent their thoughts in this way. Certainly 'motivation' or 'purpose' is expressed but it is a motivation which is attributed to the subject by another party. It is my claim that the primary function of this particle in Koine Greek is not to indicate purpose, but a representation; purpose must be inferred from the wider syntactic context or shared contextual environment.

Following on from this then, it becomes clear that in Koine ἵνα may not *primarily* signal purpose, but rather an interpretation/representation of a thought. The context may show that the interpretation of this thought as motivation (i.e. 'purpose') is the most relevant understanding of the sentence, but if the *context* does not lead us to derive such motivation, then we are on uncertain ground in claiming that ἵνα alone may do so. Both Jannaris and Mandilaras[7] state that, after the classical period, it is the *context* which gives the best indication of which kind of clause ἵνα introduces. Consequently, if ἵνα begins a sentence and there is no main verb, this cannot be a context in which purpose is expressed. That is, if ἵνα is used in a clause that is not dependent on some other verbal clause this is a distinguishable context which must be seriously considered in determining the function of this particle in such a grammatical environment. The only way in which purpose can be deduced in such a context is by positing an ellipsis which contains a suitable matrix from which such a purpose clause might follow on.

In positing an ellipsis we are drawing inferences, frequently deduced from earlier sentences. This is valid, but there must be a context from which it can be drawn. It has been pointed out to me[8] that the classical language frequently used ellipsis, in particular in the omission of the verb 'to be'. In other cases, the omitted words could be recovered either from the previous sentence or even an earlier clause. The classical language is not the focus of this study, but a quick glance through the early parts of Plato's *Republic* showed that in dialogue, which could be expected to display a high degree of ellipsis, the preceding sentence invariably gave the words to be supplied. In fact the response to a question would either involve the repetition of a word in the question, or be an indication of agreement. In the examples delineated in 3.2.1 and following, however, an entire clause would have to be supplied and in only one case could this be recovered from the previous sentence. I argue that if the writer expected his readers to infer a motivation by deriving a clause which would allow such an interpretation, he would have given them more procedural clues. It is my hypothesis that by the use of ἵνα alone he was alerting them to expect a representation of his own attitude or thought: what he wanted to happen or thought should happen.

---

[7] Jannaris (1897) §1761, 1766; Mandilaras (1973) pp. 258-265.
[8] Dr Mealand, personal communication.

In this chapter, examples to support this latter hypothesis are given not only from the Gospels and the epistles, but also from pagan Greek in the Koine period. There are so many of these independent clauses both in the NT[9] and extra biblically that a reappraisal of their interpretation is long overdue.

3.2 Use of ἵνα to Give an Answer to a Question

In conversational English replies to 'why' questions are frequently given in less than sentence form, the one replying expecting that the hearer will supply the missing grammatical forms:

Example (3a) Why are you opening that window?
Example (3b) To let some air in!

It would be redundant to state in full:

Example (3c) I am opening the window in order to let some air in.

RT claims that our actual utterances are underdetermined: they do not state everything we 'mean' because a hearer is able to infer information from the context. A fully specified sentence, such as (3c) has higher processing costs and is therefore less relevant to the hearer. Further, if (3c) *is* used, then the hearer will derive other inferences, such as [10]

There is no need to say all that.
The speaker thinks I'm stupid.
The speaker is exasperated with me.

Similarly in Greek, both in biblical and non-biblical text, this underdeterminacy may be found. Some examples of these are given below.

In the NT, there are several examples of a ἵνα clause alone giving the answer to a question. If the question asks 'why?', then an answer which gives a reason or a motivation might be inferred without the need to posit an ellipsis because the question has supplied the clause to which the answer refers. The use of 'why' invites an answer which may indicate either motivation or cause.[11]

Other interrogative pronouns such as 'what', on the other hand, do not create a context in which a purpose clause can be inferred. Consider Example (4) in which the author presents the context for the dialogue as Jesus meeting a blind

---

[9] Matthew 2:15; Mark 5:23; 10:51; John 1:8, 22, 31; 2 Corinthians 8:13; Galatians 2:10; Ephesians 5:33 as a representative sample.
[10] Recall that inferences are presented in italic font.
[11] Consider the dialogue in Luke 19:33-34 'Why are you loosening the colt?' 'The Lord needs it.'

Independent Clauses 47

man who addresses him as 'Son of David' and asks him to 'have mercy':[12]

> Example (4a) Τί σοι θέλεις ποιήσω;
> Example (4b) ὁ δὲ εἶπεν, Κύριε, ἵνα ἀναβλέψω.
> 'What do you want me to do for you (lit.:what I shall do)?'[13]
> He said, 'Lord, that I may see again.'

The reply does not directly answer the question. The blind man does not tell Jesus what he wants him to do; he merely states his wish, or *metarepresents* his thought to put it in *RT* terms. All three Synoptists use the same construction. Mark (10:51) has Ραββουνι for Κύριε, while a Matthean passage in a similar context (20:33) uses a different verb altogether: ἵνα ἀνοιγῶσιν οἱ ὀφθαλμοὶ ἡμῶν. Luke uses far fewer ἵνα clauses than the other gospel writers, but has maintained Mark's use here.[14] This is significant, given the fact that Luke *does* rework some of the material which is generally assumed to come from a Marcan source.[15] I claim that there was no need to rework this construction since it was familiar to the first readers as an indication of a speaker's desire: what he wanted to happen.

There are differing potential interpretations of the answer given in (4b), all of them involving inferencing.[16] The usual interpretation suggested is the positing of an ellipsis of such a verb as θέλω 'I want'.[17] This is derived from the question Τί θέλεις. The inference would then be: *The blind man is saying that he wants to see again.* From the fact of his addressing Jesus as 'Son of David' and the statement of his desire to recover his sight a further inference may be drawn: *The blind man believes that Jesus is able to make him see again.*

These inferences do fit the context, since it is obvious from the narrative firstly that the man *does* want to see again, and secondly that Jesus' question was posed in order to elicit faith and not information, but this does not explain the significance of ἵνα. If θέλω is assumed, however, we have to take into account the grammatical fact that in the NT, where the subject of the θέλω clause and the one following are the same, ἵνα does not seem to be used.[18] It does appear in this environment in later Greek, but in the NT it only appears to

---

[12] Luke 18:41.

[13] This is a paratactic construction: *ATR* sees ἵνα as originating with parataxis (p. 982) also Goodwin (1965 reprint) §307: δείδω· μὴ νῆας ἕλωσι 'I fear: may they not take the ships'.

[14] This comment is based on an assumption of Marcan priority, but even without such an assumption the basic point is still valid: Luke used a construction which was less usual for him than for other synoptic writers.

[15] Consider Luke's use of an infinitive after δεῖ in 4:43, rather than Mark's ἄγωμεν ...ἵνα καὶ ἐκεῖ κηρύξω in 1:38.

[16] Nolland (1993) does not deal with this use of ἵνα.

[17] Marshall (1978) 'Before ἵνα supply θέλω' p. 694.

[18] *MG* (2002) pp. 474-476.

follow θέλω if the subject is different: 'I want *you/him* to do something'. This is not an insuperable obstacle given later Greek usage and it was no doubt common in vernacular speech some time before it made its way into the written language, but it is nevertheless a relevant consideration in positing such an ellipsis.

If it is suggested that it indicates purpose, then the ellipsis would have to include a different main verb, perhaps one such as θεραπεύω or even ποιέω. The inference would then be: *The blind man tells Jesus to heal him so that he may see again.* In the context, however, the blind man treats Jesus with respect, addressing him as 'Son of David' and κύριε (Ραββουνι in Mark). He is then less likely to have used the imperative form of θεραπεύω, necessary for a purpose clause. Of course he does cry out, ἐλέησόν με earlier in the narrative, but this verb is less strident in its imperatival form. Its semantic content makes an imperative acceptable. Also the inference suggested above is not readily recovered from the context. The blind man waits for Jesus to respond; he does not tell him what to do.

It is sometimes said that this use of ἵνα with the subjunctive is 'imperatival'.[19] This would fit well with the context, being a way of framing a 'polite request', rather than giving a direct command, but the first person subjunctive alone could have achieved the same effect: ἀναβλέψω 'Let me see again!' As in other putative cases of 'imperatival' ἵνα it does not explain why the writer used this particle rather than the subjunctive alone.

My hypothesis is that ἵνα gives instructions to the reader/hearer to expect the following clause to be a representation of the thought or wish of the blind man. There is no previous clause which can support a telic interpretation for this particle in the context, while positing an ellipsis such as θέλω would create an ungrammatical Greek sentence by NT standards, and if the author had wanted us to read this as a first person imperative, he did not need ἵνα. We may still translate the ἵνα clause as 'Let me see again!' but we should recognise the procedural instruction which this particle is giving us.

3.3 Question and Answer by the Same Speaker

In addition to answers by a different speaker, the answering of a rhetorical question by the speaker himself is a common device used not only by orators, but also by historians and philosophers. It may also be found in the NT, particularly in the letters of Paul, as well as in the portrayal of Jesus' teaching by the four evangelists. In the examples below all the answers begin with an independent ἵνα clause. As noted in 3.3.1 and 3.3.2 it is possible for a reply indicating purpose to be deduced from a question which asks 'why'. The answer is not so transparent when following other interrogatives such as 'what'.

---

[19] Cadoux (1941) pp. 165ff; Moule (1982 reprint) pp. 144-5.

Independent Clauses 49

3.3.1 Examples from Polybius and Epictetus

The use of a rhetorical question, introduced by 'why', with the answer being given in a ἵνα clause is found in the *Histories* of Polybius.[20] The author has been discoursing on matters which might have seemed to some readers to indicate long windedness, and so he poses a question which may have been in the minds of some of his readers. The answer is contained in two ἵνα clauses, but there is no main clause:

Example (5a) Τίνος οὖν χάριν ἐπὶ τοὺς χρόνους τούτους ἀνέδραμον;
Example (5b) ἵνα πρῶτον μὲν γένηται συμφανὲς πῶς.......δεύτερον δ' ἵνα τὰ τῆς προαιρέσεως μὴ μόνον διὰ τῆς ἡμετέρας ἀποφάσεως, ἀλλὰ καὶ δι' αὐτῶν τῶν πραγμάτων πίστεως τυγχάνῃ,...
Example (5a) Why was I running back to these times?
Example (5b) so that, firstly, it might be clear how...and secondly, that the matter of this policy might not only appear faithful/true through our assertion, but through the events themselves...(MGS)

In this example it *is* possible for the question (5a) to function as the main clause, with the ἵνα clause in the following sentence (5b) responding to the question and indicating the author's motivation. This would be a relevant interpretation in this context. Rather than see ἵνα as merely marking purpose, however, we can view it as a procedural clue that ἵνα is being used to introduce a clause which indicates the author's thought and attitude to his arranged material. The writer is marking his thought, which is also his intention, and feels comfortable, in a formal history, with introducing a sentence with what was earlier regarded as a subordinating particle: *Firstly it should be clear that...the matter should appear...*Polybius was a native speaker of Greek, writing in the second century BCE, one who could not be accused either of writing poor Greek, or of being influenced by another mother tongue. It is my hypothesis that by the time this prose was written, the use of ἵνα as a procedural clue to mark a *representation* of the thought of the speaker/writer or another was accepted by educated native speakers of Greek in written as well as spoken form. I do not suggest that this was a conscious procedure, any more than 'I'm like…' is a conscious representation of the speaker's thought in modern informal English,[21] but that does not invalidate my argument. Speakers of a language frequently use constructions for which they have no cognitive explanation, but which hearers recognise intuitively as leading them to draw particular inferences. This extension of use of ἵνα may have originated in the spoken language and been prevalent among bilinguals, but it was *not* the uncouth vulgarism that some grammarians have suggested.

Epictetus, a Stoic philosopher from the first century CE, taught philosophy

---

[20] Book 2.42.1&2.
[21] Consider Example (15) in 2.2.2.6.

in a question and answer mode. Although his language is later and much less formal than that of Polybius, he was nevertheless a native speaker of Koine and certainly not susceptible to Semitic influence.[22] He taught in the Koine and this is how Flavius Arrian has recorded his teaching.[23] From the multiplicity of examples in which answers are given in the form of a ἵνα clause, I have selected two only:

> Example (6)[24] τίνος οὖν ἕνεκα χεῖρας ἔχεις, ἀνδράποδον;
> οὐχ ἵνα καὶ ἀπομύσσῃς σεαυτόν;
> For what reason do you have hands, slave?[25]
> Surely that you may also wipe your own nose/ sharpen your own wits? (MGS)

Here the speaker asks a question about the purpose of human hands and the answer is given in the form of a ἵνα clause. The sentence consists of nothing else. It gives the purpose for which the slave had hands but this is presented, I claim, as a representation of a potential answer which someone might give, which in turn represents his thought. It could also be interpreted as having deontic force: 'You should wipe your nose/sharpen your wits.' Epictetus in presenting a potential answer to his question may be representing his own thought or that of someone else. He may also be inviting a range of inferences by using metaphorical language here.[26]

A further example of an answer to a 'why' question:[27] is found in Book 3.10.10:

> Example (7) Τίνος δὲ ἕνεκα φιλολογεῖς; ἀνδράποδον, οὐχ ἵνα εὐροῇς; οὐχ ἵνα εὐσταθῇς; οὐχ ἵνα κατὰ φύσιν ἔχῃς καὶ διεξάγῃς;
> Why do you love learning? Slave, surely that you may go on well? Surely that you may be steady/in good health? Surely that you may conduct yourself according to nature and live your life (like that)? (MGS)

In this example a string of ἵνα clauses provides potential answers to the speaker's question. Each one is a possible thought in the mind of one of Epictetus' students, perhaps, or merely in his own mind: what he thinks they *ought* to think. Of course they may all be read as purpose clauses, if the original

---

[22] I make this point because it is so frequently stated by scholars, both ancient and modern, that any deviation from a classical norm is the result of 'Semitic Greek'.

[23] Arrian himself wrote in Attic (*LCL Discourses* 1979 reprint p. xiii), as may be seen also from his *Anabasis*.

[24] *Discourses* Book. 1.6.30.

[25] Epictetus himself had been a slave and never seems to have forgotten it. He is said to have been the epitome of humility and so he may have been representing his *own* thought in these examples.

[26] See 2.2.2.5.1 for a resume of an *RT* approach to metaphorical language.

[27] *Discourses* Book 3.10.10.

question supplies the necessary main clause for this logical connection, but I claim that a more relevant reading is of ἵνα as introducing a representation of a potential thought or response to the question. My argument is not that a purpose clause cannot follow ἵνα, but that this particle does not mean 'in order that'.

3.3.2 New Testament Examples

As stated in 3.1.1, many examples of rhetorical questions in which a speaker both asks a question and then gives his own answer, are found in the Gospels and also Pauline writings. The answer to these questions is sometimes introduced by ἵνα with the subjunctive. The example below[28] asks the question 'what' but the answer consists of an independent subjunctive clause introduced by ἵνα.

Example (8a) τίς οὖν μού ἐστιν ὁ μισθός;
Example (8b) ἵνα εὐαγγελιζόμενος ἀδάπανον θήσω τὸ εὐαγγέλιον εἰς τὸ μὴ καταχρήσασθαι τῇ ἐξουσίᾳ μου ἐν τῷ εὐαγγελίῳ.
Example (8a) What then is my reward?
Example (8b) In preaching the good news I make it free of charge so that I do not use up/abuse my right/privilege in the gospel.

The context here is Paul's explanation of both his *right* to receive some financial support for the work that he does for the benefit of the Corinthians and others, and his assertion that he has, in fact, made no use of that right. If there is no financial gain for him in preaching the gospel, someone might ask what his 'reward' is. Paul both asks this potential question and then gives his own response, introduced by ἵνα. This clause describes his 'reward'. It could be analysed grammatically as a noun clause, but it cannot be a 'purpose' clause.[29] There is simply no event for which this could be the motivation. On the contrary, the 'purpose' is actually expressed by εἰς τὸ with the infinitive, contained within the ἵνα clause itself.

Scholarly opinion[30] does not attempt to make this a statement of purpose. Conzelman:[31] 'Paul defines his reward exhaustively in the ἵνα clause' and then the particle is translated as 'that', an epexegetical infinitive. Kistemaker describes the ἵνα clause as 'appositional'.[32] Robertson and Plummer[33] do not

---

[28] 1 Corinthians 9:18.

[29] Consider a similar example from the *Discourses* of Epictetus Book.1.19.5, noted in 5.5.2 Example (21).

[30] Thiselton (2000) does not comment on the use of the particle here, nor does Fee (1991 reprint), but the former translates the particle as 'that' while Fee accepts the *NIV* translation.

[31] Conzelmann (1975) pp. 156 & 158.

[32] Kistemaker (1993) p. 304.

[33] Robertson & Plummer (1983 reprint) p. 189.

discuss the issue of this particle as independent but translate as follows: 'Why, that in preaching the Gospel I shall render the Gospel free of charge so as not to use to the uttermost my privilege in the Gospel.'

My analysis here is that the ἵνα clause represents Paul's thought, namely his belief that in his work of preaching the gospel he has the satisfaction of making the gospel free by choosing to forego the financial support to which he was entitled, as the immediate context makes clear. He is contrasting the words 'reward' and 'free'. His 'reward' is to refuse financial help. He gains by taking no money.

It is very difficult to work in motivation here, there being no action or event on which the purpose depends. The action instead is contained within the ἵνα clause, namely εὐαγγελιζόμενος followed by a prepositional phrase which gives the motivation for it. Further, the question asks what the *reward* is, not the *purpose*.

Translations[34] treat ἵνα as introducing a noun clause:

NIV Just this: that in preaching the gospel...
NEB The satisfaction of preaching the Gospel...
RSV Just this: that in my preaching I may make...
Phillips This, that when I preach the gospel, I can...
Moffat This, that I can preach the gospel...

With the exception of *NEB*, these translations all supply a minimal main clause which gives a pronomial referent which is then explicated by the ἵνα clause. *NEB* answers the question elliptically, but the inference requires to be drawn: '*the reward is...*'

In the following example from Luke 14:28-29 Luke presents Jesus as warning his followers of the cost of discipleship, telling them that they must first reckon on having all their natural priorities changed. In order to make clear the need first to weigh up what might be required of them,[35] he is shown as painting an oral picture which would be well understood in the context of the original readers, that of a man undertaking a building project:

Example (9a) τίς γὰρ ἐξ ὑμῶν θέλων πύργον οἰκοδομῆσαι οὐχὶ πρῶτον καθίσας ψηφίζει τὴν δαπάνην, εἰ ἔχει εἰς ἀπαρτισμόν;
Example (9b) ἵνα μήποτε θέντος αὐτοῦ θεμέλιον καὶ μὴ ἰσχύοντος ἐκτελέσαι πάντες οἱ θεωροῦντες ἄρξωνται αὐτῷ ἐμπαίζειν...

---

[34] This book deals only tangentially with the issue of translation, but these examples are given to illustrate the point that readers, or translators, draw the most relevant inferences from the stimulus.

[35] Nolland (1993) notes a similar passage in the *Discourses* of Epictetus (3.15.8-12) in which the philosopher advises aspiring philosophers to 'σκέψαι πρῶτον' before embarking on this career p. 763.

Example (9a) 'For which of you,[36] if he wishes to build a tower, does not sit down first and reckon up the expense, whether he has (enough) for completion?
Example (9b) Otherwise, when he has laid a foundation, but is unable to complete (it), all those looking on will begin to mock him....'

As with Paul in the previous example from 1Corinthians, Luke presents Jesus as both asking and answering his own question. In fact his answer is only partial – it assumes that the listeners' response will be: *Of course we would sit down first to count the cost.* Assuming this answer, Jesus then goes on to point out the result of not doing this. This sentence is underdetermined. A fully determined sentence would require much processing effort and therefore cease to be relevant to the hearer. There are many unstated inferences which need to be drawn before the ἵνα clause becomes clear. These might be as follows:

Everyone undertaking a building project must consider the cost of the whole.
They must do this before they begin.
If they do not know the cost, they might not have enough resources to finish.
Laying a foundation is not the whole cost.
Some building projects do not rise above the foundations.
People laugh at stalled building projects.

In this example it is just possible that the ἵνα clause is giving the motivation or purpose for the question. To paraphrase:'Someone will sit down and count the cost before building, so that people will not laugh if he has not enough resoures to finish, after laying the foundation.'

A closer consideration, however, makes this seem much less likely. The point which Jesus is making is that it is *prudent* to plan first and act later. The motivation for this is really to be able to decide whether or not this course of action should be followed, not merely that one will not be laughed at. The answer might be giving the *result* of lack of forethought, but not the motivation for planning ahead. The use of ἵνα here signals a *potential* thought of the builder. Remember that this is Luke's account of an episode where Jesus was teaching crowds who came to him and in which he had a live audience. He is presented as painting a picture for them. To show the folly of acting without careful thought, he depicts the mockery of onlookers on seeing an unfinished project.

Neither Marshall nor Nolland comment on the use of ἵνα in an independent clause, but the former does note ἵνα μήποτε as 'a strengthened form of ἵνα μή expressing apprehension.'[37] The analysis presented above does not contest this, but takes the argument further by claiming that this 'apprehension' is the

---

[36] Marshall (1978) p. 463 points out that 'the effect of this is to address the hearers personally and force them to a decision on what is being told them.'
[37] Marshall (1978) p. 594.

thought of the would be builder and that the particle ἵνα aids the reader in inferring this.

3.4 Expressing Desire and Intention

This section covers a variety of speaker desires or intentions. According to the person of the verb, it may also indicate the speaker's belief that the hearer *ought* or *should* carry out some course of action. In other words if the verb has first person marking then the speaker wants something to happen which *he* can bring about, or which affects him personally, as in Example (4b). If the morphological marking on the verb is second or third person, then he is asking someone else to do it. The overall pattern of the section, however, is of the ἵνα clause representing a thought. It may also be observed that speaker attitude comes into focus, often in expressing what the speaker feels should or ought to be done. All examples are of independent ἵνα clauses with no main clause preceding.

It has long been understood that the subjunctive indicates 'irrealis', an indefinite utterance, in contrast to the indicative mood which is felt to be descriptive of a state of affairs in the real world. In these examples, ἵνα with the subjunctive indicates a potential state of affairs which usually reflects the speaker's attitude towards an utterance. In all of these examples, the ἵνα clause is independent.

3.4.1 Johannine Examples

In Example (10) the author describes the way in which some priests and Levites, sent by Jews from Jerusalem, question John the Baptist about his identity, or more accurately about his authority[38] for preaching and baptising. After four attempts at getting an answer out of the Baptist, they say:[39]

> Example (10) Τίς εἶ; ἵνα ἀπόκρισιν δῶμεν τοῖς πέμψασιν ἡμᾶς· τί λέγεις περὶ σεαυτοῦ;
> 'Who are you? We must give an answer to the ones sending us; what do you say about yourself?'

This is not a straight question about identity: they knew his parentage. The questioners had been sent to find out why someone outside the religious establishment had the audacity to perform religious acts, viz. preaching and baptising. The Baptist seems to have known this and so gives several negative answers to their leading questions. Their first question was Σὺ τίς εἶ - who are you? John understands or infers that they are not asking him what his name is

---

[38] They knew who he was; the authority behind him was the issue.
[39] John 1:22 with 1:19-21.

and gives the answer to the inferred real question: 'I am not the Christ'.[40] That this has, in fact, been the desired information is made clear by the next question: Τί οὖν; Σὺ 'Ηλίας εἶ; 'What then? Are you Elijah?' The contextual information which both hearer and speaker shared, as well as probably the readers of this gospel, is the expectation that another prophet would come, as promised in Malachi 4:5, 'like Elijah'. The Baptist denies being a new Elijah, which gives rise to a further question: Ὁ προφήτης εἶ σύ; Are you the prophet? Again the shared contextual information is of the promise given by Moses[41] that the Lord would send another prophet like him. This is also denied and so the questioners are forced to reveal their real agenda: 'We must give an answer to those who sent us.' This is introduced by ἵνα and has the effect of making the Baptist much more forthcoming about his work.

Schnackenburg does not deal with the independent use of ἵνα, but his translation assumes a main clause such as 'tell us...: Who are you? - so that we can give an answer to those who sent us'.[42] There is no need to posit such an ellipse here, as 'Tell us, in order that...' This analysis is driven by the desire to keep the telic force for the particle, and so maintain it as a subordinating conjunction following a main verb. Certainly there may be an element of purpose in the clause, but that is not the reason for the presence of this particle with the subjunctive. Rather it is a procedural clue which alerts the reader to expect a representation of a thought – in this case the questioners' knowledge that they would be required to give an answer to those who had sent them. This might be verbalised as 'We must give an answer...' The element of obligation expresses their attitude, but behind that is the inference that 'someone' considers this to be a necessary thing to do, resulting in the use of 'ought' or 'should'. Such deontic verbs are attitudinal (note Schnackenburg's 'can'), not necessarily expressing only the view of the speaker, but also that of another, unnamed, party who considers the action to be desirable.

The ἵνα clause then gives the thought and attitude of the questioners: 'We need to give an answer...' In fact some translations[43] bring out the deontic force of the clause, which suggests that those translators did find such a translation to be relevant in the context.

There are several different representations here.[44] The author is representing the utterances of John's questioners, but these utterances represent not only

---

[40] This analysis is supported by Morris (1971), but the latter maintains that the force of the particle here is telic: 'The meaning is surely "(tell us) so that we may give an answer"' footnote 23 p.137. Bernard (1942 reprint) also sees the construction as elliptical and so maintains that the conjunction 'has full telic force' p. 35 (and 338).

[41] Deuteronomy 18:15, 18.

[42] Schnackenburg (1982) p. 291.

[43] So *NEB*.

[44] Recall the discussion of this in Chapter 2 at 2.2.2.5 and also of the use of evidentials which point to the speaker's allusion to the beliefs of others (footnote 56 of that chapter).

their own thoughts, but the instructions of those who sent them. Humans regularly do this. The use of words such as 'ought' or 'should' indicates a proposition considered to be good or desirable by someone - not necessarily by the speaker, although he may concur. It is this representation which is encapsulated by ἵνα and the subjunctive.

JOHN 9:36 FIRST PERSON REFERENCE

The context here is of Jesus healing a blind man who was subsequently interrogated by the religious leaders regarding this miracle. In the verses below[45] the author presents this man's second meeting with Jesus and his response to the latter's question:

> Example (11) Ἤκουσεν Ἰησοῦς ὅτι ἐξέβαλον αὐτὸν ἔξω καὶ εὑρὼν αὐτὸν εἶπεν,
> Σὺ πιστεύεις εἰς τὸν υἱὸν τοῦ ἀνθρώπου;
> ἀπεκρίθη ἐκεῖνος καὶ εἶπεν, Καὶ τίς ἐστιν, κύριε, ἵνα πιστεύσω εἰς αὐτόν;
> Jesus heard that they had put him out, and finding him he said, 'Do *you* believe in the son of man?'
> He said in reply, 'So who is he, sir? I *want* to believe in him.' OR
>   'So who is he, sir, that I *should* believe in him?'

As with other occurrences, an elliptical verb is usually posited so that this particle can be maintained as indicating 'purpose', viz. 'Tell me, so that I may'. Bernard claims,

> There is an ellipsis before ἵνα which has full telic force. "Who is He? *for I want know* in order that I may put my trust in Him".[46]

In fact Bernard is supplying inferences that may be drawn from the text, but this does not mean that an ellipsis is required in order to understand ἵνα. The inferences may be drawn without the need to translate this particle as 'in order that':

> *The blind man does not know definitely who the son of man is*
> *The blind man suspects that Jesus is the son of man*
> *The blind man is open to believing in this 'son of man'*
> *The blind man has spoken positively about Jesus before the Jewish leaders*
> *The blind man believes that Jesus is 'from God'*

---

[45] John 9:35-36.
[46] Bernard (1942 reprint) p. 338. This verse is cross referenced to the earlier example (10) from John 1:22. The adherence to the notion of 'telic force' seems to dominate the exegesis and make ellipsis unavoidable.

Independent Clauses 57

This type of use has been called 'imperatival' by Cadoux whose suggestion has been supported by C.F.D. Moule and others, and is said to have originated from the jussive use of the subjunctive.[47] It is also true that many verbs of command or request are followed by ἵνα with the subjunctive.[48] As in an earlier section,[49] however, it can be seen that the use of the subjunctive alone, without the conjunction would have given the meaning 'Let me'. It does not explain the use of the particle, although it could explain the use of the subjunctive alone.

Alternatively, we may consider the ἵνα clause to be representing the man's thought or attitude to Jesus' question. His inference from this question would be: *Believing in the son of man must be a good thing*. This leads on to the utterance: 'I ought to believe in him' 'Should I believe in him?'[50] As in the previous example,[51] the use of 'ought' or 'should' marks the awareness of another party's thought or belief. The blind man deduces that Jesus considers it a good thing that he believes in 'the son of man'. The writer marks the blind man's acknowledgement of this by the use of a ἵνα clause with the subjunctive.

3.4.2 Examples from Orators and Rhetoricians

A slightly different range of examples, also featuring the independence of the ἵνα clause, is found both in the NT and also in pagan rhetoricians or historians. These examples express what the speaker himself felt that he should do: note the first person marking on the verb in the ἵνα clause. Consider this example from Acts 24:4, in which the orator Tertullus is said to be addressing the governor, Felix:

Example (12) ἵνα δὲ μὴ ἐπὶ πλεῖόν σε ἐγκόπτω, παρακαλῶ ἀκοῦσαί σε ἡμῶν συντόμως τῇ σῇ ἐπιεικείᾳ.
'That I may not hinder you for longer, I urge you to hear us briefly in your goodness.'

Not only does this ἵνα clause occur at the beginning of the sentence, but it does not indicate a purpose or intention which is linked to the main clause of the sentence. It is a rhetorical aside. The motivation urged on Felix to hear Tertullus is not so that he will not hinder him, in fact it could be thought to be the reverse! Rather, the initial clause represents the orator's wish; it expresses his deferential and perhaps apologetic attitude towards Felix: 'I should not

---

[47] Cadoux (1941), Moule (1982 reprint) p.145, Moulton (1998 reprint) p. 206. Note the comments in chapter one at 1.3.2.2.
[48] These are dealt with in Chapter 4.
[49] 3.2. Example (4b).
[50] Schnackenburg (1982) does not comment on the grammar of the ἵνα clause at all, but does claim that 'in his question, the man expelled by the Jews expresses his readiness to believe; he suspects that Jesus means himself' p. 254.
[51] John 1:22.

detain you', 'Let me not detain you'. Logically, it does not provide a subordinate clause with telic force which could follow the main clause.

This type of rhetorical aside, which is *de facto* an independent clause can be seen in pagan Greek also. Consider the following Examples (13) and (14) from Demosthenes and Dionysius:

3.4.2.1 DEMOSTHENES
The following example is quoted by Smyth[52] from this orator who practised in the fourth century BCE:

Example (13) ἵν᾽ ἐκ τούτων ἄρξωμαι... 'to begin with this'

Purpose is not the issue here. It is, again, a rhetorical aside, with the speaker stating his intention or in *RT* terms representing his thought. This is probably the beginning, with a native speaker of Greek, and in fact an orator, of a much wider use of ἵνα with the subjunctive, in which speaker attitude is signalled both by the particle itself and also the concomitant subjunctive mood. To state this another way: the speaker is representing his thought of what he *should* do, which represents his own attitude or his understanding of someone else's expectation.

3.4.2.2 DIONYSIUS OF HALICARNASSUS
Consider this example[53] which presents an independent ἵνα clause in the middle of a sentence, as an aside:

Example (14) αὐτίκα τὴν ἡγεμονίαν, ἵν᾽ ἀπὸ ταύτης ἄρξωμαι, πῶς παρέλαβεν;
For example, the chief command, that I may begin from this/I should begin from this, how did he receive it? (MGS)

The ἵνα clause here cannot be indicating purpose. Even if it were to be 'let me begin', the subjunctive alone would be sufficient. The author here is signalling his thought: 'I should begin at this point' or 'I want to begin at this point.' Dionysius wrote many treatises on the works of classical authors and was himself a teacher of rhetoric. He is generally considered to be an upholder of Attic standards.[54] If he is found to use this particle in an independent environment, surely this is a clear indication that the primary function of ἵνα is no longer to signal purpose, since there is no main clause on which this depends, but to introduce a representation of the author's thought or attitude regarding what he should do.

---

[52] Smyth §2204 'The principal clause is sometimes omitted; Dem. 21.43'.
[53] Dionysius Book 3.XI.9.
[54] Mealand (1996) p. 65 'It was Dionysius who promoted the Attic revival which began in the first century BCE'.

Independent Clauses 59

3.4.3 Examples from Septuagint and Non-Literary Papyri

In this section, the context of each utterance marked by an independent ἵνα clause gives clues as to whether or not the author or speaker's wish is being communicated or his belief that the hearer ought to do something. Unlike the previous section, here the speaker wishes someone else to do certain things. Sometimes these two meanings are very close together.

3.4.3.1 SEPTUAGINT
Consider the following example from 2 Maccabees 1:9:

> Example (15) καὶ νῦν ἵνα ἄγητε τὰς ἡμέρας τῆς σκηνοπηγίας τοῦ Χασελευ μηνός· ἔτους ἑκατοστοῦ ὀγδηκοστοῦ καὶ ὀγδόου.
> 'And now, you should keep the days of the feast of booths during the month of Chislev. In the one hundred and eighty eighth year.'
> *or* 'And now, please keep the feast...'

The choice between these two interpretations of the verse is dependent on the context of the letter. The Jewish religious leaders in Jerusalem are urging the Jews in Egypt, part of the Diaspora, to celebrate the feast of booths in their local situation. They did not use an imperatival form of the verb, but chose to indicate their wish or attitude by the use of ἵνα and the subjunctive. Perhaps they felt that the issuing of a command in this instance would cause the readers of the letter to derive the wrong inferences, such as: *The Jews in Jerusalem are giving orders*. By using a more gentle construction, they were making their attitude clear, but avoiding the appearance of being dictatorial.

Since the earlier part of this letter does not indicate a reluctance on the part of those in Jerusalem to instruct the Diaspora, probably the deontic inference is the correct one: 'You ought/should'. As has been shown earlier, ἵνα is underdetermined for a specific interpretation; it gives a procedural clue to alert the reader to expect a representation. This displays speaker attitude, but it is the *context* which allows the hearer/reader to deduce the inferences which make clear which particular attitude is being communicated. Goldstein translates as 'we ask you' commenting that this is 'a good idiom in Hellenistic Greek, unparalleled in Hebrew and Aramaic.'[55]

3.4.3.2 EXAMPLES FROM THE PAPYRI
Many striking examples of this use of ἵνα introducing an independent clause or sentence are found in the papyri.[56] Of course the material is fragmentary, but a

---

[55] Goldstein (1983) p.153.

[56] Many of these examples are later, e.g. an excellent example from Oxyrhynchos, dated fourth century CE and given by Horsley (1983) p.141: ἵνα οὖν καὶ σοὶ παραβοηθήσῃς μοι τῷ ὄντι ἐπὶ ξένης καὶ ἐν νόσῳ ὄντι. 'You should help me as I am in a strange (town) and ill.' Horsley translates: 'Please send help to me...'

consistent pattern emerges in which this construction seems to be used to indicate a wish or suggestion, and to have been selected rather than an imperative verb form.

Consider the following examples:

BGU IV.1079 (A.D. 41) [57]
Example (16) ἔχομεν πολλοὺς δανιστάς· μὴ ἵνα ἀναστατώσῃς ἡμᾶς
'We have many money lenders/creditors; please, don't drive us out.'

Here the wish of the writer, who tells the recipient what he should say to Ptollarion, is expressed by ἵνα and the subjunctive, rather than the imperative. Since the excerpt is so short and the context unknown, it is difficult to discuss 'attitude', but for some reason the writer retained the particle, in his suggested approach to a superior, even though by leaving it out he could have written a perfectly normal negative imperative: μὴ ἀναστατώσῃς. As in the previous example, the use of the construction may have signalled a more gentle, respectful request: 'this is what I would like', rather than a blunt command. Even in English, speaker attitude in directional language is clearly marked. 'Would you mind closing the door?' is not a question but a request, while 'Shut the door' is only permissible when directed to family or children. On the other hand, as in Example (15), the writer could be communicating what he thought the recipient of his letter *ought* to do: 'You should not drive us out.'

Further papyri examples show the same indications:

Example (17) O.Amst.22.7-8 (II) [58]
ἵνα μίνῃς αὐτόν, ἐπὶ γὰρ ὀρτίζει πρός σε αὔριον·
'Wait for him, since he comes to you tomorrow.'

This translation treats the ἵνα clause as 'imperatival',[59] but I claim that a less imperatival rendering of 'You should wait for him' is more appropriate. This acknowledges what the writer feels that his respondent *ought* to do. As in the other examples of independent clauses, a telic interpretation is not possible. Example (18) below is quoted in Mandilaras.[60] He gives many examples of what he sees as 'imperatival' ἵνα, but many of these are dated in the third and fourth centuries and for that reason I have not include them in this analysis.

P.Fay. 112, 11-13 (A.D. 99)
Example (18) ἐπέχον τῷ δακτυλιστῇ Ζωίλωι καὶ εἵνα αὐτὸν μὴ δυσωπήσῃς.

---

[57] Example taken from Hunt & Edgar (1988 reprint) p. 296.
[58] Noted by Horsley (1981) 43 p. 86 apropos of the meaning of the verb ὀρθρίζω: 'The translation is that of the editors of that corpus.'
[59] Recall the comments at Chapter 1, 1.3.2.2.
[60] Mandilaras (1973) p. 264.

'Pay attention to the reckoner Zoilos and please don't make him embarassed.'

This example has a regular imperative form for the first verb, but for the second a more gentle request is made. Given the semantic content of this second verb, perhaps a straight command would have been rude and would have caused unintended bad inferences to be drawn such as: *The writer thinks that the recipient of the letter will be rude to this official, Zoilos.* Again, of course, a deontic interpretation would also be relevant here: 'You should not make him embarassed'. Mandilaras, on the other hand, considers the ἵνα clause in this example to be fulfilling the same function as the imperative in the preceding clause. He links Ephesians 5:33 with this usage,[61] but this assumes that the writer was not inviting a further inference by the use of a different construction.[62] The fact that an imperative occurs in the same sentence as a ἵνα clause which is not dependent on it has led not only Mandilaras, but many commentators to come to the same conclusion. There is, however, no logical reason why this should be so. The example from Ephesians 5:33 which Mandilaras uses above is dealt with in the next section.

3.4.4 Examples from the Epistles

Although the following example from Ephesians 5:33 is not an independent sentence, it *is* an independent clause, which is introduced by ἵνα with the subjunctive:

Example (19) πλὴν καὶ ὑμεῖς οἱ καθ' ἕνα, ἕκαστος τὴν ἑαυτοῦ γυναῖκα οὕτως ἀγαπάτω ὡς ἑαυτόν, ἡ δὲ γυνὴ ἵνα φοβῆται τὸν ἄνδρα.
'Only in addition, let each one of you love his own wife in the same way as (he loves) himself, but I would like the wife to respect her husband/the wife should respect her husband.'

The second half of this verse is usually taken as parallel to the first, making the subjunctive clause the equivalent of the imperative. The reasoning is that the author must have been issuing a command to wives also, perhaps because this is a regular pattern in the household code.[63] This then becomes an example of an 'imperatival' ἵνα which the author used for variety. My analysis is that the ἵνα clause indicates speaker attitude, namely a wish, representing the writer's

---

[61] See 3.4.4, Example (19).

[62] Mandilaras p. 264. On the same page he gives a further example from fourth century CE in which the writer begins with εἵνα but after an intervening 'if' clause writes an imperative πέμπε. This is several centuries later than the other examples and so I do not consider that it gives as much weight to the parallel nature of the constructions as Mandilaras suggests.

[63] Hoehner (2002) usefully points out that the instructions in the household code were given in the plural p. 781.

thought, rather than being a direct command.

The context in this chapter of Ephesians, from verse 25 onwards, is of instructions to the males in the church. The writer begins with a direct command: οἱ ἄνδρες, ἀγαπᾶτε τὰς γυναῖκας,[64] going on to explain his reasons, making the statement that men 'ought' (ὀφείλουσιν) to love their wives. The final verse of the chapter, Example (19) is a summary of this, encouraging 'each one of you' to love 'his own wife', but adding the rider that he wants 'the wife' to respect her husband. Since the focus has been on the husband's behaviour, the author lets the woman know what his attitude is: he thinks she *should* respect her husband, but he does not use an imperative form. If we insist on treating the ἵνα clause as a 'command', we lose the finer points of the choice the author has made. A speaker chooses, according to *RT*, the forms which are most relevant to his hearer. In this sentence, the subject ἡ δὲ γυνή is actually forefronted, occurring before ἵνα, both signalling a subject change and providing a link to the beginning of the section[65] where the subject is αἱ γυναῖκες. This supports my hypothesis that the ἵνα clause is not grammatically parallel to the earlier imperative clause.

There is a general belief that writers use alternative but equivalent constructions as a matter of style. In *RT*, however, a writer in making a particular choice of words or grammatical constructions is inviting the reader to make inferences, and biblical scholars do just this. One example of this is the inference drawn from the Johannine use of σημεῖα rather than δυναμεῖς for 'marvellous acts' that this is a theological statement on the part of the author.[66] The author does not claim this but readers infer this pragmatically, rather than assume that his choice of vocabulary was a matter of style. It seems then that the use of ἵνα rather than the imperative in Example (19) should at least be considered as a deliberate choice on the author's part, inviting the reader to infer his attitude rather than be consigned to being the equivalent of an imperatival form.

Hoehner gives the translation 'and the wife should fear her husband' but then seems to suggest that this is an instance of 'imperatival' ἵνα.[67] I argue that an imperatival form would result in the translation 'let the wife...' and that this could have been achieved with the third person imperative. No one is dealing with the issue of why this particle was used, rather than the subjunctive alone. This is further supported by Example (20) below from 1Corinthians 7:29-31:

Example (20)
τοῦτο δέ φημι, ἀδελφοί, ὁ καιρὸς συνεσταλμένος ἐστίν· τὸ λοιπόν,
ἵνα καὶ οἱ ἔχοντες γυναῖκας ὡς μὴ ἔχοντες ὦσιν

---

[64] 'Husbands, love your wives.'
[65] Ephesians 5:22.
[66] For example Schnackenburg (1972) pp. 154-6.
[67] Hoehner p. 783.

καὶ οἱ κλαίοντες ὡς μὴ κλαίοντες
καὶ οἱ χαίροντες ὡς μὴ χαίροντες
καὶ οἱ ἀγοράζοντες ὡς μὴ κατέχοντες,
καὶ οἱ χρώμενοι τὸν κόσμον ὡς μὴ καταχρώμενοι·
παράγει γὰρ τὸ σχῆμα τοῦ κόσμου τούτου.

'I mean this, brothers and sisters, the time has been compressed. Finally/ in short, those who have wives should live as those who do not have, those who weep as those who do not weep, those who rejoice as those who do not rejoice, those who trade/buy as those who possess nothing, those who make use of the world as those who do not make any use of it. For the form of this world is passing.'

The context here is 'the present difficult circumstances'[68] which cause Paul to advise the Corinthians to hold lightly onto anything they value. He is not giving a command, but setting out his own understanding of what is 'right' for them: what they 'ought' to do. It is possible that he is giving his *interpretation* of the 'present circumstances', but I think that this is a less relevant reading of these verses. Again, this text from 1Cor 7:29-31 is regularly taken as an example of 'imperatival' ἵνα,[69] but Fee reads it as expressing 'the purpose God has for his people in "compressing the time"'.[70] I feel that this is driven more by the conviction that this particle has 'purpose' behind it somewhere, than the most relevant understanding. Paul has said that he does not have 'a command from the Lord',[71] which would make it difficult to introduce God's purpose half way through his argument without making this fact clear. There may be a divine purpose in these exhortations, but my hypothesis is that it is *not* introduced by ἵνα.

From all the examples in this section, the speaker's choice of a subjunctive clause introduced by ἵνα seems to be directed by relevance, by a desire to inform the hearer of speaker attitude, namely what the author wishes or believes the hearers *ought* to do and perhaps, a weaker inference, to avoid unintended inferences being elicited, which might have been the case if an imperative form had been used. As in earlier sections, there is no main clause from which a purpose clause could logically follow. This leaves ellipsis as the only way in which a telic interpretation can be derived. Of course this could be supplied by inference, but the context would have to provide the information for such a derivation.

---

[68] 1Corinthians 7:26.
[69] So Moule (1982 reprint) pp. 144-5, Turner (1963) p. 95, Barrett (1987) p. 176, Robertson and Plummer (1983 reprint) p. 155, Conzelmann (1975) p. 130, Thiselton (2000) p. 581 as well as Cadoux's article which was considered in Chapter 1.
[70] Fee (1987) p. 338.
[71] 1Corinthians 7:25.

3.5 Introducing a Quotation from the Old Testament

A slightly different type of independent clause introduced by ἵνα, is that of the quotations in the gospel of John where ἵνα introduces either a quotation from the Psalms[72] or a statement reported to have been made earlier by Jesus.[73] Two of the former are in the speech of Jesus, while the latter are the author's comment on events. Matthew also uses this formula,[74] but occasionally introduces the independent subjunctive clause by ὅπως.[75] Mark uses ἵνα in this way only once.[76] Dependent clauses introduced by this formula are dealt with in a later chapter;[77] this section deals only with independent clauses which introduce a quotation from the OT.

The usual interpretation, and also the translation, of these verses is that the events(s) occurred *in order that the scripture might be fulfilled*.[78] Looked at dispassionately, such an attribution of purpose might lead one to deduce that if the event had not occurred the Scripture could not have been fulfilled. In the case of quotations from the Psalms, the source text was not a prophecy, but a commentary on the psalmist's situation or a cry to God for help. I am arguing that current events caused the observers to remember something that had been spoken of earlier. This seems to be a more logical way of viewing such an utterance, than seeing it as a claim of fulfilment. It is difficult to view an event as taking place solely to make something predicted earlier come true, while having no relevance during the lifetime of the original hearers of the prediction, particularly when the earlier writing was not in a prophetic book. Surely what we have here may be the author attributing to Jesus the realisation that in fact the event recalls words spoken earlier. The event does 'fulfil' the earlier words, but did not take place *in order to* fulfil it. I am not, therefore, disputing the element of fulfilment, but rather I view it as the application of a previous experience, in the case of the Psalms. I deny the attribution of purpose to the introductory particle.

Consider the following example from John 13:18:

Example (21) οὐ περὶ πάντων ὑμῶν λέγω· ἐγὼ οἶδα τίνας ἐξελεξάμην· ἀλλ' ἵνα ἡ γραφὴ πληρωθῇ, ὁ τρώγων μου τὸν ἄρτον ἐπῆρεν ἐπ' ἐμὲ τὴν πτέρναν αὐτοῦ.

'I am not speaking about all of you. I know those I have chosen. But the scripture should be fulfilled/completed: "The one who ate my bread lifted up his heel against me."'

---

[72] John 13:18; 15:25; 19:24.
[73] John 18:9, 32.
[74] Matthew 2:15; 4:14.
[75] Matthew 2:23.
[76] Mark 14:49.
[77] Chapter 9, 9.3.1.1.
[78] Note Moule's (1977) comments on the wider use of πληρῶ in the NT and 9.3.1.1.

Independent Clauses 65

The words quoted come from Psalm 41:9, in which the psalmist bewails the behaviour of a close friend in turning against him. Jesus is presented as recalling that psalm and seeing a fulfilment in his own life with the betrayal of Judas, who even as Jesus spoke was eating with him. Indeed this context is of the fellowship meal with all reclining together as they ate and drank. It is a 'fulfilment' or an application of Psalm 41:9, but Judas did not act the way he did *in order to* fulfil it. John may also be presenting Jesus as indicating the appropriateness of fulfilment. Recall that previous examples of the use of ἵνα in this section have shown a representation of what someone believed *should* be done. This is not the same as indicating that Judas was impelled to act as he did in order to fulfil Psalm 41:9. The question of the overall purpose of God being the driving force behind the ἵνα clause will be dealt with at the end of this section.

Consider a further example in John 15:24, 25. The author presents Jesus as commenting on the inevitability of the 'world' hating his followers, because it has already expressed its hatred for him. He points out that this hatred is not because of any wrong done, but a consequence of the world's hearing and rejecting his words. With this background of righteous actions and condemnation of evil, he recalls the words of Psalm 35:19, repeated in Psalm 69:4:

Example (22) εἰ τὰ ἔργα μὴ ἐποίησα ἐν αὐτοῖς ἃ οὐδεὶς ἄλλος ἐποίησεν, ἁμαρτίαν οὐκ εἴχοσαν· νῦν δὲ καὶ ἑωράκασιν καὶ μεμισήκασιν καὶ ἐμὲ καὶ τὸν πατέρα μου. ἀλλ' ἵνα πληρωθῇ ὁ λόγος ὁ ἐν τῷ νόμῳ αὐτῶν γεγραμμένος ὅτι Ἐμίσησάν με δωρεάν.
'If I had not done among them deeds which no one else ever did, they would not have sin; but now they have both seen and hated both me and my father. But this is the fulfilment of the word written in their law: "They hated me without a cause."' OR 'But the word written in their law must be fulfilled.'

The context of the original words is that of a righteous man hated and persecuted by those around him, almost certainly fellow Jews, although his only crime has been to contrast the lawlessness of their actions by his own righteous deeds. In Psalm 69 there is even the expressed belief that the writer is suffering because of his zeal for God. The author then understands Jesus to be seeing his own situation as a further fulfilment of this psalm, but the 'world' did not hate him *in order to* fulfil Psalms 35 and 69. This is a much wider picture of the implicit condemnation of evil, or hypocrisy, which comes from a truly good person, whose actions highlight the result of heart attitudes, rather than the outward observance of ritual alone. The author uses a ἵνα clause to indicate a representation of Jesus' thought, his attitude to the psalms he quoted, namely that they are being fulfilled in, or applicable to, his circumstances. Again, this is an independent clause with no main verb to link with a purpose. The perception of 'the purpose of God' functioning as the main clause is dealt with at the end of this section on fulfilment quotations.

As well as portraying Jesus as viewing the events around him being the fulfilment of earlier Scripture, the writer of John's Gospel also comments himself on the fulfilment both of earlier Scripture and also of the words which he notes Jesus as having spoken some time before. Firstly he sees a fulfilment or application of Psalm 22:18 in the fact of the soldiers sharing out and casting lots for Jesus' clothes at his crucifixion. He is not claiming that the soldiers did this *in order to* fulfil the psalm, but that he could see a further fulfilment in it, *beyond* the immediate reference to the situation of the writer of that psalm.

> Example (23)[79] εἶπαν οὖν πρὸς ἀλλήλους, Μὴ σχίσωμεν αὐτόν, ἀλλὰ λάχωμεν περὶ αὐτοῦ τίνος ἔσται· ἵνα ἡ γραφὴ πληρωθῇ [ἡ λέγουσα], Διεμερίσαντο τὰ ἱμάτιά μου ἑαυτοῖς καὶ ἐπὶ τὸν ἱματισμόν μου ἔβαλον κλῆρον.
> So they (the soldiers) said to one another, 'Let's not tear it, but let's cast lots for whose it will be.' This fulfilled the scripture [which says]
> 'They divided my clothes among them, and threw dice for my robe.'

Psalm 22 is referred to many times by the writers of the New Testament as having fulfilment in or application to the life of Jesus.[80] I am not denying such fulfilment, or invalidating their reading of the OT text, but claiming that the events provided fulfilment or application without having to take place *in order to* fulfil that text. This claim then allows an immediate reference in the context of the original speaker and hearers, while recognising that events in the life of Jesus could provide a further fulfilment from the new context provided by the first century CE observers, writers and readers.

In all these examples the clause introduced by ἵνα and the subjunctive gives the writer's attitude to, that is his interpretation of, the events which took place. There is no 'main clause' preceding these clauses. This should warn us against forcing this construction into the earlier classical pattern in which ἵνα almost never introduced an independent clause. These examples stand alone, indicating the writer's interpretation of events.

This use of ἵνα πληρωθῇ may also be seen in references to earlier words attributed to Jesus concerning his death. It is significant that the Evangelist here uses the same phrase to refer to the fulfilment of the words of Jesus as he does for the OT writings. When looking back on what Jesus had said earlier, the author sees fulfilment of this. That is *not* the same as saying that the event happened *in order to* fulfil the earlier words. Consider John18:8, 9, which presents Jesus as asking the guards to release his followers, and the Evangelist's response:

> Example (24a) εἰ οὖν ἐμὲ ζητεῖτε, ἄφετε τούτους ὑπάγειν·

---

[79] John 19:24.
[80] John 19:28 *inter alia*.

Example (24b) ἵνα πληρωθῇ ὁ λόγος ὃν εἶπεν ὅτι Οὓς δέδωκάς μοι οὐκ ἀπώλεσα ἐξ αὐτῶν οὐδένα.
'If then you are looking for me, let these ones go.'
This was a fulfilment of the word he spoke 'I have not lost anyone of those whom you gave me.'

The author saw Jesus' utterance marking his concern for the safety of his followers as the direct outcome of his prayer earlier,[81] and also of his assertion that it was the will of his father that none of them should be lost.[82] The clause introduced by ἵνα in 18:9 marks the Evangelist's understanding or interpretation of this utterance as a fulfilment of Jesus' earlier words, but does not indicate that the statement was made *in order to* fulfil what was spoken earlier. If we insist on an interpretation which makes purpose the focus, we miss the real significance of the particle, which is to alert the reader to expect a representation of the speaker's attitude.

In the following Example (25a,b) of the Evangelist's fulfilment interpretation, inferences require to be drawn in order to understand the point that he is making. This is further complicated by the fact that knowledge which would have been shared by the first readers of this gospel, is not immediately available to a reader of the twenty first century. Consider the passage below:[83]

Example (25a) εἶπεν οὖν αὐτοῖς ὁ Πιλᾶτος, Λάβετε αὐτὸν ὑμεῖς καὶ κατὰ τὸν νόμον ὑμῶν κρίνατε αὐτόν. εἶπον αὐτῷ οἱ Ἰουδαῖοι, Ἡμῖν οὐκ ἔξεστιν ἀποκτεῖναι οὐδένα·
Example (25b) ἵνα ὁ λόγος τοῦ Ἰησοῦ πληρωθῇ ὃν εἶπεν σημαίνων ποίῳ θανάτῳ ἤμελλεν ἀποθνήσκειν.
So Pilate said to them, 'You take him and judge him according to your law.' The Jews said to him, 'We are not allowed to put anyone to death.'
So the word of Jesus was fulfilled which he spoke, signifying by what sort of death he would die.

The following are some of the inferences which the first readers would make in order to make the verses quoted above relevant:

The Jewish leaders had authority to conduct trials according to their own laws.
The Jewish leaders were permitted to stone to death someone convicted of blasphemy. They were not allowed to crucify any one. [84]
The Jewish leaders had decided to crucify Jesus.

---

[81] John 17:12.
[82] John 6:39.
[83] John 18:31, 32.
[84] So Hoskyns quoted in Morris (1981).

The Jewish leaders required to have Pilate condemn Jesus to death, which would lead to his crucifixion.

With these inferences in his mind, the author is recognising the fulfilment of the words attributed to Jesus in commenting on his death: 'The son of man must be lifted up',[85] 'When you lift up the son of man...',[86] 'I, if I am lifted up.[87] Since the whole crucifixion event was of vastly greater significance, the leaders did not say what they did *in order to* fulfil Jesus' words earlier. Jesus is portrayed as understanding that crucifixion lay ahead of him, and indicating this to his followers by using the metaphor of 'lifting up'. Now the author is recalling those words and recognising their fulfilment. This recognition is indicated by the use of ἵνα and the subjunctive. He is not saying that the Jews spoke in order to fulfil earlier words of Jesus. What they said did fulfil those words, but the author is interpreting the action of the Jews in the light of what he remembered Jesus saying before this time, and on more than one occasion. Recall that representation presents a previous utterance or thought either by the speaker or by some other person. The particle ἵνα alerts the reader to expect such a representation.

The Jews could have dealt with Jesus themselves, on a charge of blasphemy, but their bringing him to Pilate was an indication of their intention to see him crucified with his crime being sedition. It was this bringing together of the words of Jesus reported earlier with the demands of the Jews that the Roman governor be responsible for the execution which prompted the fulfilment clause. If the Romans condemned him he would be crucified; if the Jews tried him, at most he would be stoned. The writer infers this and uses this particle with a subjunctive verb to metarepresent his thought regarding what he understood this statement ('It isn't lawful for us to kill anyone') to imply: the Jews wanted Jesus to be crucified. This in turn reminded him of what he understood Jesus to have said on an earlier occasion.[88]

3.6 Indicating Speaker's Interpretation

Example (25a,b) leads into this next section. There are several other instances of independent ἵνα clauses with the subjunctive in the gospel of John, other than those concerned with fulfilment, in which purpose is not being indicated, but rather the speaker or writer's *understanding* or *interpretation* of the purpose of some event. This was exemplified in Examples (1) and (2), for dependent clauses, which showed that although purpose was clearly indicated by the context, that purpose was *attributed* to the subject by an onlooker, rather than being stated as his own. The fact that we have independent clauses, however,

---

[85] John 3:14.
[86] John 8:28.
[87] John 12:32.
[88] John 3:14; 8:28; 12:32, 33.

makes it necessary to re-examine the traditional understanding of these as purpose, there being no main clause on which to base that logical relationship.

So in Examples (26) and (27),[89] the author is claiming that the reason for the coming of John the Baptist was 'to bear witness concerning the light.' This is either the author's own understanding of the Baptist's mission or a report of what the Baptist said about himself, or conceivably what the author presented Jesus as saying about him. The following verse then repeats that representation in the previous verse. There is no need for a main clause, but the function is not to indicate purpose but to represent again what had been asserted in the previous sentence.

Example (26) οὗτος ἦλθεν εἰς μαρτυρίαν ἵνα μαρτυρήσῃ περὶ τοῦ φωτός, ἵνα πάντες πιστεύσωσιν δι' αὐτοῦ.
Example (27) οὐκ ἦν ἐκεῖνος τὸ φῶς, ἀλλ' ἵνα μαρτυρήσῃ περὶ τοῦ φωτός.
This man came for witness, that he might witness about the light, that all might believe through him. He was not the light, but was to witness about the light.

In the first verse, there are three clauses which, traditionally, might be interpreted as telic. I suggest that only the first of these: εἰς μαρτυρίαν is giving purpose alone, but that the other two clauses are reporting the author's interpretation of the Baptist's role. This is reinforced by the repetition of the first clause in the second verse, here without being introduced by a main verb: ἵνα μαρτυρήσῃ περὶ τοῦ φωτός. Now commentators are united in positing an ellipsis here, with ἦλθεν usually being selected as the verb on which the ἵνα clause depends.[90] Burney[91] on the other hand claims a mistranslation of the Aramaic relative *di*, which would then read 'but *who* was to bear witness...' I find this interesting, not because the explanation is convincing - none of the commentators support it - but because it demonstrates the need for some explanation of this use which does not fit the usual translation/interpretation of purpose.

Morris comments on Cadoux's and Moule's suggestion of an imperatival ἵνα here, but rejects it, because

> 'he had to' (so Cadoux) is not an imperative. It sounds more like a construction based on δεῖ.[92]

It is true that 'he had to' sounds like a deontic expression rather than a third person imperative, but Cadoux is struggling to express in traditional terms what the writer is inviting his readers to infer. Instead of describing this use as

---

[89] John 1:7 and 1:8.
[90] Barrett (1965) p. 133, Bernard (1928) pp. 9-10, Morris (1981) p. 92.
[91] Burney (1922) p. 70.
[92] Morris (1981) p. 92.

'imperatival' we could more profitably and accurately describe it as an expression of what the subject believed or wished *should* happen. The ἵνα clause describes a potential rather than actual state of affairs, the subjunctive mood supporting such an analysis.[93]

It seems that scholars knew the problems which arose when a subordinating conjunction introduced an independent clause, but were reluctant to question its telic force, preferring to posit either a main verb on which a final clause could depend, or 'the divine purpose',[94] which requires no clause at all! If we consider the possibility of ἵνα introducing a representation, namely the author's understanding or reporting of the mission of John in Example (26), with the following verse referring to this, Example (27), then we do not need to introduce either an Aramaic mistranslation or another verb in order to make the verses relevant.

Another example of such an independent ἵνα clause may be found in the same book, in John 9:3, reported as the speech of Jesus:

Example (28) ἀπεκρίθη Ἰησοῦς, Οὔτε οὗτος ἥμαρτεν οὔτε οἱ γονεῖς αὐτοῦ, ἀλλ᾽ ἵνα φανερωθῇ τὰ ἔργα τοῦ θεοῦ ἐν αὐτῷ.
Jesus replied, 'Neither this man nor his parents sinned, but the works of God must be revealed in him.'

The author presents the context as the disciples' question to Jesus when they saw a man who had been blind from birth. They asked whose sin had caused this man to be born blind.[95] Jesus is presented as rejecting their analysis and giving, I suggest, a (prophetic) utterance regarding what was about to happen. The works of God were about to be shown because Jesus knew that he could and would heal this man.[96] If we insist on a meaning of purpose for the ἵνα clause, then we must provide an elliptical main clause, from the context, which will allow a logical relation to operate in the ἵνα clause. We are then still bound into the picture of a God who causes blindness so that his works can be shown many years later, assuming a main clause such as 'this happened'.

Just as the use of ἵνα in the previous verse cannot indicate purpose,[97] so here we should move beyond the traditional understanding of this particle, particularly since even the syntactic environment of the clause (independent) provides no evidence for a telic force. It is my hypothesis that in this example a barely questioned but inadequate grammatical analysis, based largely on

---

[93] *ATR* pp. 924-6; *BDF* §363.
[94] Morris p. 92.
[95] John 9:2 is dealt with in Chapter 6 Examples (4) and (5) and noted in footnote 58 of Chapter 9.
[96] Note the use of δεῖ ἐργάζεσθαι in the following verse.
[97] It is almost impossible to imagine parents sinning in order that their child will be born blind.

Classical Greek, has shaped our theological interpretation.

It seems from this section, that in order to maintain a telic force for this particle in fulfilment clauses, commentators infer, frequently without acknowledging it, a divine purpose behind all other actions:

God did this in order that...
This happened in order that...

If, however, we lay aside the telic force of ἵνα as the predominant inference to be drawn from its use, and look at this particle in all its occurrences in the NT and also pagan Greek, we should see what its use really does lead us to infer. Purpose may be inferred from the context, but that does not mean that ἵνα is signalling this, nor that it has a dictionary meaning of 'in order that'. I am not refuting divine purpose, merely presenting the hypothesis that such divine purpose should not rest on one small particle. The purpose of God is stated clearly in many passages in the NT, and more generally in the narrative of events as a whole.[98] We lose nothing by reading ἵνα as underdetermined in terms of lexical meaning, but as introducing a representation of a thought either of the speaker or of someone else. Instead we gain a greater flexibility in interpreting writer attitude and acknowledging the function of quotations from the OT.

3.7 Reporting the Thoughts or Speech of Others

Most of the examples given so far have been concerned with the speaker's attitude to an utterance, either his interpretation of events or previous utterances, or his wish or belief that something should be done, either by himself or by someone else. There are other examples, however, of a speaker indicating by his use of ἵνα what someone else has been saying. Most of these are in dependent clauses[99] but I have included below two which are not. Consider first this example of an independent clause introduced by ἵνα but with no verb at all:[100]

Example (29) οὐ γὰρ ἵνα ἄλλοις ἄνεσις, ὑμῖν θλῖψις, ἀλλ' ἐξ ἰσότητος·
For it isn't 'indulgence for others, hardship for you', but from (desires for) equality/parity.
OR It should not be indulgence for others, hardship for you, but from (desires for) equality/parity.

Paul has been urging the Corinthians to give generously to their brothers and

---

[98] Acts 2:22ff.
[99] Chapter 4 considers ἵνα clauses following verbs of request or command, these clauses indicating what the subject wanted to be done.
[100] 2 Corinthians 8:13.

sisters in the faith who are in great need. He praises their generosity and enthusiasm, but also mentions, at the beginning of this chapter, the great liberality of the Macedonians who gave 'out of great hardship...and poverty'.[101] Indeed the whole of Chapter 8 of this letter is devoted to reminding the Corinthians of their enthusiasm expressed earlier regarding giving to the needy churches, and the need for 'putting their money where their mouth was'. Given such a context, I suggest that this use of ἵνα may actually be quoting interpretively what some of the Corinthians may have been saying:

ἄλλοις ἄνεσις, ἡμῖν θλῖψις *'indulgence for others, hardship for us.'*

Because this is a highly condensed sentence, various interpretations of the clause have been offered. Hughes[102] understands it as a (negative) purpose clause, agreeing with the *ASB* translation: 'For I say not this that others may be eased...' which adds a main verb in order to achieve this. Similarly Barrett[103] has: 'the intention is not...' but points out that others 'would make it imperatival - let there not be'. The general meaning of the verse is clear: Paul is not advocating a policy of giving which makes the church in Jerusalem wealthy while the Corinthians are suffering. The question is: why has he used ἵνα here, and without a subjunctive verb, indeed with no verb at all?

On several occasions in the Corinthian letters it has been suggested that Paul is actually quoting what his correspondents, or at least some of them, have been saying.[104] I suggest that here just this very thing is recorded: Paul is alerting the readers of this letter to the fact that he is dealing with a reported complaint from some in Corinth that they are to be made poor for the benefit of the churches elsewhere, notably Jerusalem.[105] Here there is no subjunctive verb to carry the idea of speaker attitude, merely the particle alone. Surely this is showing the use of the particle as indicating a representation, or to put it another way: ἵνα is giving a procedural clue to the reader, prompting her to expect a representation of a potential state of affairs, *either* of the speaker, *or* of some third party.

We considered in Chapter 2 the different levels of representation which speakers and hearers regularly process instinctively without conscious awareness that they are doing this. If the ἵνα clause in Example (29) represents not Paul's own utterance but that of the Corinthians, then we are seeing a

---

[101] 2 Corinthians 8:1-2.

[102] Hughes (1962) pp. 305-6.

[103] Barrett (1987) p. 226.

[104] So 2 Corinthians 10:1, 10. Consider also the comments of O'Mahony (2000): p. 124 '8:13a is an example of his (Paul's) brevitas to let them know he anticipates their objection'.

[105] Bruce (1971) p. 223 'this criticism of the collection may well have been voiced at Corinth during the recent unpleasantness'. I have found no other commentators who voice this possibility, but it is surely more than plausible.

further level of representation, namely his reporting of ἄλλοις ἄνεσις, ἡμῖν θλῖψις.

To develop this further: we may infer that Paul is reporting what was being said in Corinth, while distancing himself from it (οὐ ἵνα), or that he is giving his own attitude: 'it should not be...' What requires much more inferencing for which I claim there is no real evidence, is reading a telic force for the particle which would suggest that the Corinthians, or at least a section of them, were of the opinion that the *purpose* of the collection was their own impoverishment for the enrichment of the church in Jerusalem.

Consider also another example from Galatians 2:10, again an independent clause:

Example (30) μόνον τῶν πτωχῶν ἵνα μνημονεύωμεν
Only that we should remember the poor.

Commentators view this in various ways: 'a good example of the imperatival use of ἵνα';[106] 'some such verb as ᾐτήσαντο ("they asked") or ἤθελον/ἠθέλησαν ("they desired") needs to be supplied after the adverb.'[107] Dunn does not comment on the use of the particle, but his translation is 'with the one qualification that we should remember the poor...' which in essence indicates a representation of what the 'pillars' thought Paul and Barnabas *ought* to do.[108] Lightfoot[109] points out other instances of 'ellipsis after μόνον,' such as the passages in Galatians 6:12 and 2 Thessalonians 2:7, but they do not, in my opinion, address the issue here of an ellipsis of a main clause *before* the particle ἵνα. As I have argued already: if there is no main clause there cannot be an event or action on which a purpose clause can be based. ἵνα introduces a clause which represents the articulated view of James and John concerning what they thought Paul and Barnabas should do. The particle guides the reader to infer this representation of a potential state of affairs.

3.8 Summary

This chapter has been concerned with the use of ἵνα in independent clauses. It has been shown that in these the reader is invited by its use to consider the introduction of a representation, rather than to assume that a purpose clause is following. Such independent clauses were seen to give answers to questions, to express a wish, rather than a direct command, to introduce a prophetic statement and to indicate the speaker's interpretation of events. Finally, a suggestion was made that this particle might even alert the reader to expect the representation of an echoic utterance.

---

[106] Bruce (1982) p. 126.
[107] R.N. Longenecker (1990) p. 59; so also Burton (1980 reprint) p. 99.
[108] Dunn (1993) p. 86.
[109] Lightfoot (1978 reprint) p. 110.

These independent clauses force a reconsideration of the traditional telic view of ἵνα, since there is no main clause from which, logically, a purpose may be derived as a reason for its happening. If the traditional view is maintained, then either an ellipsis has to be supplied from the context, which would also be possible as a relevant interpretation, or from an assumption of the over riding purpose of God. This latter proposal does not fit at all in many contexts, such as the passages in John 1:22, 2 Corinthians 8:13, 2 Maccabees 1:9, and certainly not in the secular literature.

My hypothesis is that this particle should be seen as giving procedural instructions to the reader inviting her[110] to expect a representation in the following clause. In other words, ἵνα is underdetermined: it does not have a fixed lexical meaning of its own, but functions with the subjunctive, and occasionally without a verb at all, to alert the reader to the representation of a thought either of the speaker himself, or of a third party. It encapsulates speaker attitude, but the specific attitude in view is determined by the context. This is considerably less prescriptive than traditional grammar is comfortable with, but it is much closer to the way in which we actually interpret utterances. We do take into account the semantics of each word, but our comprehension of utterances is driven by the drawing of inferences.

A further hypothesis is that this use was actually present in the earlier language, and was selected by a writer when he wished to represent either his own thoughts or those of someone else. Other ways of indicating purpose were available and were used more frequently than ἵνα with the subjunctive, in particular the accusative and infinitive, or the articular infinitive. It was the flexibility of ἵνα with the subjunctive, however, which gradually replaced the other telic constructions, perhaps because it allowed the subject to be morphologically marked in the verb, and more than this, could indicate speaker attitude.

---

[110] Recall that in this book the masculine pronoun is being used to represent the speaker and the feminine pronoun the hearer.

CHAPTER 4

Requests, Commands, Prayers Introduced by ἵνα

4.1 Introduction

In Chapter 3 we considered independent clauses in which ἵνα was used to introduce a speaker's wish, either as a polite request or as a deontic statement, giving the speaker's view of what the addressee 'ought' to do. The clauses dealt with in that chapter were all independent, that is, there was no main clause which preceded the clause beginning with ἵνα, and from which an analysis of purpose could logically be inferred. These requests or commands, then, formed independent clauses, and were not preceded by any introductory verb.

Of course in the Koine there are many verbs whose semantic domain itself *indicates* instructions or requests of some kind: δέομαι, ἐντέλλομαι, ἐρωτάω, παρακαλέω and many others. These occur as main verbs in a complex sentence, whose subordinate clause introduces the actual request, or 'desirable state of affairs', as we shall see. In earlier Greek, the arguments of such verbs would have been explicated either by the accusative and infinitive or by ὅπως with the indicative,[1] but in Koine they are followed by

- the accusative and infinitive,
- by ἵνα with the subjunctive,
- by a verb of saying, such as λέγω, followed by direct speech,[2]
- ὅπως is also used, but unlike the earlier language, it is always followed, at least in the NT, by a verb in subjunctive mood.

Although such constructions are noted in the traditional grammars,[3] what is not usually articulated is the fact that an utterance or thought which expresses the desire of the speaker, or the subject of the 'requesting' verb, lies behind these verbs of commanding, urging and requesting. In other words, the speaker asks someone to do something: this request, or command, represents his thought about what is desirable. Consider the following example[4] which the author presents as a report of an invitation to Jesus to eat at a Pharisee's house:

Example (1) ἠρώτα δέ τις αὐτὸν τῶν Φαρισαίων ἵνα φάγῃ μετ' αὐτοῦ.

---

[1] Goodwin (1965 reprint) pp. 128-9.
[2] *BDF* §392(i)(c)(d); *ATR* pp. 991ff.
[3] As footnote 2 above.
[4] Luke 7:36.

One of the Pharisees asked him to eat with him.

The use of the verb 'ask' presupposes an utterance such as: *'Eat with me'* or *'I want you to eat with me'*. This utterance is a representation of the Pharisee's thought: 'I want Jesus to eat with me.' The writer then, in turn, reports this utterance in the form of a ἵνα clause with a subjunctive verb. This is called 'metarepresentation'.[5] Usually the first representation is ignored by speakers: they assume that an utterance is the same as the speaker's thought. Since we do not know exactly how thoughts are transmuted into words, *RT* prefers to describe the first transfer, from thought to utterance, as a representation. The second transfer is a representation of the speaker's utterance, which is an interpretation of the original utterance.

I submit that from Hellenistic Greek onwards (300 BCE) ἵνα has been used to signal a representation of an utterance. In every use of this particle with a subjunctive verb there is an implied thought or utterance. This may indicate purpose, intention or a state of affairs desirable to the subject, but the one factor which all the uses have in common is that a representation is introduced by this particle.

Consider this example from the passage in Matthew 14:35-6:

Example (2) καὶ προσήνεγκαν αὐτῷ πάντας τοὺς κακῶς ἔχοντας καὶ παρεκάλουν αὐτὸν ἵνα μόνον ἅψωνται τοῦ κρασπέδου τοῦ ἱματίου αὐτοῦ·
...and they brought to him all those who were sick and urged him that they might only touch the edge of his robe.

Here the use of παρακαλέω - 'I urge'- assumes an utterance on the part of those who were bringing the sick. The request of these people is not given *verbatim*, but instead the author's interpretation of such speech. When we consider what those making the request might have said, we recover an utterance such as: *'Let them only touch the edge of your robe.'*
If we view this as a representation of the utterance of those approaching Jesus, then we might consider the 'desirable state of affairs' which is represented by this utterance to be: *They need only to touch the edge of his robe.*

The author could have used other constructions, as noted in paragraph two above, but I argue that he uses ἵνα with the subjunctive to make salient the representation of this utterance which indicates the 'desirable state of affairs' expected by those making the request. This state of affairs is not actual - note the use of the subjunctive - but what the speaker, or the one requesting, wants to see realised.[6] The use of a finite verb with subjunctive mood allows the

---

[5] This is dealt with throughout the book, but is explained in 2.2.2.5.
[6] Note that Mark 6:56, regarded as a parallel account, has ἵνα κἂν τοῦ κρασπέδου τοῦ ἱματίου αὐτοῦ ἅψωνται, which makes the representation of those bringing their sick friends more vivid by the use of κἄν.

writer to make explicit both the person of the subject: such as 'I', 'you', 'he', and the desirability or potentiality of the request. This would not have been the case if an infinitive, with the subject in the accusative, had been used.

4.2 Authorial Choice

A speaker or writer has a choice when he reports an utterance: he may use direct speech, in which case the resemblance to the original utterance may be a *metalinguistic* one. That is, the formal speech properties of the original utterance are repeated. Of course in the case of a speaker rather than a writer, the voice quality or accent will differ, but the general phonological and syntactic properties will remain the same:

Example (3) He complained 'I hate minestrone soup.'

Alternatively, the speaker or writer may use indirect speech, which focuses on the meaning of what was said, but does not preserve the original linguistic features, such as pronominal reference and tense:

Example (3a) He complained that he hated minestrone soup.

In saying that indirect speech focuses on meaning, we are in fact claiming that such speech interprets what someone else said. It does not claim to give the exact words of the speaker, but an interpretation of what the hearer deduced to be the meaning of his words. This may be a close or loose resemblance. Example (3a) would be a 'close' resemblance, while (3b) would be less so:

Example (3b) He was complaining about the soup.

Now indirect commands belong to the category of indirect speech in which a writer notes the fact of another's utterance as a prayer, command or request by the semantics of the main verb. In the Koine, he may choose to resemble the content of that request or command by the use of the infinitive or he may make the speaker's attitude more salient by the use of the subjunctive and ἵνα.

The semantic field of each verb assumes an utterance which indicates a desirable state of affairs from the perspective of its subject: pray, ask, urge, command etc. We will see that when this desirable state of affairs is explicated by a clause with ἵνα and the subjunctive, the speaker's desire or attitude is being expressed. Not all verbs with a semantic field of 'command' have the range of possibilities noted above for the explication of their arguments: ἐπιτάσσω for example is always followed by an infinitive in the NT, with only one example in which a speech verb follows.[7] The reason for this may be that the semantic content marks the attitude of the subject so strongly that a further

---

[7] Mark 9:25.

indication is unnecessary.

I have included on the following page a chart which delineates the type of construction which follows verbs of request or command in the four gospels. The reason for this comparison is the fact that there is so much material common to two or more of these implied authors. Even where a common source might be postulated, each author frequently has a different construction following the main, requesting, verb. Most of the verbs noted in the chart may have their arguments explicated either by

- direct speech introduced by λέγων, that may be a claim to metalinguistic resemblance[8] or by
- the accusative and infinitive, that is giving an interpretive resemblance of what was said, or by
- using a clause with ἵνα and the subjunctive which gives not only an interpretive resemblance, but also indicates speaker attitude.[9]

Since all three constructions after such verbs are used by the Synoptic writers,[10] the challenge for the interpreter is to discover what each writer was inviting her[11] to infer from the differing uses.

In the chart below I have noted those verbs whose arguments may be explicated by ἵνα with the subjunctive, by an infinitive (inf.), or by using direct speech introduced by a part of λέγω (dsp). It may be seen from this chart that such 'requesting' verbs are uncommon in John's gospel.

The verb most commonly used by the author of that gospel to introduce a request (x6) is ἐρωτάω, apart from two examples of ἐντέλλομαι. Luke's gospel, on the other hand has 32 instances of a main verb with a semantic field of 'request' or 'command', which are followed either by a clause with ἵνα (x14), or by an infinitive (x13) or by direct speech (x5). Matthew has 19 examples, two of which are followed by ὅπως[12] with the subjunctive, rather than ἵνα. We can also see more clearly from the chart those verbs whose argument is never explicated by the infinitive in the four gospels, such as ἐπιτιμάω or διαστέλλω. It should be noted that I have not included every use of these verbs in the writers mentioned, merely those whose underlying utterance has been explicated. Those occurrences of the verb which only take a

---

[8] Such a claim varies with the world view of the speaker. In academic circles quotation implies an accurate transcription of the utterance, while in a less formal setting quotation is more likely to be an interpretation, in spite of the addition of 'he said'.

[9] It has been claimed that the subjunctive in Modern Greek indicates speaker attitude (Rouchota, 1994), and this has also been claimed for Spanish, in Aherne (2004).

[10] The Johannine use is slightly different and there is no scholarly consensus regarding parallel passages, but the data has been added because of such differing use.

[11] Recall that the speaker or writer is referred to as 'he', and the hearer or reader as 'she'.

[12] The particle ὅπως will be dealt with in more detail in Chapter 8.

direct object have been excluded.[13]

Table 1

	Matthew			Mark			Luke			John		
	ἵνα	inf.[14]	dsp	ἵνα	inf.	dsp	ἵνα	inf.	dsp	ἵνα	inf.	dsp
ἀγγαρεύω	1	0	0	1	0	0	0	0	0		0	0
δέομαι	1	0	0	0	0	0	4	2	2	0	0	0
διαστέλλω	1	0	0	3	0	1	0	0	0	0	0	0
εἶπον	2	0	0	2	3	0	2	3	0	0	0	0
ἐντέλλομαι	0	1	1	1	0	0	0	0	0	1	1	0
ἐπιτιμάω	3	0	1	3	0	2	1	0	2	0	0	0
ἐρωτάω	0	0	1	1	0	0	4	2	0	4	1	1
παραγγέλλω	0	1	1	1	1	0	0	4	0	0	0	0
παρακαλέω	2	0	3	5	1	3	2	1	1	0	0	0
προσεύχομαι	2	2	0	0	1	1	0	0	0	0	0	0
Total	12	4	7	17	6	7	13	12	5	5	2	1

Chart includes all 'requesting' verbs in the four gospels, and tabulates the constructions which follow each one.

The semantic range in the chart goes from an invitation to eat (ἐρωτάω) to a compulsion to carry a cross (ἀγγαρεύω), but all may generally be considered in traditional grammar as introducing indirect commands or requests. With all of these verbs, verbal communication is presupposed between at least two parties. The fact that a speech verb, such as a participle of λέγω, often accompanies these verbs supports this presupposition.

The use of εἶπον requires some explanation. I have included only those uses which have an indirect command following. I have omitted those instances which may have an imperative form of the verb, but which then give the content of what is to be told in direct speech.[15] In other words when this verb may be translated as 'order', with an indirect command following, then those occurrences have been included. In these cases, the hearer is being told not to do something herself, but to order a third party to do something.

Further, although παραγγέλλω is not followed by a ἵνα clause in Matthew's gospel, in contrast to Mark and Luke, ἀπαγγέλλω *is* followed by such a construction in 28:10:

Example (4) ὑπάγετε ἀπαγγείλατε τοῖς ἀδελφοῖς μου ἵνα ἀπέλθωσιν εἰς τὴν

---

[13] For example Matthew 5:41 ὅστις σε ἀγγαρεύσει μίλιον ἕν 'whoever presses you (to go) one mile'.
[14] Inf. = infinitive (+/- accusative); dsp. = direct speech, introduced usually by λέγων.
[15] For example Matthew 21:5; 22:4.

Γαλιλαίαν, κἀκεῖ με ὄψονται.
'Go tell my brothers that they should go to Galilee and they will see me there.'

Since this verb usually means 'announce', it has not been included in the chart above, but Example (4) has been included because of the clause following. This verb is regularly followed by the accusative, either a nominal alone or a relative clause introduced by an accusative pronoun, which describes what is to be announced: 'they announced everything' Matthew 8:33; 'tell them how much the Lord has done for you' Mark 5:19. In Example (4), as well as in the passage in Acts 26:20, it also appears with the force of 'tell them to... '. In the former it has the argument explicated by ἵνα and the subjunctive, while in the Acts reference it is followed by the infinitive.[16]

It is generally accepted that the use of ἵνα with a verb in subjunctive mood was widely employed to indicate the content of an indirect command or request in Koine Greek.[17] Such acknowledgement, however, does not always concede that the idea of 'purpose' is not the primary inference to be drawn from such use. The clause introduced by ἵνα may of course indicate the subject's desire or intention, but it does not indicate his purpose. This particle was never used in such constructions in the earlier language,[18] where its function was much more constrained. I argue that the extension of its use to the predicate of verbs of request or command is not the result of an expansion of the notion of 'purpose', but the result of its use as a marker of metarepresentation.[19] The context of indirect command or request presupposes an utterance, that is, the request or command which is being reported. This utterance is not only a representation of the speaker's thought, but involves a further representation, namely that of the author who is reporting this. As noted in Chapter 2, this is metarepresentation,[20] and I argue that it is this which is being signalled by the particle ἵνα, together with the subjunctive mood which is appropriate in marking the desirable rather than actual state of affairs. I have selected examples from the New Testament, Dionysius and Epictetus to illustrate my analysis.

---

[16] τοῖς ἔθνεσιν ἀπήγγελλον μετανοεῖν καὶ ἐπιστρέφειν ἐπὶ τὸν θεόν... 'I told the nations to repent and turn to God'.

[17] *BDF* §392(i) (c &d); *ATR* pp. 991ff; Jannaris (1897) §1761.

[18] Goodwin (1965 reprint) describes it as 'the only purely *final* particle' p. 109.

[19] As noted elsewhere in this study, there may have been an idea of representation inherent in the choice of this construction to indicate purpose, instead of the other options available in Classical Greek, but that suggestion is beyond the scope of this book.

[20] Recall that in order to avoid the repetition of the cumbersome word 'metarepresentation' each representation will be described just in this way, with the reader assuming that different representations may be being discussed as noted in 2.2.2.5.

4.3. Synoptic Examples in Indirect Command

There are many events in the gospel narratives which are considered to be paralleled in each Synoptic writer. I have focused on several of these in order to test the hypothesis introduced above, by comparing the choices that each writer has made in recording the utterances of others. In some passages the content of the utterance[21] has been given by recording the actual speech, whereas in others the interpretation is in view. For ease of reference, the authors of each gospel are referred to as 'Matthew', 'Mark' and 'Luke', with no implication being intended regarding the actual authorship of these. The text is also being regarded as a unity in its present form, irrespective of the editorial processes which may have brought it to this form.

My point in making these comparisons is that authorial choice is not merely a matter of style,[22] but invites the reader to draw inferences from the use of a particular grammatical form. I do not suggest that this is necessarily a conscious process: that is, I do not visualise the author as consciously selecting one option as against another, but as having in mind the communicative effect which he wants his utterance to have on his readers.

The pericopes which I have chosen are: 4.3.1 the healing of Jairus' daughter, 4.3.2 the healing of a boy with a demon, and 4.3.3 the healing of a demon possessed man. In the first two examples the different forms in which the request for healing is couched will be examined, while in the third it is the request for Jesus to leave the area which will be compared in each gospel. In each section there is a desirable state of affairs which the one making the request wants to see realised, and this may be introduced by ἵνα. This is not the same as a purpose clause, but gives the content of the request, namely the state of affairs that is desirable to the speaker.

4.3.1 Healing of Jairus' Daughter; Matthew 9:18; Mark 5:23; Luke 8:41, 42

The context of these passages is the coming of a ruler to Jesus to ask if the latter will come to his house in order to heal his daughter who is on the point of death. Various details are given by one or more of the writers, but the ruler's initial request is presented in different ways, and it is on these different authorial choices that we will focus. Only Mark uses ἵνα in his account, but if the analysis suggested in this study is to be tested, then comparable contexts in which an alternate grammatical structure is used must also be examined. In

---

[21] The term 'stimulus' has been used by Gutt in an unpublished paper (2004) to indicate an original linguistic utterance. This indicates the information from which the speaker expects further inferences to be drawn by the hearer.

[22] Blakemore (1992) p. 52 'style cannot be thought of as something on top of or in addition to meaning...if he is aiming at optimal relevance, then any speaker must make assumptions about the hearer's processing abilities and contextual resources, and these assumptions will be reflected in the form of his utterance'.

short, we must ask what inferences the writer expects us to draw from the use of the form he employs.

4.3.1.1 MATTHEW 9:18

> Example (5) ἰδοὺ ἄρχων εἷς ἐλθὼν προσεκύνει αὐτῷ λέγων ὅτι
> Ἡ θυγάτηρ μου ἄρτι ἐτελεύτησεν· ἀλλὰ ἐλθὼν ἐπίθες τὴν χεῖρά σου ἐπ' αὐτήν, καὶ ζήσεται.
> Look, a ruler comes and bows down to him saying,
> 'My daughter has just died; nevertheless, come and put your hand on her and she will recover/live.'

In Matthew's very brief account, there is no 'asking' verb, but rather an 'attitude' one: προσεκύνει, together with direct speech introduced by λέγων ὅτι. The writer is claiming to give the actual words of the ruler, while the fact of his request may be inferred from the use of προσεκύνει, together with the imperative form ἐπίθες.

From a Western perspective, direct speech is often taken to be a truth claim regarding the identity of the quotation to an actual utterance. In many languages, however, direct speech is the preferred form, as opposed to indirect, because it preserves the personal referents of the original utterance or dialogue. It does not necessarily claim to be a *verbatim* report. Wilson points out that circumstances and culture determine the level of accuracy which is considered necessary for a direct report of an utterance.[23] Even direct quotation should be regarded as resembling the original utterance rather than being identical to it.[24]

In this passage we are also being invited to infer from the ruler's statement that he believes that if Jesus comes and lays his hand on his daughter, she will live. This does not require to be spelled out: it is underdetermined and a reader will readily access this inference.

The Marcan account, in contrast, gives considerably more information, but still leaves much to be drawn out by inference.

4.3.1.2 MARK 5:23

> Example (6) καὶ ἔρχεται εἷς τῶν ἀρχισυναγώγων, ὀνόματι Ἰάϊρος, καὶ ἰδὼν αὐτὸν πίπτει πρὸς τοὺς πόδας αὐτοῦ καὶ παρακαλεῖ αὐτὸν πολλὰ λέγων ὅτι Τὸ θυγάτριόν μου ἐσχάτως ἔχει, ἵνα ἐλθὼν ἐπιθῇς τὰς χεῖρας αὐτῇ ἵνα σωθῇ καὶ ζήσῃ.

---

[23] Wilson (2000) p. 142 'Particularly in academic circles the idea that direct quotation is based on resemblance rather than identity may be harder to accept'.
[24] But consider the use of the term 'metalinguistic resemblance' which attempts to deal with the issue of close identity between the two utterances, Gutt (2004) and Almazan Garcia (2002) p. 108.

> Now one of the rulers of the synagogue, Jairus by name, comes to him, and when he sees him he falls at his feet and urges him strongly saying,
> 'My little daughter is on the point of death. You should come/please come and lay your hands on her, so that she may recover and live.'

Here Jairus' attitude is also indicated by his falling at Jesus' feet, but the fact that he is making a request is shown by παρακαλεῖ. The content of that request is then given directly, introduced by λέγων ὅτι. The first ἵνα in this verse cannot indicate purpose, preceded as it is by a statement of the desperate state of the daughter. In spite of the punctuation, it is an independent clause such as those dealt with in Chapter 3. If we attempt to treat this clause as telic, then we are reading the extreme illness of the daughter as taking place in order that Jesus may come and heal her. It seems to me that a much more accessible inference is that the extreme illness of this girl is the *reason* why her father is making the request, and that the ἵνα clause actually introduces his request. As argued in Chapter 3, it gives the speaker's attitude, namely the desirable state of affairs which he wants to happen. It could be interpreted as a request rather than a command when compared with the imperatival forms in the Matthean account.

Consider also just how much inferencing is expected of one who reads this pericope, but which she does engage in without going through a lengthy logical process. The following inferences are not explicated but would be drawn by the first readers:

The ruler wants his daughter to recover.
Jesus is able to heal very sick people.
When Jesus touches sick people, they recover from their illnesses.
The ruler believes that Jesus is able to heal his daughter.

I have explicated these in order to support the contention[25] that humans readily draw inferences from utterances in order to make these relevant, but this process usually operates below the level of conscious thought. Speaker meaning, however, is heavily dependent on such an inferential process.

In the Lucan account, in contrast to that of Matthew and Mark, there is no direct speech. In its place the author interprets the ruler's implied speech and presents its content in the form of an accusative and infinitive.

4.3.1.3 LUKE 8:41, 42

Example (7) καὶ ἰδοὺ ἦλθεν ἀνὴρ ᾧ ὄνομα Ἰάϊρος καὶ οὗτος ἄρχων τῆς συναγωγῆς ὑπῆρχεν, καὶ πεσὼν παρὰ τοὺς πόδας [τοῦ] Ἰησοῦ παρεκάλει αὐτὸν εἰσελθεῖν εἰς τὸν οἶκον αὐτοῦ, ὅτι θυγάτηρ μονογενὴς ἦν αὐτῷ ὡς ἐτῶν δώδεκα

---

[25] Chapter 2 details the crucial role of inferencing in the interpretation of utterances.

καὶ αὐτὴ ἀπέθνησκεν.
Look, a man named Jairus, who was also a ruler of the synagogue, came and falling at Jesus' feet, urged him to come to his house, because he had an only daughter, of about twelve years of age, and she was dying.

The writer here does not attempt to give the ruler's request in direct speech. Rather he interprets the basic request, using the accusative and infinitive construction. The use of the verb παρακαλέω implies an utterance which includes a state of affairs which would be desirable to the subject, but the predicate is in the form of an accusative, for the subject, and an infinitive: παρακάλει αὐτὸν εἰσελθεῖν εἰς τὸν οἶκον αὐτοῦ 'urged him to come to his house'. Such a construction was less popular in Koine than in the earlier language, probably because the 'subject' of the infinitive had to take the accusative case, while the infinitive itself could not mark person or use its modality to indicate the desirability or potentiality of the request.

The author then presents the reason for the request in a clause introduced by ὅτι. I do not believe that the ὅτι clause is the author's report of what the ruler said,[26] because the tenses of the verbs in that clause are past, whereas they would be present if it was a report of speech.[27] Although the ruler's attitude is indicated by his falling at Jesus' feet, as well as by the 'request' verb, παρεκάλει, the author does not focus on his actual request, but prefers to state the reasons for this in a non reportorial clause. In an earlier incident,[28] the writer does use a clause with ἵνα and the subjunctive after this verb, but in this pericope he does not seem to choose to focus on the attitude of the speaker. In this account alone, the reason for wishing Jesus to come to the house and the serious state of the daughter is not mentioned until the very end of the sentence. The same information is given as in the other accounts, but there is no prominence given to the request. The most prominent piece of information in this account is the fact that Jairus was a ruler of the synagogue. One might deduce that for this writer, the status of this man and the fact that he bowed down before Jesus, was the information which he wanted to be most accessible for his readers.[29]

4.3.1.4 CONCLUSION
I have given three parallel pericopes to indicate the possible choices open to each author in presenting the request of this ruler who came to Jesus. The only

---

[26] Compare the use of ὅτι with a following indicative verb to indicate a representation of factual information, an actual state of affairs rather than a potential one. For a more detailed examination of this particle, see Chapter 7.

[27] Marshall (1978) p. 343 comments 'Luke turns what is part of the ruler's request in Mark into an editorial comment'.

[28] Luke 8:32, 33.

[29] Nolland (1989) supports this analysis.

Requests, Commands, Prayers 85

one who uses a ἵνα clause to encapsulate the content of the request is Mark, but, as stated above, if the analysis suggested in this book for this particle is to be tested, then comparable contexts in which an alternate grammatical structure is used must also be examined. In these examples, we can see that Mark and Matthew give the ruler's words in direct speech. Matthew puts an imperative form in his mouth, but Mark uses the particle with the subjunctive to indicate the content of his request, making salient the desirable state of affairs which the ruler wants to see realised, but presenting that request in a more gentle form. Matthew's brief account leaves the reader to make several inferences about his attitude and expectations. Luke interprets the request, noting it by the accusative and infinitive and giving the reason for such a request in a clause introduced by ὅτι. The reader is not given a signal which would invite her to consider the ruler's attitude or the desirable state of affairs which he might wish to see realised. Such an attitude may be inferred, but has not been made salient by the grammatical form chosen.

4.3.2 The Healing of a Boy with a Demon: Matthew 17:15, 16; Mark 9:17, 18; Luke 9:38, 40

This incident is presented by all three Synoptists as occurring subsequent to Jesus' coming down the mountain with Peter, James and John, after the transfiguration. The setting is slightly different in each, with the longest account, and the fullest background details being supplied by Mark. Matthew, as usual, has the shortest account, with the description of the boy's seizure being omitted. The verses I have focused on are those which detail the father's request both to Jesus and his disciples, since the constructions of each request differ, even in the same writer.

4.3.2.1 MATTHEW 17:15, 16

> Example (8) προσῆλθεν αὐτῷ ἄνθρωπος γονυπετῶν αὐτὸν καὶ λέγων, Κύριε, ἐλέησόν μου τὸν υἱόν,   ὅτι σεληνιάζεται καὶ κακῶς πάσχει· (v.16) καὶ προσήνεγκα αὐτὸν τοῖς μαθηταῖς σου, καὶ οὐκ ἠδυνήθησαν αὐτὸν θεραπεῦσαι.
> A man came to him, kneeling down and saying 'Lord, pity my son, because he is demon possessed and suffers badly... I brought him to your disciples and they were not able to heal him.'

Here Matthew chooses to give a direct speech account of a man's request for help. The father's only request is 'Pity my son', but his subsequent narrating of the boy's illness leads us to infer the nature of the 'pity' that he hopes to receive. He also states that he has already brought his boy to the disciples, again with the implication that they should do something about him, but the disciples were unable to heal him. Matthew's brief account does not use any of the 'requesting' verbs of Mark and Luke, but the reader is expected to draw inferences from the account:

The man wants Jesus to heal his son.
The man brought his son to the disciples for healing.
The man believed that Jesus' disciples should have been able to heal his son.

I have noted these inferences, not because of direct relevance to the use of ἵνα, but because the argument put forward to account for its use in the Koine is also concerned with the amount of inferencing which readers regularly engage in without being conscious of the fact! Language is typically underdetermined, with both writer and reader being able to communicate, usually, with much information left unspecified, but readily inferred. The request to the disciples is left implicit, as is the strong probability that they did attempt to heal the boy, inferred from the statement 'they were not able'.

The Marcan account does not present the father as making a direct request, but it does contain an indirect request introduced by the aorist tense of λέγω.

4.3.2.2 MARK 9:17, 18.

Example (9) καὶ ἀπεκρίθη αὐτῷ εἷς ἐκ τοῦ ὄχλου, Διδάσκαλε, ἤνεγκα τὸν υἱόν μου πρὸς σέ, ἔχοντα πνεῦμα ἄλαλον· (v.18) καὶ εἶπα τοῖς μαθηταῖς σου ἵνα αὐτὸ ἐκβάλωσιν, καὶ οὐκ ἴσχυσαν.
And a man from the crowd replied, 'Teacher, I have brought my son who has a dumb spirit to you. I asked your disciples to cast it out/ told your disciples they should cast it out, but they could not.'

The father in this account does not make a request, but merely states that he has brought his son to Jesus, indicating the boy's problem. The inference which a reader is expected to draw would be: *The man wants Jesus to heal his son.* The father then goes on to say that he has asked, or told, the disciples to cast out the spirit, but they were unable to do so. The speech verb here (εἶπα) is also used with an infinitive construction by the same author,[30] and so, in this passage, the following clause with ἵνα and the subjunctive should be seen as authorial selection, inviting the reader to infer the desirable state of affairs which the subject wishes to see realised. In fact, this state of affairs was not realised, but the author invites the reader to infer the father's desire, perhaps even his expectation, by using this construction rather than an infinitive: *The disciples should cast out the spirit.* Here ἵνα and the subjunctive mark the father's request to these disciples, and invite the reader, perhaps the implied hearers in this case, to infer his desire and expectation that they should be able to cast out demons, which he understood as being the cause of his son's epilepsy.[31]

In the Lucan account of this pericope, Example (10), there is an interesting

---

[30] Mark 5:43 and 8:7.

[31] In the sequel to this pericope the disciples are also presented as being disturbed that they could not cast out this demon Mark 9:28, 29.

contrast between a direct and indirect request, both using the same verb δέομαι, but with a different construction following each:

4.3.2.3 LUKE 9:38, 40

> Example (10) καὶ ἰδοὺ ἀνὴρ ἀπὸ τοῦ ὄχλου ἐβόησεν λέγων, Διδάσκαλε, δέομαί σου ἐπιβλέψαι ἐπὶ τὸν υἱόν μου, ὅτι μονογενής μοί ἐστιν ...
> (v40) καὶ ἐδεήθην τῶν μαθητῶν σου ἵνα ἐκβάλωσιν αὐτό, καὶ οὐκ ἠδυνήθησαν.
> Look, a man from the crowd cried out saying, 'Teacher, I am asking you to look on my son because he is my only one...
> (40) and I asked your disciples to cast it out /that they should cast it out, but they could not.'

This last account of this incident is perhaps the most interesting. As already stated, the author uses the same verb for both the direct and reported request, with only the tense changing (δέομαι, ἐδεήθην). This verb is regularly used for polite requests in contexts of respect, such as to God, to persons in authority. It may be followed either by a speech verb (not common), by a direct command (in direct speech), by an infinitive or by a subjunctive clause introduced by ἵνα or ὅπως. Luke uses all four constructions in his gospel. What follows the verb, however, is significant. When speaking to Jesus the father says 'I am asking you to look on my son...', but when reporting his interaction with the disciples he says, 'I asked them that they should cast it out.'

Now the request, again, leaves the reader to infer the father's wish that the boy be healed. All that is asked is that Jesus 'looks on' the boy, a verb reminiscent of OT language, where God 'looks on' his people, that is, he sees their trouble and helps them.[32] The father does not specify what he wants Jesus to do, apart from 'look on him'. He is, however, more specific in his request to the disciples, indicating that they should cast out the spirit. As we have seen in the earlier examples, the clause introduced by ἵνα invites the hearer to infer the following: *They should cast it out.*

Here Luke represents the father as recalling his earlier request to the disciples. In this context the force of the ἵνα clause seems to mark the previous request, in which the desirable state of affairs that he wished to see realised was the casting out of the demon. Now he is expressing what he had expected from the disciples, but they were unable to do. It indicates his previous expectation: 'they should cast it out', but also reports or represents what he has said already. The ἵνα clause is marking two different representations here: the man's original thought and also his request to the disciples. Since the verb δέομαι has been used a few sentences earlier with an infinitive following, and since I have rejected style as a reason for different syntactic forms, the question arises as to what inferences the writer was expecting his readers to draw from his use of

---

[32] Luke 1:25 ἐπεῖδεν, 1:68 ἐπεσκέψατο.

ἵνα with a subjunctive clause.

As stated earlier the use of the infinitive causes more processing effort to recover the representation. There is no person marking to indicate the subject and no mood to reinforce the desirability or potentiality of the action. When a writer uses ἵνα with a subjunctive verb, however, the desirable state of affairs becomes more easily accessible because of the person marking and the mood of the verb. *RT* does not claim that the use of such marking and the use of this particle is obligatory in the elucidating of a representation, merely that it is an option open to an author or speaker who wants to make such a desirable state of affairs salient.

4.3.2.4 CONCLUSION

In all these accounts, the father of the distressed boy never <u>asks</u> Jesus overtly to heal him. The reader must infer this from a) the statement of the boy's ailment and b) the bringing of the child, accompanied by the statement of this fact : 'I have brought my son....' (Mark), or a request articulated as 'Pity my son' (Matthew), 'I ask you to look on my son' (Luke). In contrast, the approach to the disciples does indicate a request to cast out the demon, but this is reported by the father. We may summarise these requests and the grammatical forms in which they have been encapsulated as follows:

> Matthew: to Jesus - direct request; no request to disciples: 'they were not able...'
> Mark: to Jesus - no request; to disciples: 'I told them ἵνα...'
> Luke: to Jesus - 'I ask' + infinitive; to disciples: 'I asked' + ἵνα '

Matthew chooses direct speech for the father's request, his account of the boy's suffering and the incapacity of the disciples. Since there is no 'request' verb, then there is no need to mark a representation of his desire, although there are several inferences to be drawn, as noted above.

Mark uses ἵνα and the subjunctive to indicate the representation, namely the desirable state of affairs which he wants the disciples to effect. This desire is easily recovered by this syntactic construction, and makes the resultant inability of the disciples more prominent also.

Luke first of all presents the father asking Jesus to 'look on' his son, giving the background for this request. The actual desirable state of affairs is again introduced by ἵνα and the subjunctive. It thus causes the reader less processing effort to recover the representation of the father's wish, and again, as with the Marcan account, makes the inability of the disciples more marked.

4.3.3 The Healing of the Demon Possessed Man: Matthew 8:34; Mark 5:17; Luke 8:37

The context presented in these verses is Jesus' crossing the Lake of Galilee to a non-Jewish area variously called the land of the Gerasenes, Gergasenes or the

Gadarenes (so Matthew). On disembarking from the boat he meets a man (or men in Matthew's account) who was demon possessed. Following on the healing of this man, Jesus is asked to leave by the local inhabitants. Each writer records their request in a slightly different way, according to his own particular emphasis.

4.3.3.1 MATTHEW 8:34

> Example (11) καὶ ἰδοὺ πᾶσα ἡ πόλις ἐξῆλθεν εἰς ὑπάντησιν τῷ Ἰησοῦ καὶ ἰδόντες αὐτὸν παρεκάλεσαν ὅπως μεταβῇ ἀπὸ τῶν ὁρίων αὐτῶν.
> Look, the whole town came out to meet Jesus, and when they saw him they urged him to leave their area/that he should leave their area.

The Matthean account of this incident is, as usual, the shortest of all the Synoptists' narratives. In the conclusion of this account, the author uses παρακαλέω with ὅπως and a subjunctive clause following to mark the intention of the people of this area.[33] This is a stronger indication of attitude than would have been indicated by the use of the accusative and infinitive, and it also carries person marking. In fact this author never uses the accusative and infinitive after παρακαλέω, but he does follow its use by direct speech in several verses: three out of a potential five. Here, instead of giving the actual words of the people of this region, he interprets their utterance and gives their attitude by the use of a clause with ὅπως and the subjunctive.

This was a Gentile area, and the verb the author uses suggests 'leaving these parts and moving to another area' (μεταβαίνω). In this gospel, the author uses this verb more than any other New Testament writer (x6).[34] It indicates a very definite transfer to a different area, rather than merely 'go away' which translates the ἀπελθεῖν of Mark and Luke. It seems that the Evangelist was making salient the unwillingness of this Gentile area to receive Jesus and his powerful acts, or perhaps their unwillingness to deal with the consequences of these. Matthew's gospel regularly notes Gentile participation or contrasts the attitude of Jews and Gentiles,[35] and takes this opportunity of showing, more strongly than Mark or Luke, the attitude of rejection shown in this non-Jewish area.

4.3.3.2 MARK 5:17

> Example (12) καὶ ἤρξαντο παρακαλεῖν αὐτὸν ἀπελθεῖν ἀπὸ τῶν ὁρίων αὐτῶν.
> Then they began to urge him to go away from their area.

---

[33] A fuller treatment of the function of ὅπως will be given in Chapter 8.

[34] Compare the Johannine use: x3, of which two are metaphorical.

[35] Consider the non-Jewish connections in the genealogy: 1:3, 5, 6, as well as 4:15; 6:32; 10:5, 6; 12:18, 21; 21:43.

Mark has the longest account of this incident by far,[36] with many small details being included: for example, he is the only writer who indicates that the fate of the pigs came into the discussion. He interprets what was said in indirect speech, but does not focus on the attitude of the speakers. By contrast, however, he *does* indicate the attitude of the healed man in the following verse, by using the same verb, παρακαλέω, with a following clause of ἵνα and the subjunctive:

> Example (13) καὶ ἐμβαίνοντος αὐτοῦ εἰς τὸ πλοῖον παρεκάλει αὐτὸν ὁ δαιμονισθεὶς ἵνα μετ' αὐτοῦ ᾖ.
> Then as he (Jesus) was getting into the boat, the man who had been possessed urged him that he might be with him.

When we find adjacent verses with two different constructions following the same main verb we must ask what the writer was inviting the reader to infer. This is not merely style.[37] My conclusion is that Mark does not seem to have been as much interested in the attitude of the people of the area, unlike Matthew, as he was about the attitude of the man who had been healed. The accusative and infinitive construction is used for the former but a ἵνα clause for the latter. Such a construction makes the representation of the desirable state of affairs, for the healed man, more prominent.

4.3.3.3 LUKE 8:37

> Example (14) καὶ ἠρώτησεν αὐτὸν ἅπαν τὸ πλῆθος τῆς περιχώρου τῶν Γερασηνῶν ἀπελθεῖν ἀπ' αὐτῶν, ὅτι φόβῳ μεγάλῳ συνείχοντο·
> Then the whole crowd of those living in the region of the Gerasenes asked him to go away from them, because they were seized by great fear.

In the Lucan account, a different verb is used to express the request of the people of the area: ἐρωτάω followed by accusative and infinitive. The general information presented is the same: the locals wanted Jesus to leave. The author focuses on the unanimity of this feeling (ἅπαν τὸ πλῆθος) and gives the reason for it. Of course it is possible that the indirect speech includes the ὅτι clause,[38] but the context does not really support this. Since the Evangelist has already

---

[36] Mark's account has 20 verses in comparison to 7 in Matthew and 14 in Luke.

[37] Blakemore (1992) p. 52 comments that style is also a matter of 'relevance', in that a speaker or writer chooses his words in such a way as to invite the hearer to make inferences, either about the subject matter or about the speaker himself (command of the language, etc.). See quotation at footnote 22.

[38] On this analysis the direct speech reported would be: 'Go away from here because we are filled with great fear.'

mentioned this fear in a previous verse (8:36), he seems to be focusing on the *reason* for their wishing Jesus to leave, rather on the attitude itself, again in contrast to Matthew. In this gospel, the author uses a clause with ἵνα and the subjunctive four times after ἐρωτάω, and so he clearly was accustomed to this construction. His decision[39] not to use this, but rather the infinitive, reflects the inferences which he expects his readers to draw. He interprets the people's words, rather than giving direct speech, but does not focus on their attitude.

4.3.3.4 CONCLUSION

In this pericope, we conclude that each writer has a different communicative intent which may be summarised as follows:

> Matthew: his focus is on the attitude of the local inhabitants who urge Jesus to leave: παρακαλέω + ἵνα ; no mention of healed man's request.
> Mark: attitude of healed man more important than that of local inhabitants: παρακαλέω + ἵνα for former, and accusative and infinitive for latter.
> Luke: no focus on the participants' requests. Request of healed man and that of local inhabitants both dealt with by infinitive (former) and accusative + infinitive (latter).

4.3.4 Authorial Choice in Same Context

In this section, I have selected two examples of the verb προσεύχομαι in the same locational and personal context, where the author has represented the content of the prayer by two different constructions. The reason for this selection is to demonstrate the ability of authors in handling different constructions to explicate the argument of the same verb, and in so doing to invite the reader to draw inferences from the choices they have made.

The examples below present the context of Jesus and his disciples being together at the Mount of Olives. Jesus is represented as urging his disciples, on two occasions, to pray. Example (14) has an infinitival construction, while Example (15) has a ἵνα clause with a subjunctive verb.[40]

> Example (14) γενόμενος δὲ ἐπὶ τοῦ τόπου εἶπεν αὐτοῖς,
> Προσεύχεσθε μὴ εἰσελθεῖν εἰς πειρασμόν
> Being/arriving at the place, he said to them
> 'Pray not to enter into temptation.'

> Example (15) καὶ εἶπεν αὐτοῖς, Τί καθεύδετε;
> ἀναστάντες προσεύχεσθε, ἵνα μὴ εἰσέλθητε εἰς πειρασμόν.
> and he said to them, 'Why are you sleeping?
> Get up and pray that you may not enter into temptation.'

---

[39] Recall that I do not claim that such decisions are necessarily conscious.
[40] Luke 22:40, 46.

Two different constructions follow the same verbal form προσεύχεσθε. In Example (14) there is no accusative to accompany the infinitive. This means that the identity of those who might enter into temptation has been left unspecified. It is also true, of course, that the subject of the clause could be omitted if it is the same as the subject of the main verb, i.e. 'you'. This has led some[41] to posit a source which included the pronoun με, which Luke then omitted. Marshall also suggests that the use of the infinitive here 'is unusual'.[42] My hypothesis is that the question of the identity the subject (of the 'entering') is left open by the writer deliberately. This is in contrast with an explicit mention in Example (15).

In Example (15) the state of affairs desirable to both the speaker and his hearers is stated, *You should not enter into temptation*. In this example also, in contrast with Example (14), the identity of those who should not enter into temptation is clear from the person marking on the verb. Further, the subjunctive mood makes salient what the speaker wishes his hearers to pray for. In addition, the construction used may be the writer's signal that the speaker is alerting the hearers to the repetition of the words first used to them in Example (14). They have been told this already!

Of course, both constructions which follow the verb προσεύχομαι in Examples (14) and (15) may also be interpreted as indicating purpose. I do not insist that these constructions must encapsulate the content of the prayer, rather than its purpose, but I do argue that the former is a more relevant interpretation. The English translations allow both readings by using the underdetermined connector 'that'. I propose that while in both Examples (14) and (15) the author is presenting Jesus as giving a command, Example (15) makes salient the identity of those who should be making this prayer, the state of affairs which he considers desirable, and finally the repetition of a previous utterance.

4.4 Examples from Literary Koine

Although traditional grammars recognise the use of ἵνα with the subjunctive after verbs of command and request in Koine, this is often regarded as an aberration from the earlier classical constructions: accusative and infinitive or ὅπως with the indicative.[43] That this was on the contrary a natural language change in Hellenistic Greek[44] and not merely Koine, may be seen in the way in which it is used by literary writers. In order to demonstrate this fact, I have

---

[41] Loisy (1971), quoted by Marshall (1978) at p. 830.
[42] In the NT, apart from these Lucan instances, there are 12 examples of a ἵνα clause following προσεύχομαι, but none of a following infinitive.
[43] See Turner (1988 reprint) p. 103 where a whole range of 'willing' verbs followed by ἵνα are dealt with as 'instead of almost any infinitive'.
[44] See Bradford Welles (1974) for instances of such use in official documents of the Ptolemaic period from fourth century onwards p. lxxxiii (also texts 18, 111, 141etc.).

4.4.1 Examples from Dionysius of Halicarnassus

This author, not only a native speaker of Greek, but also a teacher of rhetoric and a writer on style, has several examples of indirect command or request followed by a ἵνα clause, rather than by the ὅπως of the earlier literary language. I have included two of these here to support my contention that this use of ἵνα was not limited to non-native speakers, but was part of the process of language change observable from the third century BCE onwards.[45] Consider this example:[46]

Example (16) ἐγὼ δ' ἐπέμφθην παρ' αὐτῶν τῇ μητρὶ δηλώσων ἐν αἷς εἰσι τύχαις· ταύτην δὲ παρά σοι φυλάττεσθαι ἀκούων δεήσεσθαι τῆς σῆς θυγατρὸς ἔμελλον, ἵνα με πρὸς αὐτὴν ἀγάγοι.
'...and I was sent by them to (their) mother to make clear in what situation they were; but hearing that she was being guarded by you, I was intending to ask your daughter to lead me to her.'(MGS)
'...and I was sent by them to their mother to give her an account of their fortunes; but hearing that she was in your custody, I was intending to ask your daughter to have me brought to her.' (*LCL*: Cary)

The actual request would have been: *Please bring me to this woman/ I want you to bring me to this woman*. The ἵνα clause gives not only the content of the request, but what is the desirable state of affairs from the perspective of the speaker, the use of the optative supporting this analysis. As stated at the beginning of this chapter, the fact that a request implies an utterance makes the notion of representation, signalled by ἵνα, a most reasonable hypothesis. The fact that the speaker wants a particular state of affairs to take place is not the same as saying that he took action in order that it might take place.

Consider also the next example[47] in which a noun rather than a verb introduces the request:

Example (17) Ταῦτα λέγοντος αὐτοῦ καὶ παραχωρεῖν οἵου τε ὄντος ἀπὸ τοῦ βήματος κραυγή τε παρὰ πάντων ἐξαίσιος ἐγένετο καὶ δεήσεις μεμιγμέναι δάκρυσιν, ἵνα μένῃ τε καὶ διακατέχῃ τὰ πράγματα μηδένα δεδοικώς.
Saying this, and when he was as if about to leave the rostrum, there was a violent cry from everyone, and pleadings mixed with tears that he *should* remain and keep control of affairs, fearing no one. (MGS)
While he was speaking these words and seemed about to leave the tribunal, they all

---

[45] *BDF* §392,1.c.; *ATR,* pp.1046,1054ff; Jannaris (1897), pp. 471-2, 574-5; Mandilaras (1973), pp. 259-264.
[46] *Roman Antiquities* Book 1.83.1.
[47] Book 4.12.1.

raised a tremendous clamour, and mingling tears with their entreaties, besought him to remain and to retain control of affairs, fearing no one. (*LCL:* Cary)

Here the ἵνα clause gives the content of the 'pleadings' δεήσεις and the attitude of the speakers: *You should remain and keep control of affairs*. If the author had used an accusative and infinitive construction, the person marking and the mood indicating would be lost. By presenting his account of the crowd's reaction to the speech of Tullius using a subjunctive verb form, introduced by ἵνα, the author highlights the attitude of the crowd as well as the actual burden of their cry.[48] Again, the implied utterance is made salient by this construction.

4.4.2 Examples from Polybius

This author's work is frequently cited by New Testament scholars as an example of literary Koine. He was a native speaker of Greek, but spent approximately 40 years in Rome. His dates are 208-126 BCE. Two examples only of ἵνα following a verb of command will be given from this author:[49]

Example (18) ὁ δὲ Λυκοῦργος καὶ Πυρρίας διαπεμψάμενοι πρὸς ἀλλήλους, ἵνα ταῖς αὐταῖς ἡμέραις ποιήσωνται τὴν ἔξοδον, προῆγον εἰς τὴν Μεσσηνίαν.
Lycurgus and Pyrrhias, having interacted with one another, that they should make their exit on the same days, went forward to Messenia. (MGS)
Lycurgus and Pyrrhias, after communicating with each other and arranging to start at the same time, advanced towards Messenia. (*LCL:* Paton)

In this example, the two subjects advise one another about their strategy, viz.: *We should make an exit on the very same day*. The ἵνα clause then represents the desire of the subjects. In this example the desirable state of affairs follows not a verb of asking or commanding, but of agreeing after dialogue. Again, I argue that the utterances implied by the verbal phrase διαπεμψάμενοι πρὸς ἀλλήλους makes such a notion of representation eminently reasonable. The inference is much more readily accessible by such a construction than it would be by the use of an accusative and infinitive. The ἵνα clause marks the agreed intention of Lycurgus and Pyrrhias, but is not preceded by an action clause from which a telic interpretation can be supported.

A further example occurs in the context of the same campaign, but this time from the perspective of the opposing forces:

Example (19) Ἄρατος δέ, διαπεσούσης τοῖς πολεμίοις τῆς ἐπιβολῆς, .

---

[48] Direct speech is extremely rare in the historians and orators, apart from lengthy speeches in the former and rhetorical questions answered by the speaker in the latter.
[49] *Histories* Book 5.92.2 and 5.92.7. There are ten examples of such a construction in this corpus.

συνετάξατο πρός τε Ταυρίωνα παρασκευάζειν ἱππεῖς πεντήκοντα καὶ πεζοὺς πεντακοσίους, καὶ πρὸς Μεσσηνίους, ἵνα τοὺς ἴσους τούτοις ἱππεῖς καὶ πεζοὺς ἐξαποστείλωσι

But Aratus, the hostile attempt having failed for the enemy forces...consulted with Taurion to prepare fifty horses/horsemen and five hundred foot soldiers and with the Messenians that they should send out the equal/same number of horses/horsemen and foot soldiers to these... (MGS)

Aratus, after the failure of the enemy's project,...arranged with Taurion and the Messenians respectively to get ready and dispatch fifty horse and five hundred foot. (*LCL*: Paton)

Here the Loeb translation by Paton has taken the adjective ἴσους to mean 'same' or 'identical', while my translation reads this as 'equal to'. The idea behind both is that Taurion should prepare, but the Messenians should send the fixed number of horses and foot soldiers. Both the infinitive construction (παρασκευάζειν ἱππεῖς), and the ἵνα clause encapsulate Aratus' instructions to both parties. Moulton comments,[50] *apropos* the same quotation, that 'the equivalence of infin. and ἵνα c. subj. here is very plain.' I have tremendous respect for the scholarship of J.H. Moulton, but from a communicative perspective one must ask why the writer selected two different constructions following the same instructing verb. They may be 'equivalent' grammatically, but I would argue that pragmatically they are inviting different inferences. Although the parties involved are to prepare and send out these troops, the desired outcome of the preparations is the actual sending out of these troops (rather than the preparation). The desirable state of affairs represented is thus: *You should send out these same horse(men) and foot soldiers.*

This analysis is, I submit, supported by the rest of the sentence (not quoted) which indicates the use to which these troops were to be put, namely the protection of Messenia and the districts which surrounded it. As in earlier examples, the ἵνα clause makes salient the desirable state of affairs which the one giving the instructions wishes to see realised. It signals a representation, in this case of a desirable state of affairs. The infinitival construction may give the content of the request, but since it cannot give an indication of mood or subject marking on the verb, it does not make that information prominent in the way that the ἵνα clause does.

4.4.3 Examples from Epictetus

The *Discourses* of this philosopher seem to me to be much closer to the writings of the New Testament, particularly the letters of Paul, than the much quoted works of Polybius. When considering the use of ἵνα following verbs of request or command, however, we find that there are far fewer examples than other uses, perhaps because of the author's non-narrative style. One example

---

[50] Moulton (1998 reprint) p. 207.

only[51] is included to show that this usage may be found in philosophers also.

> Example (20) εἰ οὖν αἴσθησιν εἶχον, εὔχεσθαι αὐτοὺς ἔδει, ἵνα μὴ θερισθῶσιν μηδέποτε;
> If then they had perception, was it right for them to pray that they would never be harvested?' (*LCL*: Oldfather)

The example above has a ἵνα clause following the verb εὔχεσθαι. This clause gives both the content of the prayer and the attitude of the ones praying, in this case figuratively, since the subject is 'heads of grain': *We should not be harvested. We do not want to be harvested.* In this verse there is the quintessential deontic verb: δεῖ followed by an accusative and infinitive, together with a verb of praying with its argument explicated by a subjunctive clause introduced by ἵνα. Since the semantic content of the verb δεῖ is already marking 'necessity' or what is 'right' there is no particular reason for it to be followed by a ἵνα clause.[52] The verb εὔχεσθαι, however, may be followed either by a ἵνα clause, or by an infinitive.[53] The former construction allows person marking and a subjunctive mood to make speaker attitude more transparent.

One final example from the *Enchiridion*[54] has been included, not because the main clause contains a verb of request or command but because of the implicit communication contained in the verb of the main clause. The verb προσέχω is followed by a ἵνα clause which explicates what the subject must take care of:

> Example (21) προσέχειν οὖν ἄξιον, ἵνα αἴσθωνται, διότι ἐπ' οὐδενὶ ἄλλῳ τιμῶνται ἢ τῷ κόσμιαι φαίνεσθαι καὶ αἰδήμονες.
> So it is worthwhile to pay attention that they should perceive that they are honoured in nothing else than being seen (to be) modest and restrained. (MGS)
> It is worthwhile for us to take pains therefore, to make them understand that they are honoured for nothing else but only for appearing modest and self-respecting. (*LCL*: Oldfather)

In Classical Greek, verbs of striving, such as προσέχω would have been followed by ὅπως with the indicative. The New Testament has no example of this verb followed either by ἵνα or an infinitive. I have included this example because I believe that it demonstrates the use of this particle to introduce a clause which makes salient what the hearers *should* do. Again it represents the thought which is to be made clear to 'them'. Oldfather's translation may

---

[51] *Discourses* Book 2.6.12.
[52] I have found no examples of a ἵνα clause after δεῖ, even in the papyri, although Jannaris claims this for later Greek: Jannaris (1897) pp. 485, 574-5.
[53] Consider Examples (14) and (15).
[54] *Enchiridion* c. 40 (*LCL*).

perhaps suggest purpose in its use of an infinitive for the ἵνα clause, but the grammatical construction rather alerts the reader to expect a representation, namely of what the speaker, assumed to be Epictetus, sees as a desirable state of affairs, namely that 'ladies' should learn or understand certain things, through the agency of the hearers of his discourse: you should see to it that they should know certain information.

4.5 Summary

This chapter has considered the options open to writers in explicating the arguments of verbs which express the wish or command of a speaker. We have seen that almost all of these verbs may use three different ways of doing this:

- by a verb of saying, followed by direct speech;
- by the accusative (for the subject) and infinitive;
- by ἵνα with the subjunctive.

In fact each of the Synoptists as well as Dionysius regularly uses all three.[55]

My hypothesis is that in using ἵνα with the subjunctive[56] to indicate the content of the request after a verb of asking, commanding or praying, a writer is inviting his readers to infer the attitude of the speaker. The particle ἵνα signals the representation of the speaker's thought or utterance in the following clause. If the speaker attitude is not in focus, then the writer will use the (accusative and) infinitive. If, however, the writer wishes to present the reader with the actual words said to be used, so that it is the reader's responsibility to interpret the utterance, then he will introduce the direct speech by a form of λέγω, usually a participle.[57]

It may be argued that there is, behind the request, the notion of 'purpose' better described perhaps as intention.[58] It is certainly true that the speaker, in asking for something to be done, is indicating his wish or intention. This however is not the same as purpose which implies an action which takes place in order that something may be effected. Further, intention may still be present if an infinitival construction is used: the intention may be recovered from the semantics of the main verb which presupposes a verbal utterance describing a state of affairs desirable to the speaker. It is the context in each case which indicates intention and not the presence of ἵνα with the subjunctive. I argue that:

---

[55] *ATR* p. 371 'It was always a matter of discretion with a Greek writer whether in certain clauses he would use the infinitive or an object-clause (ὅτι, ὅπως, ἵνα)'.

[56] Or optative after historic tenses, as in Example (16).

[57] In the gospel narratives, however, even the direct speech of putative earlier sources may have already been processed by the writer in transferring the utterance from Aramaic, or Hebrew, into Greek.

[58] *ATR* p. 1046.

- The use of the latter construction signals a representation of the thought or utterance of the speaker/subject of the main verb concerning a potential state of affairs.
- When this is added to the semantics of verbs which indicate a command, prayer or request, then this potential state of affairs becomes a desirable one from the perspective of the subject.
- In choosing a construction which makes clear the person, and also the attitude of the speaker, the writer is able to invite the reader to infer the underlying thought or utterance implicit in the sentence.[59]

---

[59] *MGreek* also uses νά with the subjunctive to present indirect commands in every case, the infinitive having finally disappeared. This will be dealt with in Chapter 8.

CHAPTER 5

Noun Clauses Introduced by ἵνα

5.1 Introduction

In Chapter 3 we considered independent clauses introduced by ἵνα with the verb in the subjunctive mood. There was no introductory main verb, making the traditional analysis of 'purpose' untenable, since a true 'purpose' clause logically depends on another clause which delineates certain actions or events which take place with a purpose in view. It was seen that reading ἵνα as giving procedural instructions to expect in the following clause a representation of the thought and attitude of the speaker gave a satisfactory reading to such uses. In Chapter 4 we examined indirect commands or requests, the content of which was introduced also by ἵνα with a subjunctive verb, but preceded by a verb in the main clause with a semantic field of 'request', 'pray' or 'command'. In the latter case, we saw that the ἵνα clause represented the thought of the speaker concerning a desirable state of affairs. It gave not only the content of the speaker's thought but indicated his attitude also, his wish. This wish might not have been realised, but the speaker's desire was being communicated. The clauses dealt with in these chapters did not give information about an actual state of affairs, such as the realisation of the desire or command, but about a potential one: what the speaker wanted to happen.

In this chapter I examine those clauses which are introduced by ἵνα, but which are analysed in the traditional grammars[1] and commentaries not as purpose clauses, but as 'noun clauses'. This traditional designation identifies clauses which complement a noun in the main clause (5.3). These clauses are preceded either by stative clauses, where the subject of the verb 'to be' may be a noun, an adjective or a demonstrative, or by a main clause in which there is a noun or demonstrative which is complemented or expanded by a ἵνα clause. Some impersonal verbs, such as συμφέρει could also be considered to have clauses such as this functioning as their 'subject' (5.4). Other ἵνα clauses function as the object of a verb (5.5) The pertinent fact about the noun clauses considered here is the use of the particle ἵνα to introduce them while the verb in this clause is in the subjunctive. This is not a mere Semitic aberration since examples of all of these (5.3, 5.4, and 5.5) are found not only in the books of the NT, but also in Epictetus and the papyri, while in the works of Polybius and Dionysius of Halicarnassus there are examples of 5.3 and 5.5.

Such complements, of nouns or adjectives, could also take the form of an

---

[1] *BDF* §392, 393, 394; *ATR* pp. 991-4, Wallace (1996) p. 762.

infinitival construction, and for this reason grammars regularly speak of ἵνα clauses as 'taking the place of' the infinitive.[2] While it is true that the infinitive was becoming less common in Koine Greek,[3] the reasons for this have been only lightly dealt with. I argue that *RT* is able to give a satisfying account of this development in the language by considering the role of inference, procedural markers and the salience of representation.

Since this chapter deals with various representations as an explanation of the use of ἵνα in noun clauses, it seems necessary at this point to review what has been said on this topic in the general introduction to *RT* in Chapter 2, and also to expand on the concept.

5.2 Review of Metarepresentation[4]

In a paper which attempts to link the general accounts of 'mind reading' with a linguistic theory of pragmatics, Wilson[5] points out that

> metarepresentation ... involves a higher-order representation with a lower-order representation embedded inside it. The higher-order representation is generally an utterance or a thought.

This allows for multiple representations to be not only possible, but to be communicable between speakers. This may sound complex, but even a superficial consideration of the utterances which we interpret will show that there is real substance in this analysis. We have already seen[6] that a *deontic* expression, for example, will represent not only a thought of the speaker, but his representation of the thought of a third party. It presupposes a thought or utterance which indicates that a particular attitude is good or right. The use of 'should', as in many English translations, is the indication of *deontic* modality. Consider the following contemporary example:

Example (1) A to B 'You shouldn't drop litter on the ground.'

This utterance represents the attitude of the speaker which in turn represents the view of a third party:

Litter must not be dropped on the ground/Dropping litter on the ground is bad.

Occasionally there is no third party, but only a reference to a previous

---

[2] *BDF* §392.
[3] That is, in this context. The articular infinitive seems to have been increasing its scope, *ATR* p. 1062.
[4] Building on the general outline in 2.2.2.5.
[5] Wilson (2000) p. 130.
[6] Chapter 3.

utterance, or even thought, of the speaker.[7] This is a representation of a further representation.[8]

If, as I claim, humans really do communicate regularly using representation of several different parties, then it seems reasonable to suppose that they indicate this. I have been looking for linguistic 'clues' which would signal such a representation,[9] but it seems that languages do not usually contrast a representation which represents the speaker's own thought and one which comes from another source, by grammatical or lexical means, but rather by using contextual clues: in other words, by inference. Consider Galatians 2:9-10, in which the writer is Paul, the apostle:

Example (2) Ἰάκωβος καὶ Κηφᾶς καὶ Ἰωάννης,... δεξιὰς ἔδωκαν ἐμοὶ καὶ Βαρναβᾷ κοινωνίας, ἵνα ἡμεῖς εἰς τὰ ἔθνη, αὐτοὶ δὲ εἰς τὴν περιτομήν· μόνον τῶν πτωχῶν ἵνα μνημονεύωμεν...
James, Cephas and John ...gave the right hand of fellowship to me and to Barnabas, that we *should go* to the gentiles, but they to the circumcision; only that we should remember the poor...

From the context it is clear that the thoughts or utterances represented by both of these ἵνα clauses are not those of Paul, the writer, but of James, Cephas and John, the subjects of the main clause.[10] There seems to be no need to mark this morphologically: the only relevant authors of these thoughts are James *et al.*, although it is Paul who is reporting them. The first ἵνα clause has no verb, but the particle itself gives procedural instructions to the reader to expect a representation, even without the presence of a subjunctive verb,[11] while we may infer from the last clause 'which very thing I was eager to do', that the utterance of a third party is assumed.

In communicating we regularly represent the thoughts of others, and if these are not expressed as direct speech, or introduced by a verb of speaking, thinking or believing, the hearer has to infer the representation. It is of course

---

[7] As for example with the ἵνα clause in John 2:25 which follows another deontic clause expressed by χρεία.

[8] Recall that in this book the term 'metarepresentation' will regularly be described as 'representation', since as soon as a representation becomes public it is in *RT* terms a metarepresentation, but in a book concerned with biblical studies the repetition of technical language is unnecessary.

[9] In response to my question to him on this subject, E-A Gutt claimed that he could see no good reason for a language requiring this (personal communication).

[10] If these clauses refer to the agreement inferred, then they probably include Paul and Barnabas.

[11] There is disagreement among commentators as to whether ἵνα 'fulfils the function of classical ἐφ' ᾧτε "on condition that"' so Bruce (1982) p. 124 & Longenecker (1990) p. 58, or merely 'defines the content of the agreement' so Burton (1980 reprint) p. 96 and Dunn (1993) p. 111. The point being made here is that there are several representations.

true that by using evidentials such as 'it seems', 'evidently', 'apparently',[12] we do indicate that we are representing the opinions or utterances of a third party, but very frequently we represent without conscious thought concerning the cognitive processes involved. In this chapter we shall take the notion of representation further in considering another set of clauses which interpret a referent noted in the main clause, or which act as the subject or object of the verb in the main clause. In these the author of the utterance or thought represented may not be mentioned, but a closer look at the clause will show that different representations are involved. In terms of traditional grammar, these clauses may be grouped together as 'noun clauses'.

The Johannine writings in particular have a much more extensive use of ἵνα clauses introducing a complement, both in the fourth gospel (x18),[13] and the epistles (x9). This compares with Matthew (x6), Mark (x3) and Luke (x2), the fourth gospel then having 150% of the total occurrences in the other three gospels. Nine instances in the three short Johannine epistles is also unusual. This will be dealt with below.

Having reviewed the notion of multiple representations, I now return to the relevant examples of ἵνα clauses which explicate a noun, adjective or demonstrative in the main clause.

5.3 Explication of a Noun, Adjective or Demonstrative

Some of the instances of noun clauses introduced by ἵνα in the NT are preceded by a stative clause with a referent: noun, adjective or demonstrative, which the noun clause explicates. Although such examples may be found in all the gospels as well as 1Corinthians, this is particularly common in the fourth gospel which has 8 out of 18 examples, and which, as noted above, has a far higher percentage of all occurrences of ἵνα introducing noun clauses.

The stative clause may contain a noun, adjective or demonstrative which is expanded and explained by the use of a ἵνα clause and the subjunctive. Since stative clauses containing as they do part of the verb 'to be' do not give a logical environment in which a purpose clause can operate, such ἵνα clauses cannot be read as telic. In other words, a stative clause cannot indicate an action which took place in order that some other outcome might be achieved.

Traditional grammar has often labelled such use 'complementary' or 'epexegetic'. Of course this is technically correct: the following clause *does* explain or expand a word or grammatical unit in the main clause, but the only reason given in the grammars for the use of a ἵνα clause in this slot is the encroachment of ἵνα onto the ground covered by the infinitive in the classical

---

[12] Consider the use of οἱ δοκοῦντες in Galatians 2:6, and the inferences which are drawn from it.
[13] John:1:27; 2:25; 4:34; 6:29, 39, 40; 9:22; (9:39?); 11:50; 13:34; 15:8, 12, 13 , 17; 16:7, 30; 17:3; 18:39. Matthew: 5:29, 30; 8:8; 10:25; 18:6, 14. Mark: (4:22x2?) 6:12; 9:12; 11:16. Luke: 7:6; 20:28.

language. Why this particle and a subjunctive verb should be used is not made clear.

Earlier grammarians, such as Robertson and Jannaris described the use of a particle followed by a subjunctive or indicative mood as an analytical construction, in which the subject appears in the nominative case and the verb marks both person and mood.[14] The reason for such speaker preference, however, has not been seriously explored,[15] although Jannaris does point out the disadvantages of the infinitive. I argue that in addition to the presence of ἵνα as a procedural marker, this marking of person makes the recovery of the representation more transparent, while the mood makes salient the potential state of affairs in view.

5.3.1 Adjectives in Stative Clauses

The adjectives used in stative clauses which may be explicated in the Koine either by an infinitive or by a ἵνα clause are ἄξιος (Jn 1:27), ἀρκετόν (Matthew 10:25) and ἱκανός (Matthew 8:8; Luke 7:6) while Epictetus has πρῶτον in his *Discourses*.[16] Now these adjectives all imply a value judgement regarding the worthiness, suitability or fitness of a person or action. This value judgement may be a representation of an utterance or thought of the speaker/writer, but more commonly that of a wider community. When a speaker uses such words he is appealing to an accepted belief or understanding in the wider community that certain actions are acceptable. By using ἵνα with a verb in the subjunctive mood, a writer is signalling this representation in a way which makes its recovery easier for the reader. These adjectives may also be used with a following infinitive. There may be a representation involved in the mental processing behind such a construction also, but I argue that the use of an infinitive does not invite the reader to recover the representation.[17]

5.3.1.1 NEW TESTAMENT EXAMPLES

The NT examples are not numerous, but are interesting because some, although occurring in a pericope which is repeated in other gospels, appear in different grammatical forms. Consider the following example:[18]

Example (3) οὐ γὰρ ἱκανός εἰμι ἵνα ὑπὸ τὴν στέγην μου εἰσέλθῃς·
For I am not worthy that you come under my roof.

---

[14] *ATR* pp. 1054-1055. Jannaris (1897) pp. 572-3 as well as more generally.
[15] Horrocks (1997) notes the levelling of long vowels and diphthongs as a contributory feature in the expansion of the subjunctive, making ἵνα function as a marker of this mood, but does not deal further with this. Further discussion in 8.4.3.
[16] *Discourses* 1.10.8.
[17] See Jannaris (1987) §2063 for a succint analysis of the disadvantages of the infinitive *for a Greek speaker*, this being quoted in full at 5.7 below.
[18] Luke 7:6.

The author has elected to use this particle with a subjunctive verb to mark the attitude of the speaker, a centurion, to the thought of Jesus coming into his house. The particle introduces a representation of his thought, but this also alerts the reader to the possibility that his thought in turn reflects a general understanding on the part of the local Jewish community. This representation would be: *You should not come into my house.*

Such an interpretation fits the context well. Recall that the author does not present this centurion as approaching Jesus directly, but through the Jewish elders (7:3-4), who then, on his behalf, asked Jesus to help his slave. As the party approached the centurion's house, this man sent 'friends' to relay the message in Example (3). This message is elaborated in the subsequent verses (7:7-8). The use of ἵνα, rather than an infinitive, gives the reader procedural instructions to process the subsequent clause as a representation not only of the speaker's thought and attitude, but also of the community's understanding of what was fitting in Jewish-Gentile relations. Marshall[19] suggests that 'unworthiness like that felt by John the Baptist' rather than ritual uncleanness is in focus here, but Nolland considers both aspects to be in view.[20] He also points out the prominent position of the adjective here in comparison with the parallel passage in Matthew (8:8).

I do not argue that the author consciously signalled the representation, or that speaker attitude is always shown in this way but that the use of ἵνα and the subjunctive had become common communicative currency in indicating not only intention, but thoughts or beliefs of others in which different representations were involved. Such a construction makes the representation and attitude salient. Recall that the function of ἵνα is to alert the reader to expect a representation, while the subjunctive mood marks this as a potential, in this case desirable, state of affairs.

Now these adjectives may also be complemented by an infinitive, particularly if the subject is the same in both clauses. This is the case in Example (4) below in which Matthew,[21] Mark,[22] and Luke[23] all use ἱκανός followed by an infinitive in reporting the speech of John the Baptist. If the adjectives ἱκανός and ἄξιος represent the thought not only of the speaker himself but of a belief held more widely, then such a representation is a factor of communication whether or not it is marked by a ἵνα clause. I do argue, however, that the use of this particle with a verb in the subjunctive makes such a representation more salient, delineating as it does the person in focus and what he should or should not do. Example (4) refers to the same declaration, put in the mouth of John the Baptist by three different implied authors. In these

---

[19] Marshall (1978) p. 281 footnote.
[20] Nolland (1989) p. 317 footnote.
[21] Matthew 3:11.
[22] Mark 1:7.
[23] Luke 3:16.

utterances then, the author may neither be marking the *attitude* of the speaker, nor inviting the reader to infer a representation of a thought or understanding of another party, unlike Example (3):

Example (4) οὗ οὐκ εἰμὶ ἱκανὸς τὰ ὑποδήματα βαστάσαι·
Whose sandals I am not competent to carry (Matt 3:11).
οὗ οὐκ εἰμὶ ἱκανὸς κύψας λῦσαι τὸν ἱμάντα τῶν ὑποδημάτων αὐτοῦ.
The strap of whose sandals I am not competent to bend down and untie (Mark 1:7).
οὗ οὐκ εἰμὶ ἱκανὸς λῦσαι τὸν ἱμάντα τῶν ὑποδημάτων αὐτοῦ·
The strap of whose sandals I am not competent to untie (Luke 3:16).

From the perspective of syntax, rather than pragmatics, the infinitive may also have been used because there is no change of subject, unlike Example (3). In the Gospel of John,[24] however, this same declaration appears with a subjunctive clause, and a different adjective as complement:

Example (4a) οὗ οὐκ εἰμὶ [ἐγὼ] ἄξιος ἵνα λύσω αὐτοῦ τὸν ἱμάντα τοῦ ὑποδήματος.
The strap of whose sandals I am not worthy to untie/ I do not deserve to untie the strap of his sandals.

In this example the author is inviting the reader to infer the speaker's own thought of lack of self worth in comparison with the 'coming one': *I should not untie the strap of his sandals.* I do not claim that the marking of a representation is obligatory, but that the speaker or writer may choose, intuitively, to do so. When he makes such a choice he is inviting the hearer or reader to recover an inference concerning the speaker's attitude or the attitude/understanding of a third party. In Examples (4) and (4a), four different authors have chosen to present the declaration of John the Baptist in four slightly different ways, but only in Example (4a) does an author use a subjunctive clause with ἵνα to signal a representation of the speaker's thoughts about his own unworthiness. I suggest that the use of a subjunctive clause with ἵνα makes it easier for a reader to recover this representation,[25] since both person and mood are marked morphologically.

5.3.1.2 EXAMPLES FROM THE DISCOURSES OF EPICTETUS

This usage is not restricted to the Koine of the NT, but is also found in Epictetus, a Stoic philosopher who lectured in the years 59-120 CE. As well as

---

[24] John 1:27.
[25] Sophocles' Greek Lexicon p. 110 has an example in later Greek of ἄξιος followed by a subjunctive clause with ἵνα, such as in example (4a), whereas an infinitive follows a very similar construction in Acts 13:25: οὗ οὐκ εἰμὶ ἄξιος τὸ ὑπόδημα τῶν ποδῶν λῦσαι.

the many examples of noun clauses in his *Discourses* which are preceded by non-stative verbs, I include here for comparison one of those which does appear following the verb 'to be', explicating an adjective in that clause.

> Example (5)[26] πρῶτόν ἐστιν, ἵνα ἐγὼ κοιμηθῶ.
> The first thing is that I should sleep. (MGS)

The ἵνα clause here represents the thought uppermost in the mind of the speaker: what is first, that is most important, to him: *I must sleep*. The *LCL* translation[27] makes this clear: 'The first thing is that I get my sleep'. The use of this construction makes the representation easily recoverable, more salient than an infinitival construction such as: πρῶτόν ἐστιν μοὶ κοιμηθῆναι. He is representing his own belief by a construction which both alerts the reader to expect a representation: ἵνα, and also indicates by person and mood that this is a desirable state of affairs for him.

Now the *Discourses* of Epictetus have been recorded from his lectures by one of his students, Flavius Arrian, and are thought to be a reasonably faithful representation of the philosopher's words.[28] It may be that the fact that this record claims to be direct speech is the reason for the high occurrence of subjunctive clauses with ἵνα. In spoken Koine there may have been a stronger compulsion to signal a representation.[29] This would also be true of those examples in the NT which are presented in direct speech.

One further example from the same philosopher[30] shows a ἵνα clause explicating a comparative adjective: κρείσσων:

> Example (6) κρείσσων γάρ εἰμι τοῦ Ἀγαμέμνονος ἢ τοῦ Ἀχιλλέως, ἵν' ἐκεῖνοι μὲν διὰ τὸ ἀκολουθῆσαι τοῖς φαινομένοις, τοιαῦτα κακὰ ποιήσωσι καὶ πάθωσιν, ἐμοὶ δὲ ἀρκῇ τὸ φαινόμενον;
> What, am I any better than Agamemnon or Achilles - are they because of following the impressions of their senses to do and suffer such evils, while I am to be satisfied with the impression on my senses? (*LCL*: Oldfather)
> Am I better than Agammemnon or Achilles in that because they *followed* appearances they did such evil deeds and suffered, but the *appearance* was sufficient for me? (MGS)

---

[26] *Discourses* Book.1.10.8.
[27] *LCL*: Oldfather.
[28] The reason for this, as given in the introduction to the *Discourses* (*LCL:* Oldfather), is that Arrian himself wrote in Attic, but the Greek of Epictetus is Koine.
[29] The question of register is dealt with in 8.4.1.
[30] *Discourses* Book 1.28.31.

The logic of this argument is far from clear,[31] but nevertheless in grammatical terms a comparative adjective is explained by a clause introduced by ἵνα with a subjunctive verb following. That clause outlines the grounds on which the speaker might imagine himself superior to the heroes mentioned: *they suffered...because they followed appearance, but for me the appearance was sufficient*: that is: *I did not act upon it*. He is presenting a *potential* point of view, in other words he is representing. The example is included because of the appearance of ἵνα after an adjectival form.

5.3.2 Nouns and Demonstratives in Stative Clauses

The nouns in the NT which appear in stative clauses and are explicated by a noun clause introduced by ἵνα are found only in the Gospel of John, apart from θέλημα. This noun is found with a following ἵνα clause in the passages in Matthew 18:14, John 6:39,40 and 1Corinthians 16:12. The semantics of θέλημα indicate a representation of a thought or desire: the noun assumes that someone is expressing a desire. The verb θέλω in the NT is frequently followed by a ἵνα clause which represents the wish of its subject.[32] It is not therefore surprising that the cognate noun also should have its argument encapsulated in a ἵνα clause, which alerts the reader to expect a representation of the thought of the speaker.

Consider the following example:[33]

Example (7) οὕτως οὐκ ἔστιν θέλημα ἔμπροσθεν τοῦ πατρὸς ὑμῶν τοῦ ἐν οὐρανοῖς ἵνα ἀπόληται ἐν τῶν μικρῶν τούτων.
So it isn't the will of your father in heaven that one of these little ones is destroyed.

The clause introduce by ἵνα represents the thought of the 'father in heaven': *These little ones should not be destroyed*. In this example, there is a representation of the thought of 'the father' within the utterance of the speaker. The author shows the speaker representing what he understands to be the thought of, and desirable outcome for, a third party and by using the construction of ἵνα with a subjunctive verb he makes the recovery of this thought easier for the hearer.

As has been stated many times, these representations make clear the attitude of the one whose thoughts or utterances are in focus. If this representation were merely equivalent to indirect speech, this construction with a subjunctive verb would not be used. In Example (7), the inference in English (in italics) uses the modal 'should' to indicate this. I have not found any example of stative clauses with an accompanying ἵνα clause which are not in direct speech in the NT, or

---

[31] Epictetus is inveighing against the habit of men to act on 'sense impressions' φαινόμενα, whereas in other spheres of life they weigh and balance with great care.
[32] See Example (8) in which the subject of both clauses is the same.
[33] Matthew 18:14.

as in Example (8) in a letter which claims to be a direct address to a particular audience. Again, as noted above, the author's representation of an utterance as oral communication[34] may be a factor in making it salient and more easily accessible for a listener.

Example (8)[35] καὶ πάντως οὐκ ἦν θέλημα ἵνα νῦν ἔλθῃ·
But it wasn't his will at all that he comes now;

The writer here is Paul, but he is reporting the thought, or more probably utterance, of Apollos who has indicated his unwillingness to visit the recipients of this letter at this point in time. The ἵνα clause again represents the thought, and possibly even the utterance of Apollos: *I should not come now. I don't want to come now.* A straightforward statement: 'he doesn't want to come now', would have given the information, although leaving open the possibility that this was the speaker's interpretation of Apollos' wish. The use of the subjunctive construction by contrast marks the subject's attitude more clearly, and invites the reader to infer his thought more easily.

In these examples, the ἵνα clauses, explicating as they do the noun θέλημα, do not represent a state of affairs in the real world: they express a thought about a potential state of affairs and give the subject's attitude towards that. The subjunctive in Greek has usually been viewed as representing *irrealis*, in contrast to the indicative. This use of ἵνα with the subjunctive does not contradict that view, but rather gives supporting evidence for a further nuance which was clearly a fact of linguistic usage in the Koine. We have to consider why the writers used this construction rather than an accusative and infinitive.

It may be useful at this point to comment on the use of the verb θέλω both with an accusative and infinitive construction and also ἵνα with a subjunctive verb. In the NT if the subject is the same in both clauses, then it seems that the infinitive is used, no accusative being needed.[36] If the subjects are different, then for the subordinate clause following, the writer[37] may choose between:

accusative and infinitive: Mark 7:24; Luke 19:14; Romans 11:25 etc.,
another verb in the subjunctive with no subordinating conjunction: Matthew 13:28; Mark10:36; Luke 9:54;[38] or
ἵνα with the subjunctive: Matthew 7:12; Mark 6:25; Luke 6:31; John17:24.

The semantic content of this verb, as also the noun above, leads the reader to

---

[34] For a note on register see Chapter 8.
[35] 1 Corinthians16:12.
[36] Note *MG* (2004) pp. 474-6.
[37] This is the pattern in the NT, see Mandilaras (1973) §573. In the non-literary papyri ἵνα may be found even when the subject is the same in both clauses.
[38] That is, parataxis.

infer that the subject of that verb is contemplating a desirable state of affairs. If the writer wishes to make that fact salient, then he will use the construction with ἵνα. The clause following this verb may be considered as its object, viz. a noun clause, which is why I have included the preceding paragraph. Such clauses display features which link them to indirect requests, prayers and commands, but could also be included in the analysis in 5.5.

There is a real challenge in analysing the various uses of ἵνα in the fourth gospel and the Johannine epistles, firstly because of the frequency of such use: x145 for gospel alone, and secondly because many instances of this particle's use in this corpus have no parallel in the rest of the NT, although, as we have noted, we can find similar examples in Epictetus. Regarding noun clauses in particular, Abbott[39] insists that 'ἵνα in John is never merely appositional', but always has a positive object in view, which reflects his understanding of 'purpose' for this particle.

While I deeply appreciate Abbott's scholarship and the exceedingly careful work he expended in studying the Greek of the fourth gospel, I cannot agree with that premise. In the many examples of this particle following a stative clause, the word being explicated has frequently the idea of an utterance behind it: ἐντολή, θέλημα, συνήθεια. These examples are readily susceptible to an analysis which features representation. Each of them presumes an utterance indicating a command, wish or custom. Several other examples of nouns which occur in a stative clause and are explicated by ἵνα and the subjunctive use figurative language: βρῶμα, ἔργον, ἡ αἰώνιος ζωή. This also alerts the hearer to expect an utterance which does not reflect a state of affairs in the real world, but an interpretation of such.[40] Consider Example (9)[41] below:

Example (9) τοῦτο ἐστιν τὸ ἔργον τοῦ θεοῦ, ἵνα πιστεύητε εἰς ὃν ἀπέστειλεν ἐκεῖνος.
This is the work of God: *that* you should believe in the one whom he sent.

In this example, a stative clause, with an initial demonstrative pronoun, is followed by a clause introduced by ἵνα, the latter explicating 'the work of God.' By using ἵνα with the subjunctive, however, rather than the accusative and infinitive, which as we have seen would have been usual in earlier Greek, the writer is able to mark the person being addressed: 'you'. An infinitive construction could not do this as transparently. The 'subject' of the infinitive is usually in the accusative case, which would be awkward in this sentence. The infinitive alone: 'this is the will of God, to believe...' states a fact rather than introducing a desirable state of affairs, or what the speaker believes *should* happen. The use of ἵνα may also invite the reader to infer the attitude of the

---

[39] Abbott (1906) p.115.
[40] See Chapter 2 for an *RT* analysis of metaphorical language as metarepresentation.
[41] John 6:29.

speaker: *You should believe on the one whom he sent.*

This clause, and other similar ones, has been considered to be 'epexegetic', a reasonable description which 'fits' in this context, as in other Johannine examples.[42] In terms of traditional grammar it is indeed an epexegetic noun clause, in that it seems to explicate the content of τοῦτο, or ἔργον. Since the context dictates that the clause introduced by ἵνα cannot indicate purpose, grammarians have struggled either to fit in a 'purpose' somehow, or to find a label for this use. If we leave on one side the insistence on a telic interpretation of ἵνα, we should be able to view this clause from the perspective of its communicative function. I claim that the reader is being invited to infer the speaker's thought and attitude from such a use. In many of these examples the ἵνα clause is *deontic*, marking what the speaker thinks *should* be done.[43]

5.3.3 Nouns in Non-Stative Clauses Complemented by ἵνα Clauses
5.3.3.1 NEW TESTAMENT EXAMPLES

Non-stative clauses in this corpus have such nouns as: ἐντολή, κρίμα, χρεία, which are explicated by a ἵνα clause. The semantic content of such nouns implies a utterance, or the thought behind it. By using ἵνα the author alerts the reader to expect a representation. This reflects the speaker or writer's thought which is itself representing the thought or belief of another: a thought or belief about what is considered necessary or obligatory by a third party. Again, a deontic notion is being expressed. Consider only one example out of seven from passages in the Gospel of John:[44]

> Example (10) ἐντολὴν καινὴν δίδωμι ὑμῖν, ἵνα ἀγαπᾶτε ἀλλήλους
> I am giving you a new commandment that you love one another.[45]

Here the ἵνα clause gives not only the content of the 'new commandment',[46] but also the desirable state of affairs which the speaker wishes to see: *You should love one another.*

In Chapter 4, clauses which followed verbs of requesting, commanding etc. were frequently followed by a ἵνα clause with the subunctive, reflecting the actual thought or utterance of the subject of the main clause. Here the nominal form of some of these verbs is similarly explicated by a ἵνα clause. In other words, if a verb such as ἐντέλλομαι is always followed by a clause with ἵνα and the subjunctive, it is reasonable that the cognate noun should have its

---

[42] Schnackenburg, 1982 (vol. 3) pp. 54, 109.
[43] This was pointed out also in 3.4.
[44] John 2:25; 9:39; 13:34; 15:8, 13, 17; 16:30.
[45] John 13:34. Note very similar examples with a stative verb in John 15:12 and in 1John 3:11, with the noun being ἀγγελία.
[46] That could have been achieved with an infinitival construction.

argument explicated by such a construction also.[47]

5.3.3.2 EXAMPLES FROM DIONYSIUS OF HALICARNASSUS

Although the fourth gospel is unusual in the number of noun clauses which are introduced by ἵνα and explicate a noun in the main clause, other examples may be found not only in native speakers of Greek, but in serious exponents of style, such as Dionysius of Halicarnassus. These are not common, but they do occur. Consider the following example[48] which is given at length:

> Example (11) συνθῆκαι γὰρ ἦσαν ταῖς πόλεσιν ἐπὶ ῾Ρωμύλου γενόμεναι τά τε ἄλλα ἔχουσαι δίκαια καὶ ἵνα μηδετέρα πολέμου ἄρχῃ· ἡ δ᾽ ἐγκαλοῦσα ὅ τι δήποτε ἀδίκημα δίκας αἰτοῖ παρὰ τῆς ἀδικούσης, εἰ δὲ μὴ τυγχάνοι, τότε τὸν ἐξ ἀνάγκης ἐπιφέροι πόλεμον, ὡς λελυμένων ἤδη τῶν σπονδῶν.
>
> For treaties were in place in the cities in the time of Romulus, having both other just provisions (things) and also that *neither should begin a war,* but the one (city) making an accusation, of whatever wrong, *should seek satisfaction* from the city acting wrongly, but if it didn't get such, then it *should make war of necessity,* as if the treaty had already been broken. (MGS)
>
> For there existed a treaty between the two cities which had been made in the reign of Romulus, wherein, among other articles, it was stipulated that neither of them should begin a war, but if either complained of any injury whatsoever, that city should demand satisfaction from the city which had done the injury, and failing to obtain it, should then make war as a matter of necessity, the treaty being looked upon as already broken. (*LCL:* Cary)

I have given this example at length, not only because it is a good example of an explication of a noun, a treaty stipulation, in the main clause, but because there are variant readings in the second part of the quotation which, I think, bear witness to the difficulty of αἰτοῖ in this clause.[49] The optative may be accounted for as a third person imperative: let it (the city)...' Alternatively, it might be seen as a continuation of the ἵνα clause and for this reason, principally, I have noted the whole sentence, rather than select only the part of it which contained the relevant subordinate clause. The use of the optative in Classical Greek extended to 'indirect discourse after secondary tenses'.[50] This is not far from representation, although in earlier Greek such 'indirect discourse' would not have been introduced by ἵνα, but by ὅπως with the indicative mood.

In this example, the ἵνα clause gives the contents of the 'just provisions'; it is a representation not only of the contents of the treaty but almost certainly the

---

[47] See the chart in 4.2.1 for a display of its use.
[48] *Roman Antiquities* Book 3.3.1.
[49] δικάσαιτο B. (Urbinas 105) and δικάσεται R. (All MSS not otherwise cited).
[50] Smyth (1920) §1823 & 2619.

report of such provisions to the writer. I find it significant that a stylistic purist such as Dionysius still used the optative, which was in serious decline at the time of his *Histories,* but found no problem in introducing a ἵνα clause which was non telic, namely a noun clause. There are other examples also both in Dionysius[51] and Polybius.[52] Of course they are far less common than those in the fourth gospel, but they do occur. Such style is not merely Semitic Greek.[53]

5.4 Noun Clauses with Impersonal Verbs

Both in the gospels and Epictetus there are a few examples of noun clauses which follow an impersonal verb, or a neuter adjective with the verb 'to be', but which are introduced by ἵνα with a following subjunctive verb. These verbs are limited to συμφέρει, λυσιτελεῖ, ἀρκεῖ.[54] In traditional syntactic terms, the ἵνα clause acts as the subject of such 'impersonal' verbs. Again, the semantic field of these verbs assumes a common belief or understanding of what is fitting, expedient, useful or sufficient. This is a further representation, in addition to the thought, followed by the utterance, of the speaker. These verbs may also be followed by an infinitive. The representation is there: the belief regarding what is right, expedient, necessary, whether or not it is introduced by a procedural marker such as ἵνα. This construction is not, it seems, compulsory, but is related to authorial choice. I argue that such choice is related to communicative relevance: the author is inviting the reader to infer such a representation, and making this transparent by using a subjunctive finite verb preceded by the procedural marker ἵνα. One might say that such a construction makes personal the impersonal deontic statement.

In Matthew's gospel, the verb συμφέρει occurs four times:[55] in three of these it is followed by a clause introduced by ἵνα: 5:29, 30 and 18:6. Consider only this example:[56]

> Example (12) Ὃς δ' ἂν σκανδαλίσῃ ἕνα τῶν μικρῶν τούτων τῶν πιστευόντων εἰς ἐμέ, συμφέρει αὐτῷ ἵνα κρεμασθῇ μύλος ὀνικὸς περὶ τὸν τράχηλον αὐτοῦ καὶ καταποντισθῇ ἐν τῷ πελάγει τῆς θαλάσσης.
> Whoever offends/causes to stumble one of these little ones who believes in me, it is useful/better for him that a millstone should be hung round his neck and he be thrown into the depths of the sea.

---

[51] Book 4.11.1.

[52] Book 3.9.3: following ὑπομνήσις; Book 3.25.3&4: following ἔγγραπτον; Book 4.66.10: following ἐπαγγελία; Book 4.73.8: following πρόνοια.

[53] See 5.6 and Chapter 8 for comment on the frequency of ἵνα in the fourth gospel which is possibly unidiomatic.

[54] Note the use of a noun clause with ἵνα.

[55] Mandilaras (1973) §791(5) gives an example from a papyrus of 3rd century CE: τοῦτο συνφέρι εἴνα μὴ ἀπόληται *P.Oxy.*1220,18-19 'This is necessary that it should not be destroyed'.

[56] Matthew 18:6.

In this verse the Evangelist portrays Jesus as indicating what might be a fitting punishment for anyone who causes 'one of these little ones' to sin, or giving his attitude towards such a person: *A millstone should be hung round his neck and he should be drowned in the deep sea.*

The parallel passage in the gospel of Luke (17:2), Example (13), gives a comparison[57] between these two utterances:

> offending one of these little ones;
> having a millstone round the neck and being thrown into the sea.

Example (13) λυσιτελεῖ αὐτῷ εἰ λίθος μυλικὸς περίκειται περὶ τὸν τράχηλον αὐτοῦ καὶ ἔρριπται εἰς τὴν θάλασσαν ἢ ἵνα σκανδαλίσῃ τῶν μικρῶν τούτων ἕνα.
It is profitable for him (through whom the impetus to sin comes) if a mill stone is put round his neck and he is thrown into the sea, than that he should offend one of these little ones.

This gives the effect of alternatives: it is better to be drowned than to offend one of these little ones; the punishment of drowning is better than the punishment which would come after offending one of the little ones. The account in Matthew, on the other hand, seems to indicate that if anyone offends one of these little ones, he should be drowned. There could, however, be the inference that being drowned is more profitable than any other punishment which the perpetrator might receive. This inference may explain the rather unusual use of συμφέρει in this context. Nolland's comment that 'Luke's ἵνα (here "that") seems to find an echo in Matthew's use of the term in a different but syntactically similarly placed clause'[58] is interesting, but cryptic. The only point at which ἵνα might possibly be said to be 'syntactically similar' in both accounts is in giving a procedural instruction which guides the reader to infer in the following clause a representation of what the speaker thought *should* happen.

The impersonal verb in the Lukan example, λυσιτελεῖ, is found nowhere else in the Greek NT, although it occurs once in Tobit and three times in the Wisdom of Ben Sirach. The Lukan example, however, is the only one which explicates what is 'profitable' by using a ἵνα clause with a subjunctive verb.[59] Since Luke has only two examples of noun clauses introduced by this particle, indeed only 45 examples of ἵνα in the whole gospel, the use here is significant.

---

[57] Marshall (1978) p. 641.

[58] Nolland (1993) p. 837.

[59] Tobit 3:6; Wisdom of Ben Sirach 20.10, 14; 29:11 have infinitives following λυσιτελεῖ. Even the solitary example from the non-literary papyri is followed by an infinitive: λυσιτελεῖ μισθώσασθαι ἢ χορτάσματα ζητεῖν 'it is better to be rewarded or seek provisions' P.Hamb.I.27.17 (250 BCE), quoted in *MM*.

There can be no question of a final meaning for ἵνα. I suggest that the author is marking strongly the attitude of the speaker to the proposition expressed, namely: *No one should offend one of these little ones.* The representation of this thought is more easily accessible by the use of ἵνα, a procedural marker, and the subjunctive than the use of the accusative and infinitive, by indicating both person and mood.

Although the impersonal verb ἀρκεῖ is not followed by a ἵνα clause in the NT, there is an example in Matthew's gospel[60] of the adjective ἀρκετόν in such an environment:

Example (14) ἀρκετὸν τῷ μαθητῇ ἵνα γένηται ὡς ὁ διδάσκαλος αὐτοῦ·
It is sufficient for the disciple that he should become as his teacher.

The thought being represented here is: *The disciple should be like his teacher.*

As we have noted earlier, such representations do not indicate a state of affairs in the real world, but they do mark speaker attitude: what he thinks *should* happen. The clause then introduces a 'desirable' rather than an actual state of affairs. It also represents a general understanding of what is fitting for a disciple, namely a representation of the thoughts of beliefs of others about this topic. The author then represents the speaker as indicating a situation which others also see as being desirable.

Consider a further example:[61]

Example (15) οὐδὲ λογίζεσθε ὅτι συμφέρει ὑμῖν ἵνα εἷς ἄνθρωπος ἀποθάνῃ ὑπὲρ τοῦ λαοῦ καὶ μὴ ὅλον τὸ ἔθνος ἀπόληται.
You don't consider that it is useful/profitable that one man should die on behalf of the people, and the whole nation should not be destroyed.

The context presented here is that of a meeting of the Council of elders and chief priests to discuss what should be done about Jesus, namely the growth of his popularity. Caiaphas, the high priest, makes his contribution, Example (15). The ἵνα clause in this example gives the prophecy of Caiaphas, marked as a representation by this construction. The next verse states clearly that he was prophesying, giving utterance to words which did not originate from himself. I argue that the ἵνα clause is marking the prophecy[62] – a representation of the thought of another: *One man should die for the people and the whole nation should not be destroyed.*

Further, the *deontic* force of such a thought, as we have seen in other examples, presupposes the thought or belief of others. The semantic content of the main verb (συμφέρει) may also suggest this. If something is 'fitting' it is a

---

[60] Matthew 10:25.
[61] John 11:50.
[62] See 5.6 for further comments on prophetic utterance introduced by a ἵνα clause.

reasonable inference that more than the speaker believes this to be true. The same author repeats the content of this prophecy of Caiaphas.[63] In contrast, however, in this passage he is not claiming to record direct speech, but giving his own narrative comments. He does not focus on the representation of the prophecy, and so uses an accusative and infinitive construction:

Example (16) ἦν δὲ Καϊάφα, ὁ συνβουλεύσας τοῖς Ἰουδαίοις ὅτι συμφέρει ἕνα ἄνθρωπον ἀποθανεῖν ὑπὲρ τοῦ λαοῦ.
It was Caiaphas who advised the Jews that it was useful for one man to die on behalf of the people.

In the report here, there is no focus on the prophecy, or on the *deontic* force of what was said earlier, only on the man who made it.[64] Consequently the accusative and infinitive is an appropriate construction after this verb. The contrast of these two constructions in the work of the same implied author and dealing with the same information supports my contention that the choice of either was not merely authorial style, but was motivated by the comunicative intention of the author. The use of a ἵνα clause makes salient the interpretive nature of the utterance.

5.5 Noun Clauses which Function as Object of Main Verb

The noun clauses which will be dealt with in this section represent the content of the speech or thought which is introduced by verbs such as κηρύσσω, γράφω, μανθάνω[65] and others. The semantic field of such verbs implies a thought or utterance of some sort. Frequently these verbs are followed by a direct object which designates what was learned, preached, expected or written. It is not therefore surprising that these verbs might be followed by either a noun clause or an (accusative and) infinitive construction. Although they are not frequent, there are a number of examples, not only in the New Testament, but also in literary Koine, of noun clauses, functioning as the object of a verb in the main clause, which are introduced by ἵνα and a verb in subjunctive mood.[66] This is surprising, since it is generally considered that such clauses, if not taking the form of an infinitive construction, would be explicated by ὅτι with an indicative verb. I will show in a later chapter that the use of such ὅτι clauses may be analysed as representing an actual state of affairs, from the perspective of the speaker or writer, while ἵνα clauses, with a corresponding subjunctive

---

[63] John 18:14.
[64] Note the clefting which makes this prominent.
[65] 3 verbs (προνοέομαι, προσέχω, φροντίζω) are not found in this environment in the NT but do occur in Dionysius and Polybius with a ἵνα clause as the object as in the following footnote.
[66] Consider Dionysius 2.14.1 after προνοέω; 2.72.4 after φυλάττω; 3.10.6 after δεῖ. Polybius 2.2.8 and 5.2.8 after φροντίζω; 4.26.3 after διασαφέω; 5.21.2 after προσέχω.

verb, may be analysed as representing a potential and possibly desirable state of affairs.[67]

5.5.1 Examples from the New Testament

While it is not logically possible to describe as telic a clause which explicates a noun or adjective in another clause, it may be thought that noun clauses which act as the object of a verb could indicate purpose: he preached *in order that*. Although the motivation for such an analysis appears to be driven by a conviction that ἵνα always indicates purpose, it is just logically possible that some of the types of ἵνα clause described in this section might be telic. I argue that it is the context and not the particle itself from which a telic inference should be drawn. Consider the verb κηρύσσω whose argument[68] may be encapsulated by

- a noun - most common construction[69]
- a relative clause (ὅσα)[70]
- a ὅτι clause + indicative mood[71]
- a ἵνα clause + subjunctive mood.[72]

When this verb (κήρυσσω) is followed by a ὅτι clause, it indicates the content of what was proclaimed, presenting these as fact, as a state of affairs, from the perspective of the writer or speaker. Consider the following example:[73]

Example (17) ἐκήρυσσεν τὸν Ἰησοῦν ὅτι οὗτος ἐστιν ὁ υἱὸς τοῦ θεοῦ.
He was proclaiming that Jesus is the son of God.

The object of what is proclaimed is regarded by the subject as a state of affairs. Similarly, relative clauses introduced by ὅσα indicate a statement of fact from the perspective of the subject. By contrast, when κηρύσσω has a ἵνα clause as its 'object' (in traditional grammatical terms), there is the logical possibility of analysing this verb with the clause following either as an intransitive verb followed by a purpose clause: he preached *in order that* they might be persuaded, or as a transitive verb whose object is the content of what was preached: he preached that they should be persuaded: 'you should/must be

---

[67] This nomenclature is that of Carston (2002) p. 377.
[68] This analysis refers to the NT, since this verb is more commonly used there than in pagan writings.
[69] Many examples such as Matthew 3:23; Mark 1:4; Luke 9:2. There is an infinitive following in Romans 2:21.
[70] Mark 5:20; Luke 8:39.
[71] Acts 9:20; 1Corinthians 15:12.
[72] Mark 6:12.
[73] Acts 9:20.

persuaded'. I argue that the selection of one of these options does not depend on a fixed lexical meaning for ἵνα, but should be made on grounds of relevance, which will usually be determined by context.[74] Consider the following example:[75]

Example (18) Καὶ ἐξελθόντες ἐκήρυξαν ἵνα μετανοῶσιν...
Then going out, they announced that they/people should repent...*or*
Then going out, they preached *in order that* people might repent

Here the first translation treats the ἵνα clause almost as functioning as an indirect command. Whether it is considered in this way, or as the object of what was preached, since this verb is frequently accompanied by a direct object, this particle is analysed as giving procedural instructions to the reader to expect a representation. If taken as an indirect command, then this represents the thought or desire of the subjects of the main verb (the Twelve): *They should repent.*
The same representation might also show the content of what they announced or preached: *People should repent.* Note again the *deontic* force[76] which is seen in a clause which marks the person of the one who is to act, but which is absent when the infinitive is used.[77] Such a deontic force may also alert the reader to a further representation, viz. what they had been told to preach. This would create a further representation,[78] which it would be the responsibility of the reader to recover. The verb μετανοέω is not considered to be a Marcan favourite,[79] but a wider context would allow the recovery of such an implicature as:

Jesus told the Twelve
that they should preach that people should repent

The second translation given above is also grammatically possible: 'they preached in order that they might repent', where the ἵνα clause gives only the purpose of the preaching and not its content. Although this may certainly have been the ultimate goal of the preaching, it is not the most readily recoverable interpretation of the clause, in spite of the adherence to a telic view of ἵνα, and the major translations do not reflect this:

---

[74] Recall that it is my argument that this particle, in Koine, no longer signals a *logical* relationship, but gives the reader procedural instructions.
[75] Mark 6:12.
[76] Consider Example (1) in this chapter. If a speaker indicates that someone *should* do something he is reflecting (almost always) the beliefs of some person(s) other than himself. This is *deontic modality* and presupposes a metarepresentation of some kind.
[77] Note the difference in English between: 'They told him to go' and 'They told him that he should go.' The former gives a direct command, whereas the latter is representing the belief of some persons that going is the 'right' thing to do, or what he ought to do.
[78] Note again 5.2 and 5.2.1 as well as 2.2.2.5.
[79] The only other occurrence is at 1:15.

NIV: They went out and preached that people should repent.
KJV: And they went out and preached that men should repent.
NASB: And they went out and preached that *men* should repent.
NRSV: So they went out and proclaimed that all should repent.

The translators are thus inferring the most relevant interpretation of this ἵνα clause in the context. Perhaps they would describe this as the interpretation which 'makes more sense', but in essence it is the most relevant. Although the second translation is logically possible, the context is describing the activity of those sent out. Their preaching is mentioned in the context of other activities, such as casting out demons and healing the sick. Given that context, the ἵνα clause more naturally describes *what* was preached rather than *why*. This is reflected in the scholarly opinion of Gould, Guelich and Taylor.[80]

Similarly, the verb γράφω is followed by different constructions, which may indicate:

- the actual words written: often ὅτι with direct speech,
- a summary of direct speech: accusative and infinitive or ὅτι with the indicative,
- the purpose for which they were written: ἵνα with the subjunctive.

The latter construction, however, may also be used to represent an indirect command and it is only the context which gives the clues from which such inferences are drawn. Consider the following contrastive examples[81] of clauses which follow this verb:

Example (19) Μωϋσῆς ἔγραψεν ἡμῖν ὅτι ἐάν τινος ἀδελφὸς ἀποθάνῃ καὶ καταλίπῃ γυναῖκα καὶ μὴ ἀφῇ τέκνον, ἵνα λάβῃ ὁ ἀδελφὸς αὐτοῦ τὴν γυναῖκα καὶ ἐξαναστήσῃ σπέρμα τῷ ἀδελφῷ αὐτοῦ.
'Moses wrote for us that if someone's brother dies and leaves a wife and no surviving child, his brother should take the wife and raise up issue for his brother.'

This is the regular use of ὅτι to introduce the content of what was written, but within that content there is a ἵνα clause which cannot indicate purpose, but rather the indirect command of Moses: 'the brother...should...' The ἵνα clause then represents what Moses wants the brother to do or Moses' report of what someone else wants the brother to do, namely what he should do. Given the belief that the law was given to Moses, rather than that he was the author of it, the latter interpretation would seem to be the more relevant.

---

[80] Guelich (1989) p. 323; Gould (1896) p. 108; Taylor (1981) pp. 302, 306.
[81] Mark 12:19, Example (19) and Luke 20:28, Example (20).

Noun Clauses 119

In the Lucan[82] parallel to this verse, there is no introductory ὅτι. The quotation begins with a conditional clause, as in the Marcan example, but following, as in Example (19), there is a ἵνα clause which gives both the content of Moses' 'writing' and his instruction.[83] This example has been added here because there are other instances[84] in which the ἵνα clause following γράφω, *does* introduce the purpose of the subject of the main clause, but this has been inferred from the context and not from the use of ἵνα *per se*.

5.5.2 Examples from Epictetus

I have not found examples of γράφω, or κηρύσσω followed by ἵνα in the writings which I have taken as part of my data base, but there is one example in the *Discourses* of Epictetus whose interest lies in making a distinction between the inferences drawn from the use of a ἵνα clause which could not, I claim, be drawn from an infinitival construction. Consider the following example:[85]

Example (20) ἔμαθον ἵνα πᾶν τὸ γινόμενον ἴδω ὅτι, ἂν ἀπροαίρετον ᾖ, οὐδέν ἐστι πρὸς ἐμέ.
I have learned that I should see that everything that happens, however undesirable it might be, is nothing to me. (MGS)
I have learned to see... (*LCL*: Oldfather)

I argue that, contrary to the translation of Oldfather, the use of the ἵνα clause here with a subjunctive verb invites the reader to infer what the speaker *should* do rather than what he actually does. Oldfather, I suggest, is translating as he does because he views this particle as 'taking the place of' the infinitive. Of course the speaker could also have used ὅτι if he had been describing what he had learned,[86] in factual terms, but the use of the subjunctive with ἵνα alerts the reader to expect a representation of what the speaker *should* learn, rather than what he actually *did* learn. The proposition expressed by the ὅτι clause is a tenet of Stoic philosophy which more than Epictetus held: 'everything that happens is nothing to me'. The clause introduced by ἵνα then leads the reader to infer that Epictetus is saying that he *should* see things in this way, rather than claiming that he actually does so.

---

[82] Matthew 22:24 has no ἵνα but rather a future tense ἐπιγαμβρεύσει, as in Deuteronomy 25:5 *LXX*, the latter using different verbs.

[83] Marshall (1978) 'ἵνα...should be probably taken in the rare imperatival sense' p. 739. Nolland (1993) does not comment on the particle but translates the following subjunctive verb as 'must take', p. 962.

[84] Luke 1:4; John 20:31; Romans 15:4; 1John 5:13.

[85] *Discourses* 1.29.24.

[86] Note Acts 23:27 μαθὼν ὅτι ῾Ρωμαῖός ἐστιν in which the ὅτι clause describes what the subject learned to be the actual state of affairs, rather than a potential one; also Phil 4:11 in which the infinitive is used to describe *what* the subject learned: ἔμαθον ἐν οἷς εἰμι αὐτάρκης εἶναι.

Similarly, the verb ἐκδέχομαι when followed by a ἵνα clause indicates what the subject *should* expect, rather than what he does expect. Consider the following example from the *Discourses*:[87]

Example (21) ἐπεὶ τί ἐκδέχῃ; ἵνα τις ἀποστῇ αὐτοῦ καὶ τοῦ ἰδίου συμφέροντος;
So what do you expect? That someone should separate from himself and his own interests? (MGS)
For what do you expect? That a man should neglect himself and his own interest? (*LCL*: Oldfather).

Now we have already considered examples of an independent ἵνα clause which answers a question posed by the same speaker,[88] but here the answer is in the form of a noun clause,[89] which might be analysed as expanding the τί of the question. Typically such sentences would ask the question 'what?' with the ἵνα clause giving the answer. Grammatically this is correct, but in terms of explaining the reason for the occurrence both of ἵνα and of the subjunctive, it is inadequate. This particle is giving procedural instructions to the reader to expect a representation either of a thought of the speaker or of someone else. In this instance it would be: *Someone should separate from himself and his own interests.*

Note, however, that the speaker, by the device of a question followed by an answer which is also a question, distances himself from this thought. It seems to me that rhetorical questions regularly do this very thing. They are *echoic*,[90] stating potential opinions, or perhaps even actual ones, which the speaker wishes to articulate in order to discuss and, usually, discard. The potential thought is not one with which the speaker agrees, but he states it, subsequently asserting his own view. This is a representation of the thought, that is the expectation of the hearer to whom the question is addressed. In Example (21) the distancing is achieved by a question in the form of a clause introduced by ἵνα which has a verb in subjunctive mood. The particle functions as a procedural marker to alert the hearer or reader to expect a representation, while the subjunctive mood indicates the potential rather than the actual nature of that representation.

In the NT corpus consider how frequently[91] Paul asks rhetorical questions which are then followed by μὴ γένοιτο. The questions articulate a potential

---

[87] Book I.19.15.

[88] See 3.1.1, Examples 4 (Polybius) and 5 (1Corinthians 9:18). Also in Chapter 3, I considered examples of ἵνα clauses which were independent, but which answered a previous question.

[89] As in 1Corinthians 9:18.

[90] See 2.2.2.5.1, but also Noh (2000) pp. 94-8 for a detailed analysis of echoic utterances, and in particular of questions.

[91] In Romans.

Noun Clauses 121

point of view which a hearer might hold, but with which the speaker disagrees. The reply μὴ γένοιτο then makes such disagreement patent.[92]

5.6 Prophetic Utterance Introduced by ἵνα

This section will consider several examples of ἵνα clauses which follow the noun ὥρα and which have proved difficult to analyse, given that a telic interpretation is not possible without theological gymnastics. Translations deal with this by using 'when' as a translation of the particle, but as this cannot be the lexical entry for ἵνα, the reason for its use is not being addressed. I deal with this at length in order to address the question of 'Semitic influence' or even 'mistranslation', which, although not an issue in current scholarship, is evident in earlier commentaries on the fourth gospel.

Burney[93] has suggested that such a use of ἵνα in the Johannine writings arose from a mistranslation of the Aramaic *di*, which has a much wider semantic field than ἵνα. If this were the case, however, one would have expected to find one of the translators of the Septuagint making the same mistake,[94] but I have not discovered this particle being used to translate the Hebrew *asher* or *ci*.[95] Torrey[96] and Colwell[97] disagree with Burney's analysis, suggesting instead that the particle with a subjunctive clause is functioning as an infinitive would have in the earlier language. This of course is true, but it then raises the wider question of *why* this construction came to be more popular than the infinitive, particularly as an alternative to a noun clause. This will be dealt with in more detail in Chapter 8 which examines the diachronic use of ἵνα.[98]

Although I have not discovered Greek writings contemporaneous with the fourth gospel which also use a ἵνα clause following a noun with temporal reference such as ὥρα, it is certainly clear that later Greek did so, and with no Semitic influence.[99]

Moulton[100] quotes G.R. Driver's example from 'late Greek' of καιρὸς ἔρχεται (ἐστιν) ἵνα and Thumb[101] gives a similar use in Modern Greek of

---

[92] Romans 3:4, 6, 31; 6:2; 7:7, 13; 9:14; 11:1, 11. The phrase μὴ γένοιτο is ubiquitous in the *Discourses* of Epictetus.
[93] Burney (1922).
[94] But from a Hebrew rather than an Aramaic original.
[95] Using Hatch & Redpath (1987 reprint) with Muraoka (1998).
[96] Torrey (1933) p. 328.
[97] Colwell (1931).
[98] Jannaris (1897) §2063.
[99] Jannaris §2081 notes the verbal infinitive following ὥρα and quotes Plato *Apol.* 42A: ἀλλὰ γὰρ ἤδη ὥρα ἀπιέναι 'for it is already the hour to go away'. Mandilaras (1973): 'The Greek and Semitic languages possessed parallel usages which developed in a similar manner but independently' p. 50.
[100] Moulton (1979 reprint) p. 470.
[101] Thumb (1912) p. 187. This example is late 19th century.

ἦρθεν ἡ ὥρα νά πεθάνῃ 'the hour came to die.' It seems therefore that we have to look for an explanation outside of mistranslation or Semitic Greek for the unusual use of ἵνα in these examples. Of course it is true that a use which is acceptable to Greek speakers if used occasionally may become less natural when used to excess in the speech of a non-native speaker. Nevertheless, every unusual use of ἵνα with the subjunctive in the fourth gospel may be found in pagan Greek writers, albeit not to the same extent. It may be that we are seeing the adoption of a perfectly acceptable idiom which was favoured above the alternative grammatical structures by a writer for whom Greek was not a first language. On the other hand, it is also true that in Modern Greek νά is so common that it is regarded as a marker of the subjunctive mood.[102] It is surely unlikely that first language speakers of Greek would have adopted constructions that were patently Semitic in origin.

Further, since the author uses ὅτε following ὥρα in passages in John 4:21, 23; 5:25; 16:25, as well as ἐν ᾗ in 5:28, we have to ask if he is inviting his readers to infer something further from such a use of this particle, rather than 'mistranslating'. There are four occurrences of ἵνα with the subjunctive following the noun ὥρα. In each case the clause in question refers not only to a future event, although the main clause reads 'the hour has come'/ 'the hour now is..', but to a prophetic interpretation of such an event. I suggest that this prophetic interpretation is a representation of the author's understanding of what this utterance conveyed to those who heard it. Three of these examples are placed by the author in the speech of Jesus, while a fourth (John13:1) is the author's own comment on his view of Jesus' understanding of his future. The author is alerting the reader to several representations. The use of ὥρα in the fourth gospel to indicate a special future time, rather than just an hour of the day, is well recognised.[103] I claim that by explicating this word with a ἵνα clause, the author is inviting the reader to access the various representations involved. As noted above, he does not invariably use this construction: in fact there are as many occurrences of the word[104] which are not followed by ἵνα than those which are (5:4). I do not claim that the use of this particle is obligatory, but that when used, it gives the reader a procedural clue to assist in the recovery of a representation, or in this instance, a series of representations.[105] Consider only one example, which is not in direct speech:[106]

---

[102] See 8.5 on the diachronic use of this particle for further discussion.

[103] Occurs 16 times in this sense; 26 in total in this gospel. Brown (1966) pp. 517-8; Morris (1971) pp. 592-3.

[104] That is, where a subordinate clause follows ὥρα. In several instances a statement is made about the 'hour', in a metaphorical sense, but no clause expands the meaning: 2:4; 7:30; 8:20; 12:27 (x2); 16:4; 17:1.

[105] John 16:32, is widely taken to refer to the prophecy of Zecharaiah 13:7.

[106] John 13:1.

Example (22) εἰδὼς ὁ' Ἰησοῦς ὅτι ἦλθεν αὐτοῦ ἡ ὥρα ἵνα μεταβῇ ἐκ τοῦ κόσμου τούτου πρὸς τὸν πατέρα...
Jesus, knowing that the hour had come that he should go from this world to the father...

In this example the author uses a ὅτι clause to describe what Jesus knew, a representation of a state of affairs from the speaker's perspective, but then uses a ἵνα clause as a representation of a *potential* state of affairs: what Jesus is presented as understanding by the concept of ὥρα in this context. The author presents that understanding as being revealed[107] to Jesus, from which we infer these representations. The author has placed other examples of this construction within the speech of Jesus, and it may be seen that the reference has to be to a future time, thus adding further support to my contention that the author is marking such use as potential rather than actual, indeed as prophetic: a representation of what was revealed to the speaker by God, in biblical terms. Consider the passage in John 16:32:

Example (23) ἰδοὺ ἔρχεται ὥρα καὶ ἐλήλυθεν ἵνα σκορπισθῆτε ἕκαστος εἰς τὰ ἴδια κἀμὲ μόνον ἀφῆτε·
Look, the hour is coming and has (even) come that you will be scattered, each one, to his own place and will leave me alone.

Even if the reference to Zechariah 13:7 in this example is not accepted, it is clear that a future event is being alluded to. The Evangelist is inviting his readers to see this as a prophetic utterance from Jesus, either as a revelation from God, or a representation of an earlier prophetic utterance.

The clauses in this section may be regarded as noun clauses which explicate a noun in the main clause, but behind the explication there are various representations to which the reader is alerted by the marked use of ἵνα with a subjunctive verb. In other contexts the use of ἵνα with a verb in the subjunctive has been said to indicate a potential or desirable state of affairs. In these examples the state of affairs is still potential, but not necessarily desirable.

5.7 Summary
We have seen in this chapter the use of clauses introduced by ἵνα which may function as:

- 5.3 the explication of a noun, adjective or demonstrative in a stative or non-stative clause,
- 5.4 the 'subject' of an impersonal verb,
- 5.5 the object of a verb indicating verbal utterance,

---

[107] Not made explicit, but it is a reasonable inference.

- 5.6 the interpretation of an utterance as prophetic.

With the exception of 5.5, it is impossible, without the addition of serious theological assumptions, to interpret the ἵνα clauses in this chapter as telic. Even the summoning of these theological assumptions is driven by the persistent belief that ἵνα clauses indicate purpose.

The traditional explanation for a noun clause introduced by ἵνα is that it is 'epexegetic.' Somehow an idea of 'goal' may be attached to this. In some examples there may certainly be an idea of purpose, but this comes from inferences which are derived from information out with the sentence. The semantics of θελήμα, for example, may suggest 'goal', but in fact 'wishing' or 'wanting' frequently depends on others for realisation. To infer purpose we have to stipulate an action which occurred with a particular goal in view. Of course, if it is the will of God which is in question, theologically it may be seen as inevitably being realised. This, however, is based on inferences which are not part of the propositional content of the sentence. Such an interpretation cannot depend on the meaning of the particle ἵνα.

Certainly these are noun clauses in syntactic terms, but this analysis does not give an explanation of the use of ἵνα with a subjunctive verb in this context. In fact the use of the term 'noun clause' neatly avoids the question of why a particle which has been regarded as having a lexical meaning of 'in order to' appears in a context in which a telic interpretation is impossible.[108] Similarly the statement that these 'take the place of the infinitive' does not explain their occurrence, but refers only to the fact that both constructions are not only possible but actual in the work of one author. *BDF*[109] regards such clauses (i.e. ἵνα clauses with a subjunctive verb which seem to complement the main verb), as an alternative for the infinitive, the classical way of encapsulating such a complement. In describing an explanatory or epexegetic infinitive they note that 'ἵνα can also take the place of the infinitive, especially in John.'[110] Now it is true that the infinitive was giving way to constructions such as ἵνα with the subjunctive, and ὅτι with the indicative,[111] but the reason for this and its effect have not, it seems to me, been adequately dealt with. From a linguistic perspective, certain constructions do not merely 'give way' without indications of trends or forces which have brought this about.

---

[108] The only 'noun' clauses which might posibly be treated as telic are those which follow verbs such as κηρύσσω, 5.5, Example (18).

[109] *BDF* §392.

[110] *BDF* §394. In the same section they also point out that 'if the epexegetical phrase refers to an actual fact, Jn uses ὅτι rather than ἵνα.'

[111] *BDF* §388, Horrocks (1997) pp. 45, 75; *ATR* pp.111, 371, 996; Jannaris (1897) §1762, 1766; Mandilaras (1973) §732-4, §793.

The extended use of ἵνα clauses is often spoken of as 'non-classical.'[112] This is true, but is usually stated not to indicate an historical fact, but to assert the superiority of the earlier language, and is based on the assumption that what is classical is normative and 'correct', with any deviation being grammatically inferior. Koine Greek followed on from 'Great Attic', but the changes its speakers introduced should not be considered, automatically, as inferior to the classical language and a reflection of non-native speaker (in)competence.

> Language is not just a convenient labelling of the 'real' world. Rather it is itself a unique, pervasive constituent of our reality, and is dynamic and even creative as it mediates our relationship with each other, the world and ourselves.[113]

I maintain that it is this dynamism and creativity, rather than linguistic incompetence, which has led to the disappearance of the (accusative and) infinitive and the innovative use of clauses with ἵνα and the subjunctive or ὅτι with the indicative.[114] Jannaris points out that the lack of number and person marking on the infinitive made it indefinite:

> when it is remembered that the cardinal points aimed at in popular discourse are simplicity, perspicuity, and emphasis, and that, speaking of the Greek language in particular, these conditions have at all times ...been fulfilled by means of inflectional properties (endings, prefixes etc.), it is evident that the absence of these requisites from the infinitive often rendered it unfit for the purpose. As a natural consequence, popular discourse began as early as *G* times (Greco-Roman, 150 BCE – 300 CE) to dispense with the infinitive and replace it...by...finite moods (ἵνα with primary subjunctive, ὅτι with indicative).[115]

Neither the use of the term 'epexegetic', nor the giving of a list of lexical equivalents for this particle explains the way in which speakers used it. I claim that it was being used, by both first language speakers and those who were bilingual, as a procedural marker which alerted the reader to expect a representation of a thought or utterance interpretively used. This may involve more than one representation, for which there is no other morphological signal, but the context, as in Example (23) should make this clear. It may also indicate what a speaker thought should be done: it has deontic force. I have claimed that this implies a further representation, usually of a generally held belief or assumption.

---

[112] For example Turner (1988 reprint) p. 2: 'I have tried to expose consistently the almost complete absence of classical standards in nearly every author'.
[113] F. Young and D.F. Ford (1987) p. 142.
[114] This is mentioned in the introduction and will be dealt with in depth in Chapter 8.
[115] Jannaris (1897) §2063.

CHAPTER 6

Purpose Clauses Introduced by ἵνα

6.1 Introduction

For many biblical scholars, especially those brought up on Classical Greek, the quintessential function of the particle ἵνα is its use as a subordinating conjunction which introduces a purpose clause, that is a clause whose logical relationship to the main clause is one of purpose:[1] a participant, usually the subject of the main clause, performs an action *in order that* something else might happen. ἵνα is then a subordinating conjunction, a logical connector introducing a subordinate clause, and as such it has a fixed lexical meaning of 'in order that'.

In Classical Greek this was seen as the only function of this particle, and even in Koine Greek, although the function of ἵνα has widened considerably,[2] its use as an introducer of purpose clauses is still a prominent but not exclusive one. In this chapter then I will deal with such purpose clauses, but will demonstrate that the particle which introduces them is not a logical connector, but a procedural marker which alerts the reader to expect a representation of a thought either of the author or another person. The following extract[3] exemplifies this:

> Example (1) ἔδοξε κἀμοὶ ... καθεξῆς σοι γράψαι, κράτιστε Θεόφιλε, ἵνα ἐπιγνῷς περὶ ὧν κατηχήθης λόγων τὴν ἀσφάλειαν.
> It seemed good to me also ... to write for you in an orderly fashion, excellent Theophilus, in order that you might know the certainty of the accounts you have heard.

The writer is stating the purpose of his writing: his reader should understand the certainty of the things/accounts which he heard. We do not know if this purpose was realised, but it was the author's stated intention in writing. This intention might be stated as: *You should know the certainty of the accounts you have heard.*

Even if we ignore the particle ἵνα, the context, together with the subjunctive mood of ἐπιγνῷς would enable us to infer purpose for this subordinate clause. It is my hypothesis that this is in fact what a reader of

---

[1] Goodwin (1965 reprint) p. 311 'ἵνα is the only purely final particle'.
[2] *BDF* §369; Burton (1894) §191.
[3] Luke 1:3-4.

Purpose Clauses

Koine does in interpreting a ἵνα clause: she[4] derives purpose from the context and not from the lexical meaning of the particle.

6.2 Purpose as Indicating Intention, and Beyond

Indicating purpose involves communicating the subject's intention in carrying out a particular action: 'an intention is a mental representation of a desired state of affairs'.[5] Communicating that intention is not describing a state of affairs, but giving a representation of the communicator's own thought. Every statement of purpose is a representation of someone's thought: the motivation which led to a certain action.[6] This may be the speaker or writer's own thought, or one which he attributes to others. The resultant utterance, therefore, may reflect several representations.[7] This understanding of the way in which we communicate our thoughts is crucial for appreciating a new perspective on purpose clauses. Consider the following example which presents intention from three different perspectives:

Example (2) I'm living in Jersey to avoid paying taxes.
(2a) He says he's living in Jersey to avoid paying taxes.
(2b) He's living in Jersey to avoid paying taxes.

In Example (2), the speaker is voicing his own intention, that is, it is a representation of his own thought. In Example (2a) the same intention is voiced but as part of the reporting of the original speaker's utterance. This also is a representation of the subject's thought, but it is an interpretive resemblance of Example (2). An extra level of representation has been added. If we had not read Example (2) first, we would have no assurance that the original speaker actually said those words. Example (2b) may be interpreted as a close resemblance to the original or the speaker's interpretation of the original which the first speaker would not have accepted. In the latter case, the first speaker may have indicated that he was living in Jersey because the climate suited him, but the hearer used a strategy of sophisticated understanding to interpret this utterance. Her processing might have moved like this:

He wants me to think that

---

[4] Recall that in this book the speaker or writer is referred to as 'he' and the hearer or reader as 'she'.

[5] Sperber (1994) p. 185.

[6] Note that 'purpose' is distinguished from 'intention' in that it presupposes a certain action taking place *in order that* a result may be effected. Intention may never reach the point of action, but purpose does involve action.

[7] See 5.2 as well as Chapter 2 for a more detailed account of the levels of representation which humans regularly process in attributing intention to others, also Sperber (1994) quoted there.

> he lives in Jersey *because of the climate,*
> **but** *most expatriates live in Jersey to avoid paying taxes.*

As stated above, humans regularly attribute motives, especially malicious ones, to others on very slight evidence.

In Example (1), the writer's stated purpose in communicating is that his addressee, Theophilus, should understand the certainty of the accounts which he has heard. We do not know if this purpose was realised, merely that it was a desirable state of affairs from the perspective of the author, and further that he took action by writing to fulfil that purpose. The use of the subjunctive in Greek is said to indicate *irrealis* rather than an actual state of affairs.[8] When used with the particle ἵνα the subjunctive focuses on the attitude of the subject of the main clause, which may be his intention.[9] In Example (1) the writer is giving his own intention, that is, he is representing his own thought in the clause which follows ἵνα.

Of course we regularly attribute motives or intentions to others which have not been communicated to us. We do this either by drawing inferences from their behaviour, or by drawing inferences from our own understanding of their mental processes before these are realised in behaviour. We are seldom aware of these processes, but according to Sperber they are an intrinsic part of human intelligence:

> Humans can no more refrain from attributing intentions than they can from batting their eyelids.[10]

In looking at 'purpose' clauses in the NT, and in Koine Greek in general, we frequently observe a writer describing an intention which is *not* his own. In this case he is either

- reporting what someone else has said;
- drawing an inference from the behaviour of another;
- attributing an intention to another which may not be acknowledged by that third party.

In all these cases, however, the common factor is that of representing a thought.

It is my argument that the particle ἵνα invites the reader to infer such a representation in the clause which follows. It may be the writer's own thought or that of another but this representation indicates a desirable rather than an actual state of affairs, which accounts for the use of the subjunctive in such

---

[8] *ATR* calls the subjunctive and the optative 'the modes of doubtful statement' pp. 927-8. This is discussed in more detail in Chapter 7.
[9] See Rouchota (1994) for the claim that this mood encapsulates subject attitude.
[10] Sperber (1994) p. 187.

clauses. We draw the inference that the clause indicates the 'purpose' of the subject from the context: that is, the rest of the sentence and the wider context. The notion of purpose is not linked intrinsically to the particle ἵνα in Koine Greek.[11] In other words this particle does not have a lexical meaning of 'in order that.'

This may sound unlikely, when we have been trained to read ἵνα as a subordinating conjunction with such a lexical meaning of 'in order that', but it is the case that we identify those examples of ἵνα clauses which are perceived to indicate a relationship other than purpose by the very same method: in certain contexts purpose does not 'make sense'! It seems that the basic initial assumption of most readers of Koine Greek is that a clause introduced by ἵνα indicates purpose. If this does not 'fit', then we derive an alternative analysis from the context.

6.2.1 The Role of Context in Interpreting ἵνα

This section outlines several examples in which the grammatical and logical context forces the interpreter to consider the ἵνα clause as having a relation to the main clause which is not that of purpose.[12] As I argued in the previous section, if it is context which guides the reader to a non-purpose interpretation of this particle, then it must also be true that it is context which indicates a telic interpretation, not of the particle, but of the clause it introduces. Three examples are adduced below to support this contention.[13]

Example (3) ἐὰν ὁμολογῶμεν τὰς ἁμαρτίας ἡμῶν, πιστός ἐστιν καὶ δίκαιος, ἵνα ἀφῇ ἡμῖν τὰς ἁμαρτίας καὶ καθαρίσῃ ἡμᾶς ἀπὸ πάσης ἀδικίας.
If we confess our sins he is faithful and just *so that/in that* he forgives our sins and cleanses us from all unrighteousness.

In this example it is clear that God's faithfulness and justice are not in place for the *purpose* of forgiveness and cleansing from sin, but that the latter are possible *because of* such attributes of God. Brooke claims that

ἵνα defines the sphere in which the faithfulness and the justice are shown. In view of the usage of the writer and the frequency of definitive ἵνα in papyrus documents, it is

---

[11] I have already indicated that I suspect that even in Classical Greek this particle may have been alerting the reader to expect a metarepresentation, but further work needs to be done on this and it is not the focus of this book.

[12] In Chapter 3 I have argued that certain independent clauses introduced by ἵνα cannot indicate purpose, since they lack a main clause on which purpose could be predicated. Chapters 4 and 5 similarly have shown that clauses which indicate indirect command and those which are explications of a noun do not invite the reader to infer purpose as their most relevant interpretation.

[13] 1 John 1:9.

difficult to maintain the "telic" force of ἵνα throughout the N.T.[14]

Marshall points out in a footnote that the ἵνα clause 'is equivalent to an infinitive of result.'[15]

Translators also have assumed this understanding for reasons of context. No translation that I have found renders ἵνα as 'in order that' for this verse. Below I have noted a selection of modern versions which deal with it either by translating it as 'and' (*RSV, NIV*), by using a colon to introduce an explication of δικαίος (*GNB*), or by translating the following clause as a complement of the verb 'trust': so *NEB*, taking the passive sense of πίστος.

RSV 'he is faithful and just and will forgive our sins and cleanse us from all unrighteousness.'
NIV 'he is faithful and just and will forgive us our sins and purify us from all unrighteousness.'
GNB 'he will keep his promise and do what is right: he will forgive us our sins and purify us from all wrongdoing.'
NEB 'he is just and may be trusted to forgive our sins and cleanse us from every kind of wrong.'

I suggest that the translators whose work is reflected in these versions have viewed the clause introduced by ἵνα as an expansion of what the author means by saying that God is 'faithful and just'. In *RT* terms, they are treating the clause as a representation. This is most obvious in the *GNB* translation, where a colon is used to indicate that the particle should be viewed as epexegetic.[16] Other translations (*RSV, NIV*) use the particle 'and' to indicate, I suggest, not merely additional information, but logical progression (inferring result). Although the connector 'and' may be used in this way,[17] it gives the reader very little help in inferring the connection.[18] Finally the New English Bible translation relates the ἵνα clause most closely of all to πιστός, by reading a passive inference from this adjective and then explicating what the one who is πιστός might be expected to do.

---

[14] Brooke (1912) pp. 19-20. He gives figures of 26 and 9 for 'definitive' use (noun clauses?) in the Gospel of John and Epistles respectively.
[15] Marshall (1978) p. 114, footnote.
[16] See Chapter 5 for further treatment of clauses introduced by ἵνα which are said to be epexegetic.
[17] See Sperber and Wilson (1995) and Blakemore (2002) pp. 171ff, also Hopper and Traugott (1997) p. 73.
[18] In an *RT* analysis, connecting particles give a reader or hearer procedural clues to enable her to process correctly the information which follows, that is to draw the inferences which the speaker or author wanted her to draw. Blakemore (1987), pp.78-91; pp. 111-118.

Purpose Clauses

A further example[19] also shows the role of grammatical and logical context in determining the relationship of the clause introduced by ἵνα to the rest of the sentence:

Example (4) ʽΡαββι, τίς ἥμαρτεν, οὗτος ἢ οἱ γονεῖς αὐτοῦ, ἵνα τυφλὸς γεννηθῇ;
'Rabbi, who sinned, this man or his parents that he was born blind?'

In this example, not even the disciples understood that the man or his parents sinned *in order that* he might be born blind![20] John presents the disciples as articulating the common Jewish belief of that time that disability was the result of sin.[21] We may infer that while holding that view they were either asking Jesus to identify the immediate agent of 'sin' or, more daringly, testing out this view on Jesus. The logical relationship between the two clauses may be one of result[22] or the voicing of their thought: *why was this man born blind? he had to be born blind*. The author has embedded this question in a pericope which focuses on blindness and light, both actual and spiritual. Since the answer to the disciples' question firmly negates the idea of blindness as a result of sin, probably the logical relation should be viewed as one of result. In the answer,[23] however, there is another non telic example of ἵνα:

Example (5) ἀπεκρίθη ᾽Ιησοῦς, Οὔτε οὗτος ἥμαρτεν οὔτε οἱ γονεῖς αὐτοῦ, ἀλλ᾽ ἵνα φανερωθῇ τὰ ἔργα τοῦ θεοῦ ἐν αὐτῷ.
Jesus replied, 'Neither this man nor his parents sinned, but that the works of God should be revealed in him.'

I do not accept the interpretation of the ἵνα clause which claims that the man was born blind *in order that* the works of God should be shown in him.[24] Since blindness, even congenital blindness, was common in Palestine at this time, the view that God was obligated to make someone blind in order to show his

---

[19] John 9:2.

[20] Although it has been claimed, in order to preserve ἵνα as a telic conjunction, that the providence of God is behind its use here; so Winer (1877) 'the necessary, though not intentional, consequence of the ἁμαρτάνειν is meant' p. 574. He considers that 'Hebrew teleology' must be taken into account p. 573.

[21] Schnackenburg (1982) 'an ancient and oppressive question has been given a new answer by Jesus' p. 240. He does not discuss the possibility of a telic interpretation of ἵνα but his comments presuppose an ecbatic meaning.

[22] Burton (1894) §218, 219 suggests the use of ἵνα in this verse as 'conceived result', but this is rejected by *ATR* p. 998 who describes it as actual result. Morris (1971) also suggests result, calling it 'an unusual but not unparalleled use' p. 478. This is an understatement. It is very frequent in the papyri.

[23] John 9:3.

[24] So Bernard (1928) 'His answer ... is that the man's blindness was foreordained so that it might be the occasion of the exhibition of Divine power in his cure' p. 325.

works, seems ill-founded.[25] The works of God were displayed in this man, but the ἵνα clause indicates John's representation of Jesus' own understanding of what must happen: a representation of a representation. In denying the disciples' understanding of the relationship between disability and sin, John does not substitute another resultative connection between the man's blindness and the healing which he is to receive. Note the lack of a main verb after ἀλλ' on which either purpose or result clause could be predicated. Cadoux[26] suggested that this was an example of 'imperatival' ἵνα. I think this is on the right lines, but would rephrase this as a deontic clause: *The works of God must be revealed in him.* This shows the desirable state of affairs from the perspective of the speaker. The whole thrust of this pericope is that Jesus brings light. It would be perverse to argue that God first brought darkness *in order that* light might come by his later acts.

When the standard grammars describe the particle ἵνα as introducing final, object, predicate, complementary and result clauses,[27] it must be apparent that such an analysis can only be made from the wider context in which such clauses occur. In short, decisions on the type of clause which this particle introduces are made on pragmatic rather than syntactic or lexical grounds, although this is seldom made clear. ἵνα does not give instructions about the logical relationship between clauses, but guides the reader to process the following clause as a representation. Purpose may well be indicated in clauses introduced by ἵνα but this must be inferred from the context and not the introductory particle.

6.2.2 Purpose Attributed

I argued in 6.2 above that a writer may attribute a purpose to another. He may do this because

- he has heard the third party articulate such an intention;
- there is a common assumption concerning the relationship between certain acts and their purpose;
- he infers the intention from the subject's behaviour and believes that this was that person's intention, even though in many cases the subject would not acknowledge this.

The examples below will demonstrate a straightforward example of this:

> Example (6) I closed the window in order that the rain wouldn't come in.
> Example (6a) Peter closed the window in order that the rain wouldn't come in.

---

[25] Barrett (1978 2nd ed.) suggests 'with the result that' p. 356.
[26] Cadoux (1941) pp. 165-173. Chapter 3 deals with Cadoux's proposal and my alternative in *RT* terms.
[27] Burton (1894) p. 84, also *BDF* §369, 391, 392, 393, 394.

Purpose Clauses 133

In Example (6) the speaker is giving his own reason for his action: the closing of the window was effected so that rain would not come in. In Example (6a), it is not the speaker who is articulating his intention, but an (implied) observer who infers purpose from the desired result: no rain coming in. Although this may seem ludicrously trivial, there could be other reasons for the closing of the window: to reduce the level of noise from outside, to make the room warmer etc. Humans regularly attribute intention to others on the basis of observable behaviour. They draw conclusions based on what is for them the most relevant interpretation of the actions of another.[28]

6.2.2.1 AUTHOR'S ACKNOWLEDGED ATTRIBUTION OF INTENT
While writers and speakers regularly attribute motives to others with no indication of the reason for such inferencing, occasionally a writer may state that this is his own surmise. There are several examples in literary Koine of an author indicating that he himself has attributed such a purpose to another. I have selected the following example from the *Roman Antiquities* of Dionysius of Halicarnassus:[29]

> Example (7) καὶ τινα καὶ μοῖραν τῆς ἑαυτοῦ στρατιᾶς ἐν τοῖς πολίσμασιν ὑπολείπεται, ὡς μὲν ἐγὼ εἰκάζω, γνώμῃ ἑκουσίῳ χρησάμενος, ἵνα τοῖς ὑπὸ καμάτων βαρυνομένοις ἢ καὶ ἄλλως θαλάττῃ ἀχθομένοις ἀναπαύσεις γίνοιντο ἀσφαλεῖς καὶ καταγωγαί....
> (Aeneas) even left some part of his army in these towns. It is my own surmise that he did this by deliberate choice, to the end that those who were worn out by hardships or otherwise irked by the sea might enjoy rest and a safe retreat. (*LCL*: Cary)

Here Dionysius gives his own estimation of the intention of Aeneas in leaving some of his troops behind, using a ἵνα clause to explicate this. By contrast, however, in the next sentence he gives an alternative reason for the action of Aeneas which other historians had suggested, but he uses an accusative and infinitive construction for this. I suggest that this author makes salient his own interpretation of the actions of Aeneas by the use of ἵνα with the subjunctive, but indicates other postulated reasons by the less perspicacious articular infinitive.[30] The salient clause indicates both the person and number of the subject, whereas the infinitival construction can do neither. In RT terms, the author is inferring an intention of Aeneas and marking this by ἵνα and the optative. The subordinate clause is a representation of the thought, that is the

---
[28] Note Example (7c) in Chapter 2: 'George parked there to annoy Mary'.
[29] Book 1.52.4.
[30] As above: ὡς δέ τινες γράφουσι, τοῦ ναυτικοῦ μειωθέντος αὐτῷ διὰ τὴν ἔμπρησιν ...τὸν οὐκέτι δυνάμενον συνμπλεῖν ὄχλον ... ἀνάγκῃ καταλιπών. 'but as some say, he left them of necessity when the fleet was diminished because of the fire ... the group were no longer able to sail away.' (MGS)

intention behind the action of Aeneas as inferred by Dionysius. Of course in the subsequent sentence he is also representing the opinion of other historians as to the motivation of Aeneas, but the reader is not prompted to see this representation as important. This clause does contain a representation, as all purpose clauses do, but the author is not drawing this to our attention in the same way as he does with the representation contained in the ἵνα clause.

It is clear from the historical works of both Dionysius and Polybius that these authors attribute purpose to the historical figures whose actions they describe. Occasionally, as in Example (7), they make it plain that they themselves are inferring such intention, but on most occasions they merely state the subject's purpose. They may have been quoting an accepted understanding of that motivation or may have been given information by witnesses of the events being narrated. In the following section both of these possibilities are discussed.

6.2.2.2 REPRESENTATION OF INTENTION OF SUBJECT

In this section we will examine an author's attribution of intention which may have been gleaned from:

- the actor's own statement of intent,
- observable behaviour.

In order to support the first hypothesis, I have selected two examples from the book of Acts,[31] as well as one from the *Histories* of Polybius:[32]

> Example (8) Οὐχ οὗτός ἐστιν ὁ πορθήσας εἰς Ἰερουσαλὴμ τοὺς ἐπικαλουμένους τὸ ὄνομα τοῦτο, καὶ ὧδε εἰς τοῦτο ἐληλύθει ἵνα δεδεμένους αὐτοὺς ἀγάγῃ ἐπὶ τοὺς ἀρχιερεῖς;
> 'Isn't this the man who destroyed/ruined all those who called on this name in Jerusalem, and he had come here for this purpose in order to bring them bound to the chief priests?'

This is presented as the comment of those in the synagogue in Damascus on hearing Saul preach after his vision. They express amazement at the content of his speech, rehearsing what they know of his purpose[33] in coming to Damascus.[34] That purpose was not realised,[35] but it is reported as being the

---

[31] Example (8) Acts 9:21; Example (9) Acts 20:16.
[32] Example (10).
[33] We are led to infer that this was common knowledge among the Jews and synagogue attenders.
[34] Barrett comments 'εἰς τοῦτο anticipates and is explained by the ἵνα clause that follows.' p. 464.

desirable state of affairs which Saul wanted to see effected by coming to Damascus. The author shows the people in the synagogue as representing what they have heard about the intention of Saul.

The following example is taken from the author's account of Paul's (last) journey to Jerusalem. The author is leading us to infer that Paul had stated his own intention to his companions, in whose company he places himself by the use of first person pronouns in the narrative:[36]

Example (9) κεκρίκει γὰρ ὁ Παῦλος παραπλεῦσαι τὴν Ἔφεσον, ὅπως μὴ γένηται αὐτῷ χρονοτριβῆσαι ἐν τῇ Ἀσίᾳ· ἔσπευδεν γὰρ εἰ δυνατὸν εἴη αὐτῷ τὴν ἡμέραν τῆς πεντηκοστῆς γενέσθαι εἰς Ἱεροσόλυμα.
For Paul had decided to sail past Ephesus, in order that he might not need to spend time in Asia; since he was eager/was hurrying, if it were possible for him, to be in Jerusalem for the day of Pentecost.

Here the narrator shows Paul sailing along the coast of Asia Minor, without taking time to visit the places where he had friends and converts. Then, in order to explain this behaviour and that of the subsequent verses, he seems to show an intention which he attributes to Paul on the basis of the latter's own stated preference to be in Jerusalem by a fixed date. This is supported by the second clause which gives evidence for his intention. Further, the author by the use of first person pronouns leads the reader to infer his presence with Paul's companions at least from the time of arrival in Troas.[37] Following on from this inference the reader may infer further that as a travelling companion, the author was the recipient of information concerned with Paul's purpose in bypassing Ephesus, an action which is presented as contrary to expectation.[38]

The historians Polybius and Dionysius regularly attribute intentions to the characters whose exploits they are narrating some of which may be based on information received, while at other times they are themselves inferring or attributing such motivation with insufficient evidence. There is an example from Polybius,[39] describing the behaviour of Hannibal and the advice which he is said to have given to the Celts, regarding the benefits which might accrue

---

[35] Barrett (1994) p. 204 'pluperfect indicates a state of things that has now ceased to be' p. 464. Also Bruce (1951).

[36] I do not attempt to show that this presentation is factual, merely that this is the representation of the text as it stands.

[37] Acts 20:5-6.

[38] The use of γάρ in the second sentence of example (9) indicates confirmatory evidence for the earlier statement. Barrett (1994) discusses other reasons for Paul's behaviour, such as the comparative safety of Miletus as compared with Ephesus, especially if he was carrying the collection p. 969. Note also the D text which attributes a slightly different intention to Paul: μηπότε γενηθῇ αὐτῷ κατάσχεσις (lit. 'lest there be a hindering for him.').

[39] *Histories* Book 3, 67.7.

from their retaining Roman hostages.

> Example (10) τοὺς γε μὴν ἄνδρας αὐτοῖς ἀπέδωκε, παραγγείλας τηρεῖν ἵνα παρὰ τούτων κομίσωνται τοὺς αὐτῶν ὁμήρους κατὰ τὴν ἐξ ἀρχῆς πρόθεσιν.
> He gave the men back to them, urging (them) to keep them in order that from these they might rescue their own hostages, according to the plan from the beginning. (MGS)

In this example the ἵνα clause is part of the advice given by Hannibal, suggesting the motivation for holding on to the Roman hostages. It is presented as a report of what Hannibal said to the envoys. The desirable state of affairs, from the perspective of the envoys, was that they would be able to rescue their own hostages, by an exchange of prisoners. It is not the envoys themselves who are presented as voicing this, however, but Hannibal as he handed over the Romans into their charge. Since Polybius himself was present in Carthage for part of the Roman campaign, it may have been a report which he himself had heard from the Romans involved. This example is included to demonstrate how widespread is the representation of the intention of others, including, as here, the suggesting to them of what would or should be a desirable state of affairs, from their perspective. There are obviously several representations here:

- the thought of Hannibal
- his utterance to the envoy
- the putative report to Polybius
- the latter's written account.

6.2.2.3 PURPOSE FROM OBSERVABLE BEHAVIOUR

A writer or speaker may also attribute purpose to another on the basis of observable behaviour. Humans regularly do this, and indeed, seem incapable of desisting from such inferencing. There are many examples of this in the narrative sections of the NT, but I have selected two clear examples from John 10:31[40] and Luke 18:15:[41]

> Example (11) ἐβάστασαν πάλιν λίθους οἱ Ἰουδαῖοι ἵνα λιθάσωσιν αὐτόν.
> The Jews picked up stones again in order to stone him.

Given the fact of the Jews picking up stones, the reader may recover the intention of such an action fairly easily: it would be relevant, in the context of the original readers, in that there would be no other clear explanation for such an action as carried out by a number of people together. Probably also the way

---

[40] Example (11).
[41] Example (12).

Purpose Clauses 137

in which the stones were lifted would be seen as ostensive,[42] that is the action was designed to communicate the intention of throwing these stones at someone. The clause introduced by ἵνα gives a representation of what the writer believed the intention of the subjects to be, such belief being based on the subjects' observable behaviour.

Example (12) Προσέφερον δὲ αὐτῷ καὶ τὰ βρέφη ἵνα αὐτῶν ἅπτηται· ἰδόντες δὲ οἱ μαθηταὶ ἐπετίμων αὐτοῖς.
They were bringing young children to him in order that he might touch them, but the disciples on seeing this, were beginning to rebuke them.

Again, this was a very relevant interpretation of an observed action: in that culture the bringing of children to a respected figure would be understood as a request for blessing, usually accompanied by the placing of hands on the head of a child.[43] The disciples were certainly represented as understanding the action to be more than bringing children along as passive observers, and as reacting accordingly. The clause introduced by ἵνα represents the purpose of the parents in bringing their children, such an attribution being derived from observable behaviour and from known cultural patterns.[44]

6.2.2.4 INTERPRETATION OF BEHAVIOUR PATTERNS
In Chapter 2 it was stated that for communication to succeed, both speaker and hearer or writer and reader must share a common body of knowledge. This may be commonly shared contextual assumptions or encyclopaedic information which both parties would expect the other to be aware of. We observed that inferencing is a crucial part of successful communication and inferencing assumes such commonly shared knowledge. The following example contains information which would be readily available to all residents of the United Kingdom:

Example (13) Police install cameras in shopping centres in order to reduce crime.

The purpose clause here is a commonly held belief regarding the intention of the police force in installing such cameras. It is not derived primarily from observable behaviour, although this may be pertinent in some cases, but from general knowledge, gleaned from the media, neighbourhood information or notices placed in public places. By contrast, the purpose clause contained in

---

[42] Recall the discussion of ostensive behaviour in 2.2.2.7.

[43] Mark 10:16 makes this plain, as well as many OT passages such as Genesis 48:10-20; also Marshall's (1978) suggestion p. 682 'The background to the story appears to be the practice of bringing children to the elders or scribes for a prayer of blessing upon them on the evening of the Day of Atonement'.

[44] These were described in Chapter 2 as commonly shared contextual assumptions.

Example (14) is derived from a very different source:

Example (14) Police install cameras in shopping centres in order to spy on people they don't like.

In this example the intention of the police force is not derived from general knowledge but from a strongly held belief about the intentions of law enforcement officers. The contextual assumptions from which such a belief was drawn would not be shared by the police officers, who would deny the intention attributed to them. The hearer of Example (14) might question the speaker about the evidence for his belief, before she accepted this attributed intention, if her own contextual assumptions did not allow her to substantiate it. In Example (13), however, the information on which the attribution of intention is based is widely known and easily verifiable. Again in Koine, such attribution of intention inferred from shared contextual assumptions and knowledge is a frequent feature of certain types of dialogue, particularly in parabolic material, as Example (15)[45] shows:

Example (15) Οὐδεὶς δὲ λύχνον ἅψας καλύπτει αὐτὸν σκεύει ἢ ὑποκάτω κλίνης τίθησιν, ἀλλ' ἐπὶ λυχνίας τίθησιν, ἵνα οἱ εἰσπορευόμενοι βλέπωσιν τὸ φῶς.
'No one lights a lamp and hides it in a container or puts it under a bed, but puts it on a lampstand in order that those coming in might see the light.'

This intention is presented as information which both speaker and hearers would be aware of.[46] It was part of their shared contextual assumptions about the behaviour of someone who took the trouble to light a lamp. The intentions involved in such an action would be clear. Based on this contextual knowledge and the intention which could be drawn from known behaviour patterns, a lesson is about to be given. This seems to be a recurrent pattern in many parables. The hearers can readily infer the intention of the participants in the parabolic dialogue, because of shared contextual knowledge.

Consider also a further example:[47]

Example (16) καὶ ἐὰν δανίσητε παρ' ὧν ἐλπίζετε λαβεῖν, ποία ὑμῖν χάρις [ἐστίν]; καὶ ἁμαρτωλοὶ ἁμαρτωλοῖς δανίζουσιν ἵνα ἀπολάβωσιν τὰ ἴσα.
'And if you lend (to those) from whom you hope to receive, what credit is that to

---

[45] Luke 8:16.
[46] Marshall notes that Luke inserts a purpose clause, whereas Matthew 5:15 uses parataxis 'and it gives light...' p. 329. The use of ἵνα and the subjunctive 'constrains' the interpretation, making the inference of intention more readily accessible than the connective καί in the Matthean account.
[47] Luke 6:34.

Purpose Clauses 139

you? Even sinners lend to sinners in order to receive the same again.'

The second sentence in this example would only have made sense to the implied listeners if they shared the contextual assumptions of the speaker relating to the behaviour of those who lend money. 'Sinners'[48] lend money with the expectation of receiving their loan again, or, alternatively, receiving the same facility from the borrower at a future date. The motivation or intention of 'sinners' in lending money is represented by the ἵνα clause: *they should receive the same again.*

This representation must have been readily accessible to the implied listeners, who would recognise that lending was carried out with a certain intention in mind. It was also part of the shared context between (implied) speaker and (implied) hearer that the law forbade the taking of interest from fellow Jews,[49] although OT texts suggest that this went on in spite of the Mosaic prohibition.[50] The reference could have been to interest free loans. This latter interpretation of course would make no sense if ἵνα is taken in a strongly purposive sense: 'in order to'.[51] It is unclear, however, that this is the only possible interpretation. If we leave aside the assumption that this particle indicates purpose then the reference could have been either to obtaining similar loan facilities when needed,[52] or to receiving the principal (with or without interest). The larger argument draws on this shared information in order to point out the lesson: lend with no expectation of repayment (or no expectation of interest?) One final example[53] employs an argument which is unintelligible without shared contextual assumptions regarding certain aspects of the law. It refers back to a healing miracle which took place on the Sabbath, but which is not mentioned in the immediate context of this dialogue presented as between Jesus and the Jewish leaders. It supports what has been asserted in the examples above, that shared contextual assumptions are the basis for drawing inferences about behaviour:

Example (17) εἰ περιτομὴν λαμβάνει ἄνθρωπος ἐν σαββάτῳ ἵνα μὴ λυθῇ ὁ

---

[48] I have used quotation marks round this word because it seems that Jesus is being presented as using it echoically: this term was used by the religious leaders of that time to refer to the common people who did not aspire to observe all the minutiae of the law.

[49] Exodus 22:25; Deuteronomy 23:19-20.

[50] Nehemiah 5:1-12.

[51] Marshall (1978) points out that lending to fellow Jews without asking interest was especially virtuous, but 'this view still falls foul of ἵνα' p. 263. He takes the reference to be receiving the same facilities in return, i.e. receiving a loan (interest free?) when needed.

[52] So Marshall (1978) and also Nolland (1989) p. 299. Plummer (1981 reprint) thinks that it more probably refers to 'repayment in full', i.e. with interest, in view of the fact that in secular Greek δανίζω always meant 'lend at interest' p. 187.

[53] John 7:23.

νόμος Μωϋσέως, ἐμοὶ χολᾶτε ὅτι ὅλον ἄνθρωπον ὑγιῆ ἐποίησα ἐν σαββάτῳ;
'If a man receives circumcision on the Sabbath in order that the law of Moses might not be broken, (why) are you angry with me because I made a whole man well on the Sabbath?'

Here the motivation for circumcising on the Sabbath, i.e. 'working' was that the law of Moses must not be broken, namely the stipulation that a child should be circumcised on the eighth day. This understanding of the importance of the eighth day allowed, probably prescribed, the circumcising of an infant on that exact day, even if it happened to be a Sabbath.[54] The argument is only relevant if those listening knew and understood the intention behind circumcising on the Sabbath which might be seen as breaking another commandment by working on the seventh day of the week. The desirable state of affairs introduced by the ἵνα clause would be: *The law of Moses should not be broken.*

John presents those to whom this comment was addressed as Jewish leaders who would have a very clear understanding of the finer points of both the written and oral law. The ἵνα clause represents the intention of those prescribing circumcision on the Sabbath, but this representation would have been part of the contextual assumptions of the listeners. There was, therefore, no need to spell out the argument. If circumcision - which technically took something away from a man - could take place on the Sabbath, why could not an act which made a man whole?

6.2.2.5 ATTRIBUTION OF INTENTION WITHOUT EVIDENCE

We have considered those attributions of intention which a speaker or writer may have inferred from the subject's own admission, from commonly held motivations or from observable behaviour. In the NT corpus, approximately 40% of all ἵνα or ὅπως[55] clauses which indicate the subject's purpose, describe an intention which the writer has attributed to the subject himself. In other words, the writer imputes a motive to the subject which the latter might not acknowledge. One very obvious example of this may be seen in Example (18).[56] Paul, the writer, has been urging the believers in Galatia that, contrary to what some people were advocating, circumcision was not a necessary rite for them in order to be part of the people of God. He goes further and attributes quite a different intention behind the desire of a section of the community to see these non-Jews circumcised:

Example (18) οὐδὲ γὰρ οἱ περιτεμνόμενοι αὐτοὶ νόμον φυλάσσουσιν ἀλλὰ

---

[54] Schnackenburg p. 134 quoting Rabbi Eliezer in *Tos.Sabb.* 15,16: 'He supersedes the sabbath for one of his members, and shall he not supersede the sabbath for his whole self (his life being in danger)?'
[55] ὅπως will be dealt with in Chapter 8.
[56] Galatians 6:13.

θέλουσιν ὑμᾶς περιτέμνεσθαι, ἵνα ἐν τῇ ὑμετέρᾳ σαρκὶ καυχήσωνται.
'For not even the ones being circumcised are themselves keeping the law, but they want you to be circumcised in order that they may glory/boast in your flesh/body.'

The subjects here: 'they' of θέλουσιν, would have strenuously denied such an intention. Although the desired action would have been common ground between all three parties: 'they want you to be circumcised', the writer represents their thought as the motivation for this: *They want to boast in your flesh.* This certainly would not have been acknowledged. The writer is inferring this intention from his analysis of the situation in the churches of Galatia, as well as his interaction with other Jews in similar contexts. This seems to be a very general human response.[57] The earlier part of the verse negates what would perhaps have been presented by the opposing party as the reason for insisting on circumcision: 'they should keep the law', and substitutes the writer's own attribution of intention.

It is fairly straightforward to distinguish those instances, as in Example (18), where the attributed intention would not have been accepted by those to whom it was attributed. In many cases, however, it is not possible to distinguish a writer's own attribution of intention from his reporting of what was generally believed by those present during the events being narrated. The reasons for certain behaviour are usually inferred from observers, although not always accurately.[58] The example below[59] fits well here:

Example (19) παρετηροῦντο δὲ αὐτὸν οἱ γραμματεῖς καὶ οἱ Φαρισαῖοι εἰ ἐν τῷ σαββάτῳ θεραπεύει, ἵνα εὕρωσιν κατηγορεῖν αὐτοῦ.
The scribes and Pharisees were watching him (to see) if he would heal on the Sabbath, that they might have (something of which) to accuse him.

The context here is a synagogue in which is present a man with a shrivelled (and presumably useless) hand. Since the incident is shown to be a public one, many people could watch the reactions of the scribes and Pharisees. Their thoughts are represented by the ἵνα clause, which may be an attribution by the author, or presented as a generally believed assumption by the onlookers, based on what follows. The truth of this attribution is substantiated by the rest of the story which notes Jesus as 'knowing their thoughts.' The use of the word διαλογισμός in the following verse makes it clear that the ἵνα clause does in fact claim to represent the thoughts of the subjects, perhaps even their utterances: it is a representation. The subjects of this sentence, however, might

---

[57] Consider again Sperber's comment at 6.2 footnote 5.

[58] John 11:31 has a good example of mistaken inference: the Jews who were present with Mary, on seeing her get up quickly and go out, inferred that she was going out to weep at her brother's tomb.

[59] Luke 6:7.

have rejected this attribution, but the response which Jesus is said to have made is dependent on such an attribution. He brings into the open the potential accusation (κατηγορεῖν) by challenging what is or is not 'lawful' behaviour on the sabbath. Note again the different representations here.

If a writer or speaker attributes an intention to another, he may of course be wrong. He may have inferred a purpose from observable behaviour which is not in fact the real intention behind such behaviour. Consider the following example[60] in which the disciples are described as watching a brief interaction between Jesus and Judas Iscariot, after which Judas leaves the room. They then attribute an intention to Judas, in the normal human fashion, based on shared contextual knowledge: Judas was the treasurer for the group and alms were regularly given at Passover time, and on dialogue which they saw but did not hear:

> Example (20) λέγει οὖν αὐτῷ ᾽Ιησοῦς, ῝Ο ποιεῖς ποίησον τάχιον. τοῦτο [δὲ] οὐδεὶς ἔγνω τῶν ἀνακειμένων πρὸς τί εἶπεν αὐτῷ· τινὲς γὰρ ἐδόκουν, ἐπεὶ τὸ γλωσσόκομον εἶχεν ᾽Ιούδας, ὅτι λέγει αὐτῷ [ὁ] ᾽Ιησοῦς, ᾽Αγόρασον ὧν χρείαν ἔχομεν εἰς τὴν ἑορτήν, ἢ τοῖς πτωχοῖς ἵνα τι δῷ.
>
> Jesus said to him, 'What you are doing, do quickly.' None of those reclining knew what he said to him. For some thought, since Judas held the money bag, that Jesus said to him, 'Buy what we have need of for the feast,' or that he should give something to the poor.

This extract shows the human propensity for inference from contextual information. The dialogue was not understood, but the disciples are shown to infer the conversation anyway. The first supposition is clearly marked by ἐδόκουν followed by ὅτι, but the second inference is marked by ἵνα clause with the subjunctive. This inference could be: *He should give something to the poor.*

I have included this example because it is a demonstration of Sperber's assertion that humans cannot stop inferring intention from the behaviour of others. In other words, humans represent the thoughts and intentions of others. In this case the inferences were wrong, but the disciples are seen to be representing what they understood to be the intention of Jesus as he talked to Judas. Similarly the author attributes thoughts to those who were present. I am arguing that the function of ἵνα is to give procedural instructions to the reader to read the following clause as a representation of those thoughts: what the disciples understood as the intention of Jesus in speaking to Judas.

6.3 Other Ways of Expressing Purpose

This section deals with alternative ways of expressing purpose, namely infinitival constructions. The infinitive regularly indicates purpose in Classical

---

[60] John 13:27-29.

Purpose Clauses

Greek and Koine[61] as in English, not in the NT alone, but in Koine writers in general, particularly when it completes certain verbs such as 'want', 'intend'. We have already seen in Chapter 4 that θέλω in Koine is followed either by ἵνα with the subjunctive, or by the infinitive, the latter being the usual construction when the subject of both clauses is the same.[62] In addition to the infinitive alone, the articular infinitive together with certain directional prepositions indicated 'goal'. Such constructions, however, had several disadvantages, the predominant one being that the subject of the purpose clause was either omitted (if the same as the main clause) or appeared in the accusative case, while the verb contained no person marking at all. Jannaris, in discussing the falling into disuse of the infinitive points out several ways in which it was less flexible than alternative constructions.[63] The main disadvantages which he notes are the lack of person and number indications, and 'often also no precise time', factors which make the infinitive 'unfit' for producing the 'simplicity, perspicuity and emphasis' which popular discourse requires.[64]

We have stated that the notion of purpose involves the representation of a thought about a potential rather than an actual state of affairs. This is true whatever construction is used to represent the thought. I am arguing that the use of the particle ἵνα with the subjunctive mood in the examples cited in this section makes salient the representation of the intention which is being reported or attributed. The subject is clearly marked and the mood indicates the nature of the utterance, being a desirable rather than an actual state of affairs.

It is true that one can see in certain of the NT writings a variation between the use of the infinitive and a ἵνα construction to indicate purpose, even in the same sentence. The incredible sentence in the text of Ephesians 3:14-19 is a notable example of this. Even in this very complex sentence, however, the ἵνα clauses stand out as representing unambiguously who is involved as the subject in each section, and what the desirable state of affairs for each would be. By contrast the accusative and infinitive constructions are much less perspicacious. This passage is presented in Example (21):

Example (21) τούτου χάριν κάμπτω τὰ γόνατά μου πρὸς τὸν πατέρα,
ἵνα δῷ ὑμῖν ...δυνάμει κραταιωθῆναι...
κατοικῆσαι τὸν Χριστὸν διὰ τῆς πίστεως ἐν ταῖς καρδίαις ὑμῶν
ἐν ἀγάπῃ ἐρριζωμένοι καὶ τεθεμελιωμένοι
ἵνα ἐξισχύσητε καταλαβέσθαι σὺν πᾶσιν τοῖς ἁγίοις

---

[61] *ATR* pp. 489-90, p. 989; *BDF* §388.
[62] Note Matthew 2:18; 14:5 for θέλω and Mark 2:17; Luke 19:10 and John 4:7 for ἔρχομαι.
[63] Jannaris (1897) §2063. The quotation in full appears at 5.7.
[64] The infinitive has disappeared in Modern Greek, which Mackridge (1998) says is 'periodically lamented' by some Greek writers (p. 282), but the flexibility which the alternative finite constructions offer could be said to outweigh this.

γνῶναί τε τὴν ὑπερβάλλουσαν τῆς γνώσεως ἀγάπην τοῦ Χριστοῦ
ἵνα πληρωθῆτε εἰς πᾶν τὸ πλήρωμα τοῦ θεοῦ.
For this reason I bow my knees before the father...
that he might grant to you ...to be strengthened with power...
that Christ might live in your hearts through faith,
that, being rooted and grounded in love, **you might be strong** to comprehend with all the saints......to know the love of Christ which is beyond knowledge
that you may be filled with all the fullness of God.

The third line of Example (21) has an accusative and infinitive to represent a purpose clause:[65] κατοικῆσαι τὸν Χριστὸν ... ἐν ταῖς καρδίαις ὑμῶν, the 'subject', τὸν Χριστὸν, being in the accusative case. By contrast, the clauses introduced by ἵνα are much more salient because of their grammatical form which allows the reader to identify the subject clearly, and to read the mood as indicating a desirable state of affairs.

6.4 Disputed Purpose Clauses

Having considered purpose clauses which are both attributed and non-attributed, I now examine several ἵνα clauses which have proved to be contentious among biblical scholars. The issue is usually articulated as whether or not such clauses are 'telic' or 'ecbatic', in other words whether ἵνα is giving the motivation for an action taking place, or the result.[66] I wish to consider first the example from Luke[67] before examining the parallel passages in Matthew[68] and Mark.[69]

Example (22) ὁ δὲ εἶπεν,' Ὑμῖν δέδοται γνῶναι τὰ μυστήρια τῆς βασιλείας τοῦ θεοῦ, τοῖς δὲ λοιποῖς ἐν παραβολαῖς, ἵνα
βλέποντες μὴ βλέπωσιν
καὶ ἀκούοντες μὴ συνιῶσιν.
But he said 'You have been granted to know the mysteries of the kingdom of God, but to the other people (they are) in parables that
"seeing they might not perceive
and hearing they might not understand."'

If ἵνα is taken as introducing a purpose clause then the text is read as follows:

---

[65] Of course this could also be interpreted as an indirect command, dependent on either δῷ (3:16) or κάμπτω τὰ γόνατά μου (3:14). In either case, there is a representation of a desirable state of affairs, which is less easily accessed by an infinitival construction than by a ἵνα clause.

[66] ATR pp. 997-9, Burton (1894) pp. 92-5.

[67] Example (22) Luke 8:10.

[68] Example (23) Matthew 13:13.

[69] Example (24), Mark 4:12.

Jesus was stating that he was teaching in parables in order that those who 'see and hear' might not 'understand'. This has seemed to be unreasonable to many, not least because the peripatetic ministry of Jesus included in its scope many whom the Jews would have seen as outside the kingdom as they viewed it. Further, the parable of the sower - the very teaching about which the disciples raised these questions - describes the wide and general sowing of seed which was variously received. Commentators have suggested alternative readings to avoid this 'harsh' reading, such as treating the particle as indicating result[70] or cause.[71] Marshall[72] suggests that the function of ἵνα in this context may be neither the indication of purpose, cause or result, but giving 'a clear allusion to the OT… "so that (the Scripture is fulfilled which says that…)"'. This matches rather neatly with the parallel passage in Matthew.[73] It also fits with my claim that ἵνα introduces a representation, but that of course is not what Marshall is suggesting here! His point is that the very parable under discussion describes, not proscribes, the result of the dissemination of the 'seed' in various environments. The logical relation of the ἵνα clause to the rest of the sentence should not contradict that general picture.

Nolland[74] seems to agree that the fulfilling of Scripture is the issue rather than the deliberate obscuring of the message, pointing out that 'nowhere else does he (Luke) treat Jesus' use of parables as having any obscuring function.' It is true that the form of the sentence contrasts 'you' with 'the rest', but the context is presented as an open one with the disciples asking about a parable told earlier, for the very reason that they did *not* understand it. Green, while not commenting on the ἵνα clause *per se* does see the boundaries between these two groups as 'porous' and the 'importance of interpretation' in understanding as expressing one of the important points of Luke's theological purpose.[75] This may seem to soften the harshness of the ἵνα clause and interpret it as the result of the lack of illumination rather than a deliberate attempt to exclude certain groups. Plummer many years earlier seems to take the same line, holding to a telic understanding of the particle.[76] Fitzmyer also reads the particle as telic but sees Luke's omission of the end of the quotation from Isaiah as deliberate because he felt that this would seem to suggest that Jesus was impeding the turning to the Lord of which the prophet spoke![77] That of course is the very issue with which these scholars are wrestling. Luke's omission of the end of the

---

[70] *BADG* II.2 allows for this, but claims that in the passage above ἵνα 'is surely to be taken as final.'

[71] Note *BADG* but also Turner (1988 reprint) p. 102, Jannaris (1897) §1714, Mandilaras (1973) §590, Caragounis (2004) p. 222.

[72] Marshall (1978) pp. 322-3.

[73] Matthew 13:14.

[74] Nolland (1989) p. 380.

[75] Green (1997) p. 326.

[76] Plummer (1981 5th Ed.) pp. 219-20.

[77] Fitzmyer (1981) pp. 708-9.

quotation does not seem to me to be avoiding the problem which arises because of an insistence of a telic meaning for this particle in this context.[78]

The quotation in this verse is of course from the passage in Isaiah 6:9-10, the original prophecy being clearly ironic. The *RT* definition of irony is an utterance which echoes someone else's thought or statement, but which the speaker disagrees with; it expresses a dissociative attitude.[79] This is well exemplified by the comment credited to Jesus in Mark 7:9: 'You have a fine way of rejecting the commandment of God in order to keep your tradition!' This is widely interpreted as ironic, because the context indicated that Jesus did not believe this, but what is not usually recognised in the interpretation is the fact that those to whom it was addressed *did* think that it was 'fine' to employ casuistry to circumvent the law but uphold the tradition. Jesus' reported comments echo the thoughts of some of the hearers, but dissociate him from that opinion. This account of the trope is much more intuitively satisfying than the traditional one which identifies irony as saying the opposite of what one means. It is difficult to distinguish that explanation from telling lies and to decide also what contextual effects it might be expected to offer the hearer, apart from confusion. Irony, of course, is notoriously difficult to identify with certainty.[80] If the speaker is saying something that he expects the hearer to identify as different from his own beliefs, then she should interpret the utterance as echoing someone else's thought or statement, while at the same time dissociating the speaker from that thought.

To return to the quote from Isaiah: the context there is clearly *not* literal but figurative speech. The prophecies before and after indicate clearly that the prophet's work was to recall the people to follow the Lord their God, not to hinder that process. The people had 'heard' and 'seen' for many years, but they had not changed their ways. The passage in effect presents in poetic form both the present state of the nation and the result of the prophet's work. When the author presents Jesus as quoting this prophecy he is inviting his readers to draw the same contextual effects as did the hearers of the original prophecy, namely that there will always be observers and hearers who do not understand the significance of what they have seen and heard. The use of the ἵνα clause guides the reader to expect a representation. In this context it seems to be a representation of what the prophet Isaiah 'said' in a similar context of disbelief.[81]

If we wish to infer purpose from this clause, we must find it in the context,

---

[78] It has been suggested by Professor Marshall that Luke has reserved the final lines of the quotation for the mixed reception given to Paul's message in Acts 28:26-27.

[79] Noh p. 94-8; also 5.5.2 Example (21) and 2.2.2.5.1.

[80] Note the earlier reference to Tom Stoppard's suggestion that there should be a special typeface for irony: MacKenzie (2002) p. 220 note 12.

[81] Note the comments of Marshall and Nolland above which are not substantially different, although not employing *RT* terminology.

Purpose Clauses 147

not in the use of the particle ἵνα. I claim that the notion of purpose is lacking from that context. The parallel passage in Matthew 13:13 supports this interpretation:

Example (23) διὰ τοῦτο ἐν παραβολαῖς αὐτοῖς λαλῶ, ὅτι βλέποντες οὐ βλέπουσιν καὶ ἀκούοντες οὐκ ἀκούουσιν οὐδὲ συνίουσιν
'For this reason I speak to them in parables, because/that seeing they don't perceive and hearing they neither hear nor understand.'

The author then goes on to present Jesus as claiming that this (deliberate) lack of understanding was a fulfillment of the prophecy of Isaiah which is then given at length, ending with the words: 'But your eyes are blessed because they see and your ears because they hear.' I contend that both passages are set in the context of disbelief, where 'seeing' and 'hearing' are more than visual and aural experiences.[82] It is often said that the Matthean account 'softens' the harshness of Luke and Mark. This assessment is based on the assumption that the particle ἵνα indicates purpose, in other words that the speaking in parables took place with the purpose of creating a lack of understanding on the part of the hearers. On the contrary I argue, as above, that the Matthean passage explains that the reaction of the crowd fulfills the prophecy in Isaiah, but does not attribute Jesus' use of parables as a way of intentionally preventing some of his hearers from understanding his teaching. The passage in Isaiah quoted in Matthew 13:15 clearly gives the hardness of heart of the λαός as the reason for the lack of understanding. The use of γάρ clarifies this: it gives supporting evidence for what has preceded it.

The final parallel passage is in Mark 4:11-12, which by the addition of a further line from the original prophecy in Isaiah makes the irony more apparent:

Example (24) ἐκείνοις δὲ τοῖς ἔξω ἐν παραβολαῖς τὰ πάντα γίνεται, ἵνα
    βλέποντες βλέπωσιν καὶ μὴ ἴδωσιν
    καὶ ἀκούοντες ἀκούωσιν καὶ μὴ συνιῶσιν,
    μήποτε ἐπιστρέψωσιν καὶ ἀφεθῇ αὐτοῖς.
'But to those outside these things are in parables, that
    "although seeing they may observe and not perceive
    and although listening they might hear and not understand,
    lest they turn round and be forgiven."'

Since both the original context in Isaiah and the one implied in Mark is of the action of God in bringing his people back to him, the clause introduced by

---

[82] Note the recurrent refrain at the end of many pericopes of parables or teaching: 'he who has ears to hear, let him hear', which refers to obedience rather than an aural experience.

μήποτε has to be ironic: it echoes a belief that God does not want people to repent and be forgiven, but dissociates the speaker[83] from that belief. By reading ἵνα in these passages[84] as giving procedural instructions to the reader to interpret the following clause as a representation, in this case of the echoic utterance of the Isaiahic prophecy, the question of whether or not this particle indicates a purpose or a consecutive clause is irrelevant. If interpreters wish to infer purpose in the representation then it has to be proved from the context. I argue that the context does not provide evidence for such an interpretation.[85]

6.5 Summary

In this chapter we have seen that purpose clauses are representations of someone's desire. That person engages in certain actions with a view to a particular result coming into effect. The actual purpose clause is a representation of the thought of the desirable state of affairs which the subject would like to see implemented. This representation may be presented as

- the subject's own utterance,
- the utterance of another party based on the first party's statements or actions,
- the utterance of someone who attributes that desire to the first party.

That person may not accept that attribution, but it seems that humans do attribute intentions to others as a matter of course, with no conscious awareness of the different representations which such attribution implies.

In stating that purpose represents someone's action in order to fulfil his desire, we are describing a cognitive process and also relating two events: the action (main clause) and the desired result of the action (purpose clause). Note that this latter clause does not indicate that the desired result was actualised, merely that the subject regarded it as a desirable state of affairs. Although I have argued that ἵνα clauses may represent the desirable state of affairs which someone wishes to see realised, purpose is not obligatorily marked in this way. The utterance which represents that process may be verbalised in different syntactic forms. The use of an infinitival construction may indicate purpose, but the infinitive itself is underdetermined: it does not indicate a specific logical relation to the main verb in the sentence. When a preposition is added to the

---

[83] Recall the original context in which this is presented as the Lord's command to the prophet, Isaiah 6:10 and note the *LXX* translation from which the Matthean quotation is drawn.

[84] Examples (21), (22), (23).

[85] Sim (2009) forthcoming has a more detailed treatment of the passage in Mark's Gospel.

infinitive it guides the reader in her interpretation.[86] Although a representation may lie behind an infinitive, the form itself does not guide the reader to interpret the information in this way.

By contrast, I submit that a ἵνα clause *does* alert the reader to process the following clause as a representation of a state of affairs desirable to the subject. The use of ἵνα gives the reader instructions for processing a clause as a representation. Whether that representation indicates purpose or not is derived from the context. The use of a finite verb in subjunctive mood further encourages this interpretation, and, in contrast to an infinitival construction marks the subject unambiguously.

In summary, these are the points at issue:

- Purpose is a representation of someone's thought which is linked to an action;
- it may be uttered by the one whose thought it is or by someone else who attributes it to that person on the basis of behaviour, stated intention or other unidentified inferences;
- such attribution might not be accepted by the subject;
- ἵνα guides a reader to expect a representation of a state of affairs which is desirable to someone (but not actual);
- although ἵνα signals a representation it does not indicate 'purpose' through its lexical meaning: that is, it does not mean 'in order to';
- ἵνα is underdetermined and the interpretation of a ἵνα clause as one of 'purpose' must be inferred from the context, that is the text itself, or the shared contextual assumptions of both author and reader;
- ἵνα may also introduce clauses which represent:
  what the subject wants some one else to do (indirect commands);
  what the subject understands a desirable state of affairs to be;
  what the subject views as a desirable state of affairs from the perspective of another (prophetic statement).

Although purpose is a representation, it is not obligatorily introduced by ἵνα with a subjunctive verb. It may also take the form of an infinitive, especially after certain verbs. I argue that such constructions do not give procedural clues to the reader to expect a representation, whereas ἵνα together with a subjunctive[87] verb, does give such clues. These clues make the representation salient and communication more relevant.

---

[86] εἰς, πρός give instructions to read the infinitive as indicating purpose, while ἐν, μετά indicate a temporal relationship etc.

[87] Several examples of ἵνα clauses from the works of Dionysius of Halicarnassus use a verb in optative mood as in the older Attic.

CHAPTER 7

Investigating ὅτι

7.1 Introduction

In investigating the scope of ἵνα in Koine Greek, we have observed that the use of the infinitive for complement constructions was declining in favour of subordinate clauses.[1] Although the focus of this book is the use of ἵνα, another conjunction or particle which is relevant to this development is ὅτι. Clauses introduced by ἵνα have been the subject of Chapters 3 to 6, but to complete the picture of relevant language change in Koine we will now consider other subordinate clauses which are introduced by ὅτι. Before moving on to consider the function of this particle in the Koine, we should briefly examine its use in the earlier language so that the increase in use may be seen in this context, as well as its status as a procedural marker indicating a representation.

7.2 Classical Greek

Although infinitival constructions were popular in this period for the expansion of the content of verbs of saying, thinking and knowing, subordinate clauses introduced by ὅτι could also be used. There were three ways in which this functioned:[2]

- to introduce direct speech 7.2.1;
- to introduce indirect speech 7.2.2;
- to introduce a causal clause 7.2.3.

7.2.1 Direct Speech

This type of ὅτι clause seems to be less common in the classical authors, but is still perfectly acceptable. Goodwin notes Xenophon, Thucydides, Herodotus and Demosthenes as using this particle to introduce direct speech.[3] In effect, it acts as a marker of direct speech, functioning much as modern quotation marks, and is untranslatable. It gives procedural instructions to expect a quotation, as this example from Xenophon[4] shows:

---

[1] Some grammarians (*BDF, ATR* pp.1054-5; Jannaris pp. 572-3, Mandilaras, Horrocks) describe this as analytical constructions taking over from syntactic constructions.
[2] Goodwin (1965) §662-676, 711, 712-714. *BDF* §396, 456.
[3] Goodwin §711.
[4] *Cyropaedia* VII. 3,3, in Goodwin §711.

Example (1) Ἀπεκρίνατο ὅτι 'Ὦ δέσποτα, οὐ ζῇ.
He answered 'Master, he isn't alive.'

This is not the common use of this particle at this period, unlike later Greek, but it may be found in the works of those authors who are regarded as good writers of the language. Obviously direct speech could never be reported by infinitival constructions, but when an author wanted to use direct speech, he could introduce it by ὅτι or begin the quotation immediately after a verb of saying (usually λέγω). The use of the particle gave a clearer signal to the reader, although the pronomial reference, together with the vocative, also indicated a direct quotation. Unlike later Greek, direct speech, in classical authors, was less common than indirect apart from the long and contrived speeches in Thucydides and Xenophon.

> Direct quotation is more frequent in primitive language, in the vernacular, and in all vivid picturesque narrative. It is the dramatic method of reporting speech.[5]

7.2.2 Indirect Speech

> The term *indirect discourse* ... includes all clauses which express indirectly the words or thoughts of any person (including those of the speaker himself), after verbs which imply thought or the expression of thought. [6]

Indirect speech, in Classical Greek, could be encapsulated in an infinitival construction with the subject appearing in the accusative case, as a participial clause, particularly after verbs of perception, or by a subordinate clause introduced by ὅτι or ὡς.[7] It is the particle ὅτι which we shall consider here. Goodwin[8] discusses the advance of this particle from ὅ τι to its use in a sentence such as οἶδα ὅ τι κακὰ μήδεται which moved from its original meaning of 'I know as to what he plans evil' to 'I know that he plans evil.'

It is clear that this particle by introducing the thought or words of a speaker gives procedural instructions to the reader to expect a representation, that is a representation of a representation which is an utterance or a thought.[9] In

---

[5] *ATR* p. 1027.

[6] Goodwin §666.

[7] *ATR* makes the interesting comment, quoting Reeb, that 'Demosthenes uses ὡς for what is false and ὅτι for what is true' (p. 1032). Smyth (1956) claims that φημί 'is almost always followed by the infinitive, but by ὅτι in the later language' §2017a.

[8] Goodwin §663.

[9] Recall that in this book the first order representation will be assumed and the term 'representation' will be used for all representations, rather than the theoretically correct 'metarepresentation'.

considering the particle ἵνα we saw that the representation which that particle signalled was of a desirable state of affairs. ὅτι by contrast, introduces a representation which reflects, or claims to reflect, an actual state of affairs, that is a state of affairs in the real world. Now the speaker may be mistaken, or even be untruthful, but he is presenting the representation as factual. The use of the indicative mood supports this assertion.[10] After secondary tenses the optative could be used, but this was optional rather than obligatory. Goodwin suggests[11] that the choice here depended on the author's presentation of the quotation in the original form (as far as possible) or in his own words, the latter frequently using the optative mood. This suggests strongly that the optative mood was used to indicate a level of representation which was interpretive.

7.2.3 Causal Clauses

This type of clause could be introduced not only by ὅτι, but also by ἐπεί. The indicative was the usual mood, but Goodwin[12] points out that when the reason given was not asserted by the author but by some other person, the optative might be used. He gives the following example from Thucydides:[13]

> Example (2) Τὸν Περικλέα ἐκάκιζον, ὅτι στρατηγὸς ὢν οὐκ ἐπεξάγοι.
> They abused Pericles, because being general he did not lead them out.

If Thucydides himself had been supplying the reason, the verb would have been in indicative mood: ἐπεξῆγεν, but as he is giving the reason supplied by the Athenians, then he uses the optative. Smyth concurs with this:

> Causal clauses denoting a fact regularly take the indicative after primary and secondary tenses ... but causal clauses denoting an alleged or reported reason ... take the optative after secondary tenses[14]

I note this because it supports the assertion that communicative acts regularly employ representation both of the author's own thoughts or words and those of others. Languages frequently also indicate, by evidentials or mood, that more than one representation is involved in the communication.[15] In Classical Greek it seems that the use of the optative could also signal a representation, namely that the thought expressed, or reason given in this

---

[10] Levinsohn (2003) makes the different uses of this particle relate to descriptive or interpretive use.
[11] Goodwin §670.
[12] Goodwin §714.
[13] Thucydides 2.21.
[14] Smyth (1956) §2241 and 2242.
[15] Recall the discussion of evidentials in 2.2.2.5, as well as footnote 56 and Ifantidou (1994).

Investigating ὅτι 153

context, was not that of the author but another, as suggested in 7.2.2 above. In addition it seems that it may also signal the author's disagreement with or his distancing himself from the reason stated.

7.3 Koine Greek

Blass' claim that 'analytical constructions with ἵνα and ὅτι have developed into serious rivals of the infinitive'[16] is particularly apposite in relation to the latter particle. Almost all the uses of ὅτι in Koine are found in the earlier language, but the extent to which they are used, rather than an infinitival construction, is the most noticeable factor of language change. As noted in 7.2 this particle may introduce:

- direct speech;
- indirect speech;
- causal clauses.

7.3.1 Direct Speech

Jannaris estimates that there are 'about 120' instances[17] of this use of ὅτι in the NT. Although it was used in the classical language in this way, it is difficult to find instances of it in literary Koine, probably because the works of Polybius and Dionysius have lengthy speeches, introduced only by λέγων, but no dialogue. It is used frequently, however, before direct speech in the *Discourses* of Epictetus, often in dialogue with an imaginary respondent, where some responses will be signalled by this particle while others are not. There may well be different inferences which a reader is expected to draw from the introduction of a quotation without this particle, but as this is not the focus of my current study I have not examined this in depth.

The first book of the *Discourses* has 192 instances of ὅτι. Of these, 25 introduce direct speech. In several instances the particle introduces a dialogue which then continues without an introductory particle:

Example (3)[18] ἀπηγγέλη αὐτῷ ὅτι " κρίνῃ ἐν συγκλήτῳ." –
" Ἀγαθῇ τύχῃ. ἀλλὰ ἦλθεν ἡ πέμπτη ..."
Word was brought him, "Your case is being tried in the Senate." - "Good luck betide! But it is the fifth hour now…" (*LCL*: Oldfather)

The dialogue continues (after the fifth hour and the visit to the baths) with an introductory ὅτι followed by several short comments from both Agrippinus and

---

[16] *BDF* §388.
[17] Jannaris (1897) §2032.
[18] Book 1.1.28-29. The punctuation is reproduced from the *LCL* edition.

his respondent, none of which are introduced by this particle.[19] Occasionally there is ambiguity as to whether or not the speech is reported or direct, this being felt by the editor and translator also, who marks the English translation as direct, but not the Greek.[20]

> Example (4) λέγει ὅτι ὁ θάνατος οὐκ ἔστι κακόν, οὐδὲ γὰρ αἰσχρόν· λέγει ὅτι ἀδοξία ψόφος ἐστὶ μαινομένων ἀνθρώπων.
> He says, "Death is not an evil, since it is not dishonourable"; he says, "Ill repute is a noise made by madmen."[21] (*LCL*: Oldfather)

It is clear that this report could be either direct or indirect, since there is no pronominal reference, that is first or second person marking on the verb, to guide the reader. The translator has chosen the former. What is true whether the speech is direct or indirect is that a representation is signalled by this particle. What is not so clear is whether or not the writer was claiming to represent the exact words of the speaker[22] or to interpret them. Since it was the practice of teachers such as Epictetus to use the Stoic writings as their text,[23] with their own questions as stimulation for the students listening, it is difficult to be more certain about the claim to such a metalinguistic representation.

The NT writers on the other hand regularly claim to record dialogue, frequently introducing this with ὅτι *recitativum*. 'By far the most common form of complement with verbs of saying is *direct* discourse which can be introduced by ὅτι.'[24] Modern Greek also uses πῶς to introduce direct speech.[25] Robertson[26] notes Matt. 19:9 and Mark 10:11 as being more or less parallel, but whereas Matthew has ὅτι, Mark has direct speech without an introductory particle. The two examples, however, are not exactly parallel, since the Matthean account presents the saying *within* direct speech already, and following the set phrase λέγω δὲ ὑμῖν which seems to be frequently followed by ὅτι.

Mark's proclivity for using the particle in this sense is acknowledged:[27] out of 102 instances of ὅτι, 34 introduce direct speech, whereas in Luke there are

---

[19] Book 1.1.29-30.
[20] *LCL*: Oldfather. The Greek text in the *LCL* edition marks direct speech in Greek with quotation marks, but no initial capital letter.
[21] *Discourses* Book 1.24.6.
[22] A metalinguistic representation; recall 2.2.2.5 and footnote 55 of that section.
[23] *LCL*: Oldfather, p. xv.
[24] *BDF* §397(5). This quotation does focus on constructions after verbs of saying. It is not concerned with the much more frequent occurrence of the particle following epistemic verbs such as knowing, thinking, seeming etc.
[25] Thumb (1912) p. 192, and text II.6; Jannaris (1897) p. 472.
[26] *ATR* p. 1028.
[27] *BDF* §470: ‘Ὅτι *recitativum* is most common in Mk' and (2) 'It is quite impossible for a NT author to do what is so common in classical Greek...namely, to maintain indirect discourse in an extended passage.'

only 33 examples of ὅτι introducing direct speech, out of the 174 occurrences of the particle in that gospel. In Chapter 4 we considered the ways in which similar events are presented in Matthew, Mark and Luke: direct speech, indirect speech or straight narrative with no claim to representation. There may also be ambiguity, as noted above. The report of Herod's musing on hearing of Jesus' miracles is a case in point:[28]

Example (5) ἔλεγον ὅτι Ἰωάννης ὁ βαπτίζων ἐγήγερται ἐκ νεκρῶν·
They said 'John the Baptist has been raised from the dead.' *or*
They said that John the Baptist had been raised from the dead.
Example (5a) διηπόρει διὰ τὸ λέγεσθαι ὑπό τινων ὅτι Ἰωάννης ἠγέρθη ἐκ νεκρῶν·
He was perplexed because it was said by some that John the Baptist had been raised from the dead. *or*
He was perplexed because it was said by some 'John the Baptist has been raised from the dead.'

The tense of the latter example: ἠγέρθη, could be used in either.[29] The point is that in both examples the implied author is claiming to report what had been said. They claim to give a representation of the words of a speaker. Whether or not this is a claim to a metalinguistic resemblance (very unlikely) or an interpretive resemblance is not signalled by the text. In both Example (5) and (5a), a verbatim report would not have been considered necessary. The modern preoccupation with giving a speaker's exact words did not trouble the ancients.[30] On a more formal level, authors regularly lifted the words of others without acknowledgement, while both Polybius and Dionysius designed speeches for historical characters to fit the situations in which they found themselves. *RT* claims that *all* reported speech is an interpretive resemblance of the original utterance,[31] and in Koine, as we have seen, the same particle may introduce direct or indirect speech, with pronominal reference and context being the only indicators by which these might be distinguished.

There are five textual variants, in Matthew, Mark, Luke and John, with insertion or omission of ὅτι, three being before direct speech, one before an OT quotation and one after the set phrase λέγω δὲ ὑμῖν. Since the particle is preceded by λέγω or γράφω, this may reflect its optional nature before direct

---

[28] Mark 6:14 Example (5), and Luke 9:7 Example (5a).

[29] Greek of course, both Classical and Koine, maintains in indirect speech the tense of the original utterance. Note the ἐγήγερται of Example (5).

[30] Cadbury (1927) p. 160 '...in the unacknowledged use of written material, they had no inkling of our modern demand for quotation both verbatim and acknowledged'.

[31] More recently, Noh (2000) and Gutt (2004) have acknowledged the place of 'metalinguistic representation', in which an utterance is repeated verbatim. This implies that such use is descriptive rather than interpretive.

speech. I am arguing that it was a procedural marker, alerting the reader to expect a representation. Its use was optional. If it was not used, the reader could use contextual clues to infer a representation, but the use of the particle was a constraint on the interpretation of the words or clause which followed. As in the *Discourses*,[32] it seems that in dialogue, the first utterance is regularly introduced by this particle, while the second and following are not.[33] Consider the follow example:[34]

> Example (6) καὶ ὡμολόγησεν καὶ οὐκ ἠρνήσατο, καὶ ὡμολόγησεν ὅτι Ἐγὼ οὐκ εἰμὶ ὁ Χριστός. καὶ ἠρώτησαν αὐτόν, Τί οὖν; Σὺ Ἠλίας εἶ; καὶ λέγει, Οὐκ εἰμί. Ὁ προφήτης εἶ σύ; καὶ ἀπεκρίθη, Οὔ.
> So he admitted and didn't deny, but admitted[35] 'I am not the Christ'. Then they asked him, 'What then? Are you Elijah?' He said, 'I am not.' 'Are you the prophet?' He replied, 'No.'

When the dialogue in Example (6) has been introduced, the particle is not used again during the interchange of question and answer. I submit that this is because the reader can easily infer, from context and pronominal references, who is saying what. The constraint of the particle is not required.

7.3.2 Indirect Speech

I note in 7.3.1 that the most common use of ὅτι after a speech verb, such as λέγω, is to introduce direct speech. This, however, does not take account of the frequent use of this particle after verbs of thinking, knowing, seeing and even (in Koine, but not Classical) believing.[36] The particle introduces a representation of what the subject reportedly thought, knew or saw, that is, perceived. There are examples of the particle following verbs such as λέγω also, but the bulk of the examples of ὅτι in indirect speech refer to a mental representation of the thought of the subject. When a speaker says 'I thought' he is articulating a mental representation.[37] Because this utterance resembles his thought, it is already a representation of a representation. This particle then gives procedural instructions to the reader to expect this. Of course there may be other signals in the context, but the use of the particle makes salient this representation. Examples of the particle in this role may be found in Polybius and Dionysius, but they abound in the *Discourses* of Epictetus.

---

[32] Note the comment and examples above.
[33] Consider also Luke 20:5-6, but the parallel passages in Matthew 21:25-26 and Mark 11:31-32 have direct speech without the particle.
[34] John 1:20-21.
[35] In Matthew 14:7 the verb ὁμολογέω is followed by the infinitive.
[36] *BDF* §397(2); *ATR* pp. 1036, 1055; Mandilaras (1973) §801, 802.
[37] Recall that although *RT* describes this as a 'metarepresentation', in this book it will be referred to as a 'representation'.

7.3.2.1 EXAMPLES FROM PAGAN WRITERS: EPICTETUS AND POLYBIUS

I have included several examples from pagan writers in order to show that the increased use of this particle ὅτι, like ἵνα, is part of the general change which can be seen throughout the Koine. It is not merely a Semitic aberration. Both Epictetus and Polybius, although living outside of Greece for much of their lives, were quite outwith a context in which there might have been Semitic influence. An interesting comparison can be made between the *Discourses* of Epictetus, recorded by Arrian, and Arrian's own *Anabasis*. Consider the following example:[38]

> Example (7) ἔνθα δὴ ἄγγελοι ἀφίκοντο αὐτῷ Κλεῖτόν τε τὸν Βαρδύλεω ἀφεστάναι ἀγγέλλοντες καὶ Γλαυκίαν προσκεχωρηκέναι αὐτῷ τὸν Ταυλαντίων βασιλέα·
> There messengers reached him with the news that Clitus, son of Barydis, was in revolt, and that Glaucias, king of Taulantians, had joined him. (*LCL:* Brunt)
> Messengers reached him there announcing Clitus, son of Barydis, to have revolted and Glaucias, king of the Taulantians, to have joined him. (lit. MGS)

In this example an accusative and infinitive construction in good Attic style follows the participle ἀγγέλλοντες, unlike the style of the *Discourses*.

As noted in 7.3.1.1, there are 192 examples of ὅτι in the first book of the *Discourses* of Epictetus, with 140 of these being examples of indirect speech or thought. Of these 140, 27 follow speech verbs such as λέγω, ἀποκρίνομαι, ἀντέρομαι while the remainder (113) indicate the thought, belief, supposition of the speaker or subject. Consider the following example:[39]

> Example (8) τί γὰρ ἐστιν ἄλλο τὸ λέγον ὅτι χρυσίον καλὸν ἐστιν;
> δῆλον ὅτι ἡ χρηστικὴ δύναμις ταῖς φαντασίαις.
> For what else is it that tells us that gold is beautiful?
> Clearly it is the faculty which makes use of external impressions. (*LCL:* Oldfather)

Here the content of the participle λέγων is explicated by the clause introduced by ὅτι: 'Gold is beautiful'. This is a representation of a generally held belief. Epictetus introduces it in the course of his argument as an utterance which represents a proposition in the minds of most of his audience, in fact most of his world, at that time. Humans seem to do this regularly. We assume that certain propositions are held as beliefs by those who share our cultural and contextual environment. When moving out of that environment, we cannot

---

[38] *Anabasis* Book 1.5.1. Recall that Arrian himself wrote in Attic Greek, even in second century CE.
[39] *Discourses* Book 1.1.5.

continue to make such assumptions.[40]

The following example, in the speech of Epictetus, presents Agrippinus as reporting his own (potential) utterance, introduced by ὅτι after the aorist tense of λέγω:

Example (9) πότε οὖν σοι εἶπον ὅτι μόνου ἐμοῦ ὁ τράχηλος ἀναπότμητός ἐστιν;
Well, when did I ever tell you that mine was the only neck that could not be severed? (*LCL*: Oldfather)[41]

The context of this example indicates that the subject, Agrippinus, never made this utterance, but he reports it as a belief that was held by those to whom he was speaking. (That is: they thought that he had said it, or might have said or at least thought it.) He did not agree with it, and so repeats it as a rhetorical question in order to disabuse his followers, who thought that he could not be executed, of that belief.

As well as speech verbs, of course, this particle in the *Discourses* more usually follows epistemic verbs such as:

αἰσθάνομαι I.5.7	ἀξιόω I.9.24	γινώσκω I.3.2.
δείκνυμι I.19.9	δῆλον I.2.30	δοκέω I.4.16
ἐλπίζω I.20.13	ἐπινοέω I.11.40	εὑρίσκω I.28.20
καταλαμβάνω I.5.6[42]	μανθάνω I.2.2.	μαντεύομαι I.23.10
μιμνήσκομαι I.27.14	οἶδα I.22.4	οἶμαι I.3.1
ὁράω I.17.23	πάσχω I.2.3	πείθω I.8.9
προηγοῦμαι I.9.5	φαίνομαι I.28.2	φαντάζομαι I.18.13

In clauses which are followed by ὅτι the proportion of speech verbs to epistemic verbs is 20:111, showing that the most common construction introduced by ὅτι in the *Discourses*, in the first book at least, is a clause which explicates the thoughts of the subject: what he knows, remembers, thinks, sees, concludes, hopes. This is a representation of these thoughts which claims to be related to an actual state of affairs. As stated earlier, the subject may be mistaken or may be lying, but he is presenting the information as a representation of a state of affairs.

One final small addition to the evidence in this section is the few examples in which the title introducing a chapter of the *Discourses* is introduced by ὅτι. Consider Chapter 18[43] for example:

---

[40] Although we do make such assumptions, and in such circumstances communication often fails.
[41] *Discourses* Book 1.1.24.
[42] With the meaning 'conclude'.
[43] Book 1.18.

Example (10) ὅτι οὐ δεῖ χαλεπαίνειν τοῖς ἁμαρτανομένοις
'That we ought not to be angry with the erring.' (*LCL*: Oldfather)

This heading introduces a topic which is subsequently dealt with by Epictetus. There are very few examples of independent clauses introduced by ὅτι, apart from replies to questions and these are often best analysed as giving reasons, namely 'because' clauses. It is therefore worth considering the function which this particle has here. The title seems to give a summary[44] of the material which is to follow. I am arguing that the function of the particle here is to signal the representation of the editor's thought which summarises this material: *One should not be angry with those who err/ It is not fitting to be angry with those who err.*

There are four further examples in Book 3, almost all of which[45] feature δεῖ or οὐ δεῖ. This 'ought' clause gives the view of Epictetus concerning certain actions: what is right or necessary and what is the opposite. The introductory particle, however, gives the editor's belief concerning what the material consists of. The δεῖ clause gives the thought of the speaker, represented as Epictetus, as to what *should* be done, that is a potential state of affairs, while the ὅτι clause gives the editor's summary of what the material consists of: an actual state of affairs. Again he may be mistaken, misguided or deceitful, but he is presenting his thought as a state of affairs. The different representations which human communication seems to handle effortlessly are well exemplified here.

The historian Polybius has far fewer examples of ὅτι than Epictetus. I found 46 in the first four books of his *Histories*, with 4 of these introducing 'because' clauses and the other 42 introducing indirect speech, or rather the thought, presumption, knowledge of someone else. There are only 3 examples among these 42 of this particle following a verb of saying: one after λέγω and two after ἀποκρίνομαι. There are, however, several examples of a ὅτι clause giving the content of a noun which presupposes a verbal utterance, such as ἀγγελία. It is clear from these figures that the predominant function of this particle is to introduce a representation of the thought of someone else, rather than an actual utterance. I include one example only, and that because it shows a ὅτι clause following πιστεύω, a construction which does not seem to be found in Classical Greek:[46]

Example (11)[47] ὁ δ' Ἄρατος ἐπιμείνας δύο ἡμέρας, καὶ πιστεύσας εὐήθως ὅτι ποιήσονται τὴν ἐπάνοδον καθάπερ ὑπεδείκνυσαν...
Aratus waited two days: and thinking foolishly that the Aetolians would return by the

---

[44] From the perspective of the editor Arrian?
[45] 3 out of 4 instances.
[46] *BDF* §397(2). Note comment at 7.2.2 and footnote 32.
[47] *Histories* Book IV.10.1.

way they had indicated ... (*LCL*: Paton)

The relevant clause reads literally as 'believing foolishly that ...' The evidential[48] used here, εὐήθως, shows that Polybius knew that Aratus' belief was unfounded, but he represents what Aratus thought or believed was fact, an actual state of affairs. The point at issue is the use of this particle following the verb πιστεύω which is a regular construction in NT Greek,[49] but not in the earlier language. It is clear that the whole sphere of this particle was widening in the Koine, and not merely in NT writers, who are regularly accused of using Semitic Greek whenever their practice diverts from a perceived classical norm. Recall that the dates of this author are estimated as 208-126 BCE, at least two centuries before the NT writings.

7.3.2.2 EXAMPLES FROM THE NEW TESTAMENT

Apropos of indirect speech, Blass Debrunner comment that 'in contrast to ὅτι the (acc. with) inf. has strongly retreated in NT authors outside of Luke and Paul.'[50] This refers to constructions with verbs of saying, believing, showing, indicating, seeing. Robertson[51] gives an extensive list of all the verbs which precede a ὅτι clause in the NT, but points out that some verbs such as ἀκούω, γινώσκω, λογίζομαι, οἶδα, ὁμολογέω could be followed either by an infinitive or a ὅτι clause. Consider the following examples:[52]

> Example (12) ἠκούσατε ὅτι ἐρρέθη τοῖς ἀρχαίοις, **Οὐ φονεύσεις**·
> You have heard that it was said to the people of old, 'Don't murder.'

Note the different representations here, marked by ὅτι and then by direct speech.

> Example (12a)[53] ἤκουσαν τοῦτο αὐτὸν πεποιηκέναι τὸ σημεῖον·
> They heard that he had performed this sign/miracle.

These examples are significant because the infinitival construction comes, not in Matthew, who has only 102 examples of ὅτι, but in John, who has 271. If the use or otherwise of this particle is based only on authorial style, then one would have expected the opposite evidence. The usual construction after ἀκούω in the NT is a ὅτι clause.[54] The Johannine Example (12a) is unusual, particularly in an

---

[48] Recall the use of such as presented in 2.2.2.5, footnote 56 and Ifantidou (1994).
[49] Mark 11:24; John 11:27; Romans 10:9.
[50] *BDF* §397(3).
[51] *ATR* p. 1035.
[52] Matthew 5:21 Example (12), but note also 5:27, 33, 38, 43.
[53] John 12:18.
[54] *ATR* p. 1036.

author who uses the particle so frequently. I have argued that the use of this particle gives procedural instructions to the reader to expect a representation. If the author does not choose to give this instruction, he is leaving the reader to infer the representation without a constraint to guide her.[55] In the context of this example, however, the author has already made it clear from his perspective that the crowd was reacting to Jesus' sign in the raising of Lazarus. I claim that there was no need to make the content of what they heard more salient. As we have already claimed, the use of a procedural marker to indicate representation is not obligatory: it is an optional aid to inferencing.

It may be seen that with counts such as those in John's gospel (x271) and Luke (x174), the frequency of this particle has increased considerably since the time of Polybius. It is not, however, very much different from the *Discourses* of Epictetus, in which there are 192 occurrences in the first book alone.

As with ἵνα,[56] if the subject of the dependent clause is the same as that of the main clause, then it is more likely that an infinitive will be used to give the content of the main verb, that is what the subject thought, hoped or believed. Consider the following examples:[57]

Example (13) καὶ ἐὰν δανίσητε παρ' ὧν ἐλπίζετε λαβανεῖν...
So if you lend (to those) from whom you hope to receive...
Example (13a) ἡμεῖς δε ἠλπίζομεν ὅτι αὐτός ἐστιν ὁ μέλλων λυτροῦσθαι τὸν Ἰσραήλ·
But we hoped that he was the one who was going to redeem Israel.

In other words, although in Koine the accusative and infinitive seems to have been less popular as a construction for the description of thoughts and beliefs, the infinitive alone was still in current use, but predominantly by Paul and Luke.[58] This is not surprising because the ambiguity of having both subject and object with the same case marking made the proposition expressed less than transparent,[59] although the context makes it clear which accusative is the subject (human referent) and which the object (inanimate). Consider the following example:[60]

---

[55] Recall that we are referring to the speaker/writer as 'he' and the hearer/reader as 'she'.
[56] Consider θέλω, which in the NT only has a following ἵνα clause if the subject of the subordinate clause is different from that of the main clause.
[57] Example (13) from Luke 6:34; Example (13a) from Luke 24:21.
[58] *ATR* p. 1033 'The use of the inf. in indir. discourse takes quite a subordinate place in the N.T.' 'Luke' is used as shorthand for the author of the gospel of Luke and the book of Acts. Consider also Philemon 22: ἐλπίζω ὅτι ... χαρισθήσομαι, where the subject of both clauses is the same.
[59] As in Example (12a).
[60] Acts 28:6.

Example (14) οἱ δὲ προσεδόκων αὐτὸν μέλλειν πίμπρασθαι ἢ καταπίπτειν ἄφνω νεκρόν.
But they expected him to swell up or fall down dead.

together with the following:[61]

Example (15) ἦλθον λέγουσαι καὶ ὀπτασίαν ἀγγέλων ἑωρακέναι.
They came saying also that they had seen a vision of angels.

In Example (14) the infinitive μέλλειν is intransitive, as are the two verbs which depend on it, πίμπρασθαι and καταπίπτειν, which makes the clause unambiguous: αὐτὸν must be the subject. The verb προσδοκάω is invariably followed by the infinitive, both in the NT and the papyri. In Example (15), however, λέγω is unusually followed by an infinitive. I found only 31 examples of such in the NT, 14 of which were in Luke and Acts. In almost all of these examples λέγω has the sense of 'claiming' to be something.[62] The author in each case, however, does not choose to make the claim more prominent by the use of a clause introduced by ὅτι. With these exceptions, noted below,[63] it seems that when an infinitive follows λέγω, it is the infinitive of the verb to be (εἶναι or γίνεσθαι).

This section has been added to make clear the options open to a writer of Koine Greek at this period. Indirect speech, including verbs of knowing, perceiving, showing, was regularly introduced by ὅτι with an indicative verb, but certain writers, notably the author of Luke and Acts, occasionally used the infinitive, even after λέγω. When the particle ὅτι introduces a clause, the writer is constraining its interpretation as a representation of what was said, thought or believed. When the author selects an infinitival construction, he places no constraint on the interpretation, but the reader may infer the representation from the context.

Representation is an obligatory feature of communication after verbs of saying, believing, thinking, knowing, etc. These verbs have as part of their semantic content the notion of a mental proposition in someone's mind. This is made salient when the author uses a ὅτι clause, but it is there even if the infinitive is used to encapsulate the representation. In the latter case the subject and often the temporal reference has to be inferred from the context. By contrast, such subject and temporal reference is transparent in the use of the

---

[61] Luke 24:23.

[62] Support for this is found in Luke 9:18 where the two uses of λέγω in the same sentence have diferent constructions following: ἐπηρώτησεν αὐτοὺς λέγων, Τίνα με λέγουσιν οἱ ὄχλοι εἶναι; 'he asked them saying, 'Whom do the crowds say/claim that I am?'

[63] There are 4 examples of negative prohibitions after λέγω: Matthew 5:34, 39; Acts 21:21 and Romans 2:22.

Investigating ὅτι 163

indicative, while the introductory particle gives procedural instructions to the reader to expect a representation of someone's thought, the indicative rather than the infinitive showing clearly the subject and tense.

7.3.3 Causal Clauses

It was pointed out in 7.2.3 and 7.3 that both in Classical and Koine Greek ὅτι, together with other particles, could introduce a clause which gave the reason for an action. By the time of Koine, however, 'all other causal particles are insignificant beside ὅτι which grew steadily in use'.[64] At the heart of this use is the implied thought of the subject which is presented as his understanding of a real state of affairs. At first consideration it may seem as if this use is not so much factual as potential, or putative, but the essential issue is that the writer is presenting a thought as his belief that it is an actual state of affairs. As with indirect speech, the thought might be wrong or be represented deceitfully, but the presentation is of a state of affairs. This will be developed further in the following sections.

7.3.3.1 EXAMPLES FROM EPICTETUS AND POLYBIUS

I found only 4 examples of causal ὅτι in the first four books of the *Histories* of Polybius, but for Epictetus there were 25 in the first book of the *Discourses* alone. The two hundred years which separate these two works may account for the increase in the use of this particle. The different register of these works should also be taken into account. This is developed further in 8.4.1.

I present only two examples from Polybius both of which illustrate the reportative, or representational nature of such clauses:

> Example (16)[65] οὐδ' Ἀντιγόνῳ προσαπτέον οὐδ' Ἀράτῳ παρανομίαν, ὅτι λαβόντες κατὰ πόλεμον ὑποχείριον τύραννον στρεβλώσαντες ἀπέκτειναν...
> Nor should we charge Antigonus and Aratus with criminal conduct, if, having captured him in war they had tortured and put to death a tyrant. (*LCL*: Paton)
> Literal trans.: Nor is it necessary to attach illegal behaviour to Antigonus or Aratus, because they killed a tyrant, having captured him in war and tortured him while he was in their hands. (MGS)

This example has a ὅτι clause which both explains what Antigonus and Aratus did, but also presents the reason for a charge of 'illegal behaviour': παρανομία. In other words, the clause gives a reason why someone might accuse them of lawbreaking, but it also explicates the lawbreaking. This clause represents a potential thought on the part of someone: *It is illegal for Antigonus and Aratus to capture a tyrant and while he was in their hands to have tortured and killed him.*

---

[64] *ATR* p. 964.
[65] *Histories* 2.60.2.

When the main clause is also considered we can infer a causal relation between it and the ὅτι clause. The many examples both in pagan and NT Greek which are ambiguous should invite us to consider just what factor drives us to infer a causal relationship. Interestingly, Paton's translation[66] reads the ὅτι clause as potential, although no one has ever suggested that the particle might have a dictionary meaning of 'if'. This clause is clearly representational of a thought, as indicated above, which might lead, potentially, to an accusation.

Consider one further example from the same author which again demonstrates representation:

Example (17) πρὸς δὲ Καρχηδονίους διεπέμπετο, πυνθανόμενος τί δεῖ ποιεῖν, ὅτι Ζακανθαῖοι πιστεύοντες τῇ Ῥωμαίων συμμαχίᾳ τινὰς τῶν ὑφ' αὑτοὺς ταττομένων ἀδικοῦσι.
He (Hannibal) sent to the Carthaginians, asking what he should do, because the Zakanthians (Saguntines), trusting in the alliance with the Romans, were badly treating some of those placed under them (i.e. the Carthaginians) / subject to them.[67] (MGS)

In this example the writer has not made explicit whether the ὅτι clause is part of Hannibal's communication to the Carthaginians, or his own understanding of the reason behind Hannibal's communication.[68] If we accept the former interpretation, then Hannibal is asking for instructions on the basis of the ill treatment of a certain people group by the Zakanthians. If we accept the latter, then the author is giving his own thought concerning Hannibal's request for instruction. In both cases the representation is clear: *The Zakanthians, trusting in the alliance with the Romans, are mistreating some of those placed under them.*

With only the sentence above to guide our interpretation, it is difficult to be certain to whom that representation should be ascribed. In the wider context, however, it appears that not only was this representation that of Hannibal and the one that he presented to his masters in Carthage, but that, according to the author, it was not the real reason for his request. In other words, Hannibal presented this as his own thought and on the basis of the behaviour described, was asking what he should do. He was presenting this information as fact, as a state of affairs, but according to Polybius he was pretending.[69] He wanted the Carthaginians to think that *the Zakanthians are mistreating those placed under them* and on the basis of this information to give him instructions to fight. He

---

[66] *LCL* as footnote above.
[67] *Histories* Book III.15.8 The centre of Hannibal's operations at this point was Spain.
[68] This is a frequent ambiguity in English fiction. Consider Wilson (2000)'s comments (p. 144) on various literary analyses of certain passages in Jane Austen's *Persuasion*.
[69] 'He did not allege the true reasons, but took refuge in groundless pretexts.' Book III.15.9 (*LCL*:Paton).

had also previously attacked the Zakanthians, not because of the representation given above, but because of his enmity to Rome, under whose protection these people had been placed. Humans seem to be able to cope easily not only with several different representations, but also to use what *RT* theorists call a strategy of 'sophisticated understanding' in the interpretation of these.[70] My point in giving this example is to support my assertion that some logical relationships in sentences are inferred rather than being part of the dictionary meaning of certain particles. The particles ἵνα and ὅτι give procedural instructions to the reader to expect a representation: they do not mean 'in order that' or 'because'. The logical relationship between clauses, which may well be one of purpose, or reason in this case, is inferred from the context.

Out of 192 examples of ὅτι in the first book of the *Discourses* of Epictetus 25 relate to causal clauses. I have selected only two of these to support the contention that this particle introduces a representation, even in those clauses which might be analysed syntactically as causal. Example (18) shows a clause which explicates a verb implying utterance, ἐπιτιμάω, indicating the content of the rebuke, but which also, by inference, contains the reason for the utterance:

Example (18) ἐπεί τοι τοῦτ' αὐτὸ καὶ ἐγὼ ʽΡούφῳ εἶπον ἐπιτιμῶντί μοι ὅτι τὸ παραλειπόμενον ἓν ἐν συλλογισμῷ τινι οὐχ εὕρισκον.
Indeed this is the very remark which I made to Rufus when he censured me for not discovering the one omission in a certain syllogism.[71] (*LCL*: Oldfather)
Literal trans.: Since I said this very thing to Rufus as he rebuked me because/that I did not find one thing which was left out in a syllogism. (MGS)

Rufus' rebuke could be represented as: *You did not find the one omission in a syllogism*. Epictetus, whose own utterances are being represented by Arrian, represents the above rebuke in the ὅτι clause: *I did not discover the single omission in a certain syllogism*. As well as giving the content of the rebuke, the ὅτι clause may also lead us to infer that this, that is the omission, was the reason for Rufus' rebuke. We can do this without assigning a meaning of 'because' to the particle. In fact Oldfather translates it as 'for ...not', which also gives the idea of reason, but in different words. I am arguing that the function of this particle is to give procedural instructions to the reader to expect a representation. It is obvious that there are several representations involved here. One of those might be analysed as providing a reason for the introductory verb ἐπιτιμάω, but it does not thereby attach a causal meaning to the particle itself: that comes from inference.

Consider also the next example in which the clause introduced by ὅτι answers the question 'why':

---

[70] Recall the discussion of these strategies for interpretation in 2.2.2.3, Wilson (2000) p. 138 and Sperber (1994) pp. 196-8.
[71] *Discourses* Book. I.7.32.

Example (19)[72] διὰ τί; ὅτι σὺ σεαυτὸν ἡγῇ μίαν τινὰ εἶναι κρόκην τῶν ἐκ τοῦ χιτῶνος.
Why not? Because you regard yourself as but a single thread of all that go to make up the garment. (*LCL:* Oldfather)
Literal trans.: Why? Because you think yourself to be one thread of those of the garment. (MGS)

In the ὅτι clause Epictetus[73] answers a question and by so doing gives a reason. He also represents what he thinks the questioner believes: *I think I am one thread of those in the garment*. The content of the belief clause is described in an accusative and infinitive construction. Recall that we have already seen that in the NT the content of clauses following λέγω which have the sense of 'claim to be' is encapsulated in an infinitival construction.[74] There is a representation here also: *I am one thread of those in the garment* but this is found in an infinitival construction and is not marked by a particle which then introduces a clause with an indicative verb. Representation is present whenever there is implied utterance or thought. This may be described by an infinitival construction, but it is made salient when it is encapsulated in a clause the significance of which in turn is marked by ὅτι. The particle marks the clause as a representation, while the indicative mood allows the subject to be clearly indicated. I suggest that in this construction the representation is more easily processed by the reader. In Example (19) the person also is emphasised by the pronoun σύ.

The ὅτι clause then gives a representation of Epictetus' thought, which in turn represents his student's thought. Since this clause is also an answer to διὰ τί we may infer that it is giving a reason for a previous action. The function of the particle, however, is not to indicate causality, but representation. As we have stated, causality may be inferred but it is not part of the intrinsic meaning of that particle, which functions as a procedural marker.

7.3.3.2 EXAMPLES FROM THE NEW TESTAMENT

Since there are 1296[75] instances of ὅτι in the NT, this section will focus only on the process by which a reader decides whether or not to infer a causal relationship from its use. From sections 7.2.1.2 and Examples (5) and (5a), we have seen that there may be ambiguity in deciding whether or not a ὅτι clause introduces direct or indirect speech, in particular in those cases where the subject of the clause is in the third person. I have also argued that the Examples (16) to (19) show this particle as marking a representation, although we may also infer from the context, but not the meaning of the particle itself, that the

---

[72] Book I.2.17.
[73] As always, represented by Arrian.
[74] Consider p. 10 Example (14) and footnote 34.
[75] *Hermeneutica*, also *MG*, pp. 778-790.

clause represents the reasoning process of some person, his own or one attributed to him.

This use may also be ambiguous after verbs such as λέγω, for example in a sentence such as that in John 20:13, in which the punctuation varies with the editor, based on inferences.[76]

Consider also the following example which has an independent ὅτι clause which is variously interpreted:

Example (20) ὑμεῖς ἐστε οἱ δικαιοῦντες ἑαυτοὺς ἐνώπιον τῶν ἀνθρώπων, ὁ δὲ θεὸς γινώσκει τὰς καρδίας ὑμῶν· ὅτι τὸ ἐν ἀνθρώποις ὑψηλὸν βδέλυγμα ἐνώπιον τοῦ θεοῦ.
You are the ones who present yourselves righteous before human beings, but God knows your hearts; because the pride which is in people is a detestable thing before God *or* (that) what is esteemed among men is detestable before God.

Marshall says

the force of ὅτι is doubtful, unless we assume that "knows your hearts" carries the implicit consequence "and judges them", *because* he hates pride.[77]

Plummer[78] similarly suggests an ellipsis after ὅτι "'But God knoweth your hearts [and He seeth not as man seeth] because that which is exalted...'" Nolland[79] suggests that the clause 'may have existed as a saying in its own right: it has the antithetic exaggeration of a Semitic proverb and fits slightly awkwardly into the syntax here'. If we accept that the use of this particle invites the reader to infer a representation, then Nolland's suggestion is particularly attractive. The particle would then be alerting the reader to the echoic use of this saying. What we can perceive clearly is that the commentators' interpretation of the particle in this verse is dependent on inference, rather than the assumption that it has a fixed dictionary entry of 'because'. For the particle to be translated as 'because', certain other inferences would have to be drawn, as Marshall suggests. As claimed before, the function of ὅτι is to mark a representation; any causal relationship with another clause has to be inferred from the context.

Joel Green, while not dealing with the use of ὅτι in itself does link that clause causally to the preceding sentence, on the basis of Luke's earlier

---

[76] John 20:13 λέγει αὐτοῖς ὅτι ἦραν τὸν κύριόν μου, καὶ οὐκ οἶδα ποῦ ἔθηκαν αὐτόν.
She said to them, '(because) they have taken my Lord and I don't know where they have put him.'
[77] Marshall (1978) p. 626.
[78] Plummer (1981 reprint) p. 388.
[79] Nolland (1993) p. 810.

inclusion of 'hypocrisy' in the description of the Pharisees.[80] He notes:

> the reference to God as the one who "knows hearts"... cannot be read as a judgement against the Pharisees as though their inner dispositions were at odds with their outward behaviour...Instead Jesus is calling into question a way of life embraced by the Pharisees, one that is focused on the quest for external approval rather than on character and behaviour that are valued by God.[81]

The inferencing here is from a much wider context, but it does seem to be a relevant interpretation of this difficult clause. Luke is contrasting a difference in the value system of the Pharisees with the teaching of Jesus. Although the Pharisees are called 'hypocrites',[82] they do in fact show in their attitude to money just what their priorities were. Their sneering[83] is presented as the cause of Jesus' rebuke to them.

In conclusion, I suggest that the particle ὅτι in this context is giving procedural instructions to the reader to interpret the clause it introduces as a representation. If we infer, as Nolland, a well known saying, then it is a representation of a commonly known belief. If, on the other hand, we infer an implicit judgement in the use of the verb 'know', as Marshall, then it is a representation of the reason for the judgement.[84] Finally, if we draw on a wider context, including Luke's presentation of wealth and greed in contrast with generosity, as Green, then it is a representation of the condemnation[85] of those who seek human rather than divine approval, together with the concomitant values assumed in each.

A further ambiguous example may be seen in the text of Mark 8:16-17, resolution of which is often made to depend on the parallel passage in Matthew 16:5-12. The issue of the translation of this particle is present in the Matthean account also, but the more crucial interpretative issue regarding ὅτι is found in the Marcan passage. I will consider this in the example below:

Example (21)[86] καὶ διελογίζοντο πρὸς ἀλλήλους ὅτι ἄρτους οὐκ ἔχουσιν. καὶ γνοὺς λέγει αὐτοῖς, Τί διαλογίζεσθε ὅτι ἄρτους οὐκ ἔχετε;
They were discussing with one another (the fact) that they did not have bread. So knowing this he said to them, 'Why are you discussing (the fact) that you don't have bread?'
or They were debating with one another because they didn't have any bread. So

---

[80] Luke 12:1.
[81] Green (1997).
[82] Luke 12:1.
[83] Luke 16:14.
[84] That is, presumably, in the mind of God.
[85] Again, presumably, God's condemnation.
[86] Mark 8:16-17.

knowing this he said to them, 'Why are you debating because you don't have bread?' *or* They were debating with one another why they didn't have bread.[87]

There are serious textual variants for 8:16, which add λέγοντες and change the person marking on the verb ἔχομεν so that the particle introduces direct speech: λέγοντες ὅτι ἄρτους οὐκ ἔχομεν. This is generally regarded as an attempt to harmonise this verse with Matthew 16:7. Gould[88] and Plummer[89] base their exegesis on this reading, as does *RSV*. Vincent Taylor[90] on the other hand sees the reading of λέγοντες as 'very attractive, but textually unsound. Moreover they interpret Mk in the light of Mt rather than Mk in itself.' In general it seems to be older commentators who accept this reading.

There is substantial variation in the interpretation of this particle by commentators and translations, even apart from the variant reading. There are serious issues of exegesis involved, and the translations reveal inferences that require to be clearly articulated. Vincent Taylor[91] comments:

> The issue is important; it affects the interpretation of the narrative as a whole, not merely the exegesis of 16.

If the particle is taken as introducing a causal relationship, and also with the text which supplies λέγοντες then an ellipsis of 'it is' has to be posited. The motivation for such an interpretation is the desire to tie the saying of verse 15: 'Beware of the yeast of the Pharisees and the yeast of Herod', into the rest of the pericope. The ὅτι clause would then give the disciples' own comments on the remark which Jesus has just been portrayed as making (8:15).

Gould[92] also points to the context of the Pharisees asking for a sign (8:11-12) and relates this to Jesus' exasperation with his disciples' inability to read the signs they have already received. He sees the link as inferred in the Marcan passage but overt in the Matthean. Gould likewise reads ὅτι as causal in 8:17. Lane, on the other hand, does not accept the reading of λέγοντες....ἔχομεν but does link the logion in 8:15 with the rest of the pericope, agreeing with C.H. Turner's analysis of ὅτι as an indirect interrogative: 'why'. He also has an interesting footnote which suggests, on the basis of an article by Negoita and Daniel, that in first century CE the Aramaic for 'leaven' and 'teaching' would have been homonyms. This would also provide a better link with the logion.[93]

---

[87] This involves taking ὅτι as an indirect interrogative as Turner.
[88] Gould (1896) p. 146.
[89] Plummer (1914) p. 198.
[90] Taylor (1966, reprint 1981) p. 366.
[91] In respect of 8:16, p. 366.
[92] Supporting the readings in A C L X etc.
[93] This is countered by the fact that Mark so often translates an Aramaic phrase for his readers. It also infers a misinterpretation, or mishearing by all of the disciples. In regard

Guelich[94] seems to regard the issue as irrelevant. It seems, however, that the question of what they were discussing *is* relevant in so far as it may serve to link the logion of 8:15 with 8:14, 16. He does make a point concerning the contextual application of independent logia which is relevant here:

> To survive, an independent logion must convey a certain intelligible meaning in itself. Yet its applicability to various contexts reflects an inherent ambiguity as well.

This is exemplified, he claims, by the Lucan identification of the 'yeast' with 'hypocrisy',[95] while Matthew identifies it with teaching.[96] 'Mark, however, leaves the meaning of the "leaven" for the reader to identify.'[97] Nevertheless it is this very lack of identification which raises the question as to whether the logion of 8:15 is independent or the topic of the disciples' debate, and this comes back to the function of ὅτι. This particle introduces a representation, but the reader will draw the inferences which are most relevant for her. An 'ambiguous' logion invites different interpretations, according to what is more or less relevant for a reader.

Gundry,[98] on the other hand, discusses in depth the use of ὅτι in both 8:16 and 8:17. His conclusion, briefly, is that since the ὅτι clause of 8:17 is epexegetic, because a causal use 'would leave an ambiguity', 'we have a parallelistic reason to treat the one in v 16 as epexegetic, too.' Now if this is pressed to its logical conclusion, it gives support for the reading of λέγοντες...ἔχομεν in 8:16, in order to avoid ambiguity and also to maintain the parallel in 8:17, a position which Gundry avoids. This seems to be a rather circular argument. He does claim in his comments on 8:16[99] that the arranging of 8:15 and 8:16 supports his contention that 'Mark thinks the warning prompted (the response) and that he portrays the disciples as thinking so.' He then goes on to claim that the inference which the disciples draw is that they should not buy bread from the Pharisees. Although I have not found other scholarly support for this view, it does on the surface represent a very reasonable inference and ties the logion of 8:15 with both 8:14 and 8:16. While

---

to 'teaching' Gundry (p. 414) points out that this is the Matthean setting - it is not in the Marcan context at all.

[94] Guelich (1989) p. 418 'This rendering takes ὅτι as introducing a noun clause. It could also be causal, since it is uncertain and moot whether this clause tells us what they were discussing or why they were discussing it'.

[95] Luke 12:1.

[96] Matthew 16:12 τότε συνῆκαν ὅτι οὐκ εἶπεν προσέχειν ἀπὸ τῆς ζύμης τῶν ἄρτων ἀλλὰ ἀπὸ τῆς διδαχῆς τῶν Φαρισαίων καὶ Σαδδουκαίων. Then they understood that he did not tell them to beware of the yeast of bread, but of the teaching of the Pharisees and Sadducees.

[97] Guelich (1989) p. 423.

[98] Gundry (1993) pp. 413-4.

[99] Gundry p. 408.

it should not be used to explain Mark, the Matthean version of this pericope does present the disciples as understanding the logion of 8:15 literally, while the author presents it as being metaphorical, and even comments 'then they understood that he didn't tell them to beware of the yeast of loaves, but of the teaching of the Pharisees and Sadducees.'[100]

In examining the views of scholars, it seems that their prior interest, before assigning a function to ὅτι, is in deciding whether or not 8:15 is intrinsic or independent.[101] If it is the former, then 8:16 has to be linked to it, and one way of doing this is by inferring a causal understanding of this particle, which relates the clause to the disciples' reasoning about 'the yeast of the Pharisees and Herod'. Their discussion would be: *He is saying this because we didn't bring any bread.* If the disciples are seen to be inferencing in this way then it seems that either they see the metaphorical meaning of the logion and choose to ignore it because of the more pressing need to locate a bread source, or they read it as literal: 'yeast of the Pharisees' being bread which they have (to sell?).[102]

Another possible approach from the perspective of verse 8:15 being intrinsic is to read ὅτι as 'why', an indirect interrogative, reflecting a dispute on the part of the disciples as to whose fault it was that bread was lacking, this arising through interpreting 8:15 as a rebuke for this lack (so Lane). This involves considerable inferencing, and an adversarial view of the semantics of διαλογίζομαι, but is based on the belief that the logion is integral. καὶ the usual Marcan connector, which precedes διελογίζοντο πρὸς ἀλλήλους is thus assumed to link the logion. The phrase may then be read as the disciples' debate contingent on the implied rebuke by Jesus. In *RT* terms Mark presents the disciples as taking the most relevant inference from Jesus' comment. It is, however, difficult to see how 8:15 could be seen as a rebuke: a warning certainly, perhaps even a very strong warning (Ὁρᾶτε, βλέπετε), but the element of rebuke is not apparent in the statement. The verb which introduces the logion - διαστέλλομαι - in both Classical and NT Greek has a meaning of 'warn' or 'command', but 'rebuke' is not a part of its semantic field.

The reader in turn is seeking the most relevant understanding of the disciples' response. The Matthean account, as stated earlier, pinpoints the failure of communication on the part of the disciples as being because they interpreted the statement/warning of Jesus literally rather than metaphorically.

---

[100] Matthew 16:12.

[101] The decision here regarding the status of the logion is not relevant to my argument and so is not developed. I am presenting the inferences which a reader draws in order to come to her understanding of the function of ὅτι. I show that these begin with inferences about the placing of the logion in this context by Mark.

[102] This interpretation relies heavily on rabbinic evidence for the claim that 'yeast' could be shorthand for 'leavened bread'. Strack-Billerbeck quoted in Lane (1974) p. 281 footnote 39.

RT analyses metaphorical language as part of echoic use. 'Leaven' is taken by scholars as a 'common metaphor for evil'. As I have noted above, the passage in Matthew (16:12) specifies this evil as 'teaching', while Luke using the same phrase: 'the leaven of the Pharisees' identifies it as hypocrisy (12:1). It is conventionally assumed that the link between leaven and evil which makes the metaphor work, is the prohibition of leaven in the days around the celebration of Passover. The use of a metaphor rather than a literal expression gives rise to richer implicatures: the reader is invited to draw a wider range of inferences from the picture provided. Of course there is the danger of the metaphor failing in its purpose, as seems to be the case in the Matthean account. I have, however, found no scholar who treats the logion as a literal caveat, in spite of Lane's observations regarding the wider meaning of 'yeast' as 'leavened bread'.

If, on the other hand, the logion of 8:15 is taken as a saying independent of the Marcan context and unrelated to it, then the discussion in 8:16 relates only to the failure to buy bread, while Mark's presentation of Jesus as exasperated with his disciples relates to their focus on the lack of bread and their inability to consider the earlier feeding miracles.

I have included the differing scholarly views here to show that in every case there are assumptions and inferences which are not always clearly identified but which are used in order to give a relevant reading of these verses. It also supports my contention that the ascription of a causal meaning to ὅτι is derived from these inferences and assumptions and not from the dictionary meaning of this particle.

7.4 Summary

In this chapter I have presented the particle ὅτι as giving procedural instructions to the reader to expect a representation of a state of affairs from the perspective of the writer or subject. This is parallel to the analysis of ἵνα in this book giving instructions to the reader to expect a representation of a *potential* or *desirable* state of affairs from the perspective of the writer or subject. As with ἵνα, there is no logical semantic content of 'because' attached to this particle. It may introduce a representation which gives a cause for a previous thought or action, but this is *inferred* from the context and is not part of the 'meaning' of the particle.

It may be argued that there are three different meanings of ὅτι, that is: the issue is one of polysemy, or homonyms. Although it may seem a reasonable hypothesis, I would argue that it is purely descriptive and does not reflect the way in which a hearer or reader disambiguates such 'meaning'. There cannot be three intrinsic dictionary entries for this particle, only three contexts in which it operates. It is by inferencing from the context that a reader is able to select those instructions which the speaker or writer is leading her to expect. Further, the use of this particle to introduce direct speech does not involve 'meaning' at all, but introduces an utterance usually in conjunction with a speech verb.

Investigating ὅτι

This analysis fits the three differing contexts in which the particle has been used from classical through to the koine period, and also gives a plausible explanation for its development as a 'causal' marker. The fact that there are many ὅτι clauses which are ambiguous as to whether or not they mark direct or indirect speech, indirect thought or cause gives supporting evidence for my claim that this particle functions as a procedural use marker which alerts the reader to expect a representation, rather than having an intrinsic lexical meaning of 'that' or 'because'. The verb in the main clause gives signals to the reader also: saying verbs, especially λέγω lead the reader to expect a statement, whether in direct or indirect speech, epistemic verbs such as ἐπιγινώσκω, οἶδα, δοκέω invite the reader to expect the outlining of the subject's thought, while an absence of either of these categories invites an assumption of a cause being proposed. Consider also those instances in which a verb such as εὐχαριστέω may invite the reader to infer either the content of the thanksgiving or the reason for it. Both interpretations are a possibility with this verb.[103] The analysis proposed here encompasses all of these.

---

[103] This seems to be parallel to the ἵνα clauses which follow verbs such as προσεύχομαι, παρακαλέω. These may be interpreted grammatically either as the content of the prayer or exhortation or an indirect command: what the subject would like to see happening or what he thought *should* happen. This is dealt with in Chapter 4.

CHAPTER 8

Diachronic use of ἵνα

8.1 Introduction

In this section I trace briefly the development in the use of ἵνα from its function in Classical Greek to its use in the Koine, with a brief summary of the particle νά in Modern Greek. A wider diachronic account of the development of the Greek language during this period may of course be found in some of the major grammars, such as Robertson, Jannaris and Thumb, while Horrocks gives a broad-ranging account of the historical and linguistic environment in which such developments took place. Caragounis from the perspective of a speaker of Modern Greek as well as a scholar familiar with classical, biblical and medieval texts insists on the integrity of the Greek language and claims that it should be approached 'holistically and historically, as a living organism evolving and developing.'[1]

The purpose of this chapter is to set the *RT* account of the use of ἵνα in Koine Greek within a broader diachronic perspective. Such a perspective supports but does not prove the hypothesis postulated in the earlier chapters, namely that the change in the use of the particles ἵνα and ὅτι was in process for several centuries before the writings of the NT came into being. Further, this chapter gives evidence for the argument that the increase in the use of ἵνα with a subjunctive verb was not derived from Semitic or Latin influence, but may be detected in the writings of literary authors such as Polybius and Dionysius of Halicarnassus. In addition, from this period onwards there were phonetic changes in the quality of the vowels which in turn influenced the morphology of the verb. As I stated in the introduction, I cannot agree that the change in the structures used in Koine Greek marks that language as inferior to its classical antecedent. Living languages are always changing, not only in terms of lexicon and phonology, but also in their syntactic structure. In this chapter I argue that the features which may be observed in NT Greek were incipient even at the end of the classical period.

As this chapter gives merely a brief synopsis of the development of the Greek language over a few hundred years of its use, I limit my focus to three periods:[2] Classical (500-300 BCE), Hellenistic (300-150 BCE) and Graeco-

---

[1] Caragounis (2004) p. 4. He also insists on its unique development in contrast to the other Indo European languages which broke into distinct families pp. 2, 17.

[2] These categories are taken from Jannaris (1897) p. 2, and refer to the Attic dialect from which, together with Ionic, Koine developed.

Roman (150 BCE – 300 CE), with only sparse comments on the current use of να in Modern Greek.

8.2 Classical Greek 500-300 BCE

This was the golden age of Greek language and culture, with the authors of this period being widely known, at least in translation, and in NT studies it seems that their language and its register is the criterion against which all later Greek is judged.[3] Jannaris points out that the works of the well known authors of this period did not reflect the language actually spoken at that time, not even by the literary elite. It is important to recognise this as later periods of the language show different registers, while this period shows extant texts of a literary nature only:

> ...the classical writings of the Greeks...are of necessity artistic and artificial productions different from the common and popular, as well as from the plebeian or rustic speech[4]

This point is made much more forcefully by Caragounis[5] who insists not only on the parallel development of the spoken alongside the literary language from early times until the present day, but also on the interaction between the two registers.

Grammars of Classical Greek such as Goodwin and Smyth[6] give a detailed account of the particles ἵνα, ὅπως and ὡς and their use in this period. Here I give a brief synopsis only, with a view to seeing a pattern in the use of these particles together with the verbal mood which they introduce.

There were three particles used to introduce final or purpose clauses in this period, namely ἵνα, ὅπως and ὡς.[7] Of these, ἵνα was 'the only purely final particle',[8] since the other particles could be used to introduce 'object clauses'. μή with a following subjunctive verb was also used after verbs of fearing, and this continued to NT times, but will not be developed in this book. In purely final clauses, the verb could be either in the subjunctive (after primary tenses: present, perfect or future) or optative (after secondary tenses: imperfect, aorist and pluperfect). There could be interesting exceptions to this. If the purpose was treated as the actual speech of the subject then the clause encapsulating this

---

[3] Turner (1963) p. 2 'I have tried to expose consistently the almost complete absence of classical standards in nearly every author'.
[4] Jannaris (1897) p. 5.
[5] Caragounis (2004) p. 65 'the literary form of Greek constantly informed the language of the people.'
[6] Goodwin (1965 reprint) pp.105-116; Smyth (1920) pp. 493-499.
[7] This particle was not used in a final sense outside of this period, although Josephus does use it in this way, and so it will not be considered in this book.
[8] Goodwin p.109.

would be in the mood which reflected the subject's actual words.⁹ This accounts for the frequent use of the subjunctive after past tenses even in the classical period. This fact is noted because the logic behind it reflects the role of representation in reporting intention.

A further interesting point is that the indicative, rather than the subjunctive mood would be used in purpose clauses which were not realised, because the action on which the purpose depended did not take place. Consider the following example from Dinarchus the orator given by Goodwin:¹⁰

Example (1) ἐχρῆν αὐτοὺς τὴν προτέραν ζήτησιν ζητεῖν, ἵνα ἀπηλλάγμεθα τούτου τοῦ δημαγωγοῦ...
They ought to have made the previous investigation, in order that we might have been already freed from this demagogue (but we have not been freed).

This seems to resemble a conditional clause: 'if they had...we would have...' but the protasis did not take place and therefore the apodosis is not affected. The ἵνα clause then resembles a desirable state of affairs which is no longer possible.

The particle ὅπως was regularly used for 'object clauses' which is Goodwin's term for clauses which follow verbs of striving, asking, commanding. Although this particle could be followed by subjunctive or optative, the most regular mood was indicative, with a future tense: 'as the original form of the thought.'¹¹ In *RT* terms this would indicate a representation. In other words, the subordinate clause represents the thought of the subject: what he thinks should happen. If this can be seen as part of the cognitive process even in classical times, then it is not astonishing that the language developed further along such lines by using procedural markers such as ὅπως or ἵνα to introduce representation in a more general way. The change from indicative to subjunctive mood would further emphasise the desired as against the actual state of affairs in view.

Goodwin also notes ὅπως as 'the most common final particle' in Thucydides and Xenophon (see chart below), in spite of what has already been said about the exclusive use of ἵνα in a final context. It is also used more as a final particle than anything else in these authors. In Herodotus, Plato and other writers, however, ἵνα comes to be used to introduce final clauses, while ὅπως is restricted to object clauses. Aristotle is said¹² to have used ἵνα almost exclusively for purpose clauses, with only a few examples of ὅπως.

I have inserted below a truncated version of a table which Goodwin presents

---

⁹ Goodwin p. 114.
¹⁰ Goodwin pp. 120-1, Dinarchus 1.10.
¹¹ Goodwin p. 122.
¹² Jannaris (1897) p .417, footnote.

to give the statistics of the use of final particles in pure final clauses.[13] This of course does not deal with the use of ὅπως in object clauses, but it does make clear the decline of the latter as a final particle, even in classical times. I have totalled the figures given by Goodwin so that the great increase in the use of ἵνα may be seen within the classical period.

Table 2

	ἵνα	ὡς	ὡς ἄν	ὅπως	ὅπως ἄν
Sophocles	14	52	5	31	2
Euripides	71	182	27	19	7
Aristophanes	183	3	14	18	24
Herodotus	107	16	11	13	5
Thucydides	52	1	1	114	0
Xenophon	213	83	8	221	14
Plato	368	1	0	23	25
Ten Orators	579	3 or 4	0	42	12
Demosthenes	253	0	0	14	4
Total	**1830**	**342**	**66**	**495**	**93**

Statistics for the use of final particles in pure final clauses by classical authors

From the chart it will be observed that the orators and Plato account for much of the change from the earlier preference for ὅπως. When the Aristotelian usage, as mentioned above, is added to this it would seem reasonable to draw the conclusion that by the end of the fourth century BCE the pattern of particle use had already changed in the direction which was to become more common in Hellenistic Greek. This is a very important fact to keep in mind in considering the ubiquitous use of ἵνα in the Koine.

The infinitive also could be used to introduce purpose clauses, but in general this was limited to verbs of choosing, appointing, giving, taking or sending. In these instances the 'subject' of the infinitive would appear in the accusative case, but would also be the object of the main verb: ἔπεμψεν αὐτοὺς προσφερεῖν ... he sent them to bring.[14] Later Greek, by contrast, uses the infinitive much less frequently while the NT regularly uses a ἵνα construction after such verbs, e.g. ἀποστέλλω.[15]

---

[13] Goodwin states that the table he presents is based on statistics given by Dr Philip Weber, p. 398.
[14] Also Plato Ap 28E οἱ ἄρχοντες οὓς ὑμεῖς εἵλεσθε ἄρχειν μου 'the rulers whom you chose to rule me.'
[15] John 1:19; 3:17; Luke. 16:24; 20:10, 20.

8.3 Hellenistic Greek 300-150 BCE[16]

The historical background of this period is the conquest of Alexander the Great, which spread both the language of Greece and those who spoke it to Egypt, Asia Minor and beyond. Greek became the *lingua franca* of the ancient world of that time, but already its form was changing. It was no longer pure literary Attic, but the speech of the educated classes. Jannaris describes this as 'panhellenic Greek'.[17] Horrocks claims that this 'Great Attic' or 'Koine' was 'the only written standard, and the spoken language of the Greco-Macedonian aristocracy.'[18] Of course, there were lower registers, but it is important to keep in mind the fact that Koine was not predominantly the language of uneducated people, but in fact described a wide spectrum of use from official documents to everyday affairs. It was the *lingua franca* of that period; by this term I intend to describe the medium in which business and state affairs were carried on. The term 'Koine' itself is generally used to describe the language of a much wider period than the Hellenistic era alone, but I have separated this period so that the changes in language use may be seen before the emergence of other factors which are often viewed as the crucial ingredients for the emergence of the features which are prominent in the NT and the papyri.

By the end of the fourth century BCE, Greek was the official language of bureaucracy in Macedonia, in the conquered territories from Egypt to Syria and Persia. In denying the status of Koine as 'creole', Horrocks points out that this development of 'Great Attic' was

> essentially the established language of commerce, diplomacy, and officialdom, a variety distinct even from the Attic vernacular of the Athenian lower classes let alone the kind of pidgin put in the mouth of a Scythian archer by Aristophanes in the *Thesmophoriazousae*.[19]

With this perspective in mind, I have selected some inscriptions from the official pronouncements of that period which display features of both the classical language and the changing structures of Hellenistic Greek. We can see from the Royal Letters[20] of the Seleucid and Attalid kingdoms that although ἵνα (x13) in this selection is less popular than ὅπως (x26) as a particle introducing a purpose clause, a feature seen in many of the fifth century writers, the former particle, even in the third century, was taking over some of the functions of the

---

[16] Horrocks (1997) p. 33 marks this period from 323 to 31 BCE, i.e. from the death of Alexander to the battle of Actium. Jannaris (1897) pp.3-11 subdivides into Hellenistic and Graeco-Roman.
[17] Jannaris (1897) pp. 6, 8.
[18] Horrocks p. 37. He describes Koine as developing from Great Attic, with the incorporation of forms from other dialects, notably Ionic.
[19] Horrocks p. 34.
[20] Welles (1934).

latter in introducing object clauses, particularly after verbs of requesting or commanding. The subjunctive mood was used in such clauses, whereas in the earlier period ὅπως with a future indicative would have been the usual formation. Consider the following example[21] of a ἵνα clause which follows the verb συνεπιμελήθητε 'join in taking care':

Example (2) συνεπιμελήθητε οὖν ἵνα γένηται κατὰ τρόπον.
Join (him) then in taking care that it happens in the customary way.

Welles describes such use as 'a Koine development, an encroachment on the field of ὅπως'[22] but notes that half of the uses of ἵνα in his corpus refer to such constructions after verbs of 'taking care' or 'being eager to do'. The locations of these inscriptions are outwith Palestinian influence, and show that the language, in a register which could not be regarded as illiterate, was changing in the way that these particles were used. ὅπως also in half of Welles' examples follows verbs which either mean 'take care of' or indicate a request or command, but unlike Attic usage, they are followed by a subjunctive verb. I include one other example only, a letter of Mithridates the Great to Leonippus 88/7 BCE and again from Asia Minor:[23]

Example (3) κήρυγμα ποιῆσαι ὅπως ἐάν τις ζῶντας ἀγάγῃ Χαιρήμονα ἢ Πυθόδωρον ἢ Πυθίωνα, λάβῃ τάλαντα τεσσαράκοντα, ἐὰν δέ τις τὴν κεφαλήν τινος αὐτῶν ἐνένκῃ, λάβῃ τάλαντα εἴκοσι.
Make a proclamation that if anyone brings Chairemon or Pythodorus or Pythion living, he will/should receive 40 talents, but if anyone brings the head of any of these, he will/should receive 20 talents.

Again the provenance of this inscription is the wider Greek speaking world, with no acknowledged Semitic influence. The particle ὅπως also was extending its use and changing the mood which was used with it. In this example it was giving the reader procedural instructions to interpret the clause as a representation of the potential proclamation. Note that this inscription does not give the proclamation, but only an indication of what it should announce. There are several different representations here: Mithridates gives a representation of his thought of what Leonippus *should* say in his proclamation, namely what the desirable state of affairs might be, from the perspective of the King.

Polybius in his *Histories* shows a similar extension of the use of ἵνα which has taken over from ὅπως not only as the only final particle in his writings, but to introduce other clauses also. He does not use ὅπως at all to introduce final or

---

[21] Letter of Seleucus I to Miletus, 288/7 BCE, inscribed on a marble stele and discussed by Welles (1934) note 12 pp. 33-40.
[22] Welles p. lxxxii.
[23] Inscription noted in Welles p. 295.

object clauses. Examples of these extended uses of ἵνα have been noted in other chapters,[24] but it is clear from a survey of the first five books of his *Histories* that of the 63 instances of ἵνα found there, ten (and perhaps eleven) of these do not introduce purpose clauses, but what Goodwin would have called 'object clauses', that is clauses which follow verbs such as φροντίζω, παρακαλέω, προσέχω, διαπέμπω, συντάσσω as well as nouns such as ὑπόμνησις, ἐπαγγελία, πρόνοια. This is a sizeable proportion of non telic clauses: at least 16% if not 17.4%. There is no question of Semitic influence in the writings of Polybius, and so it must be concluded that the Greek language, as used by native speakers, was changing both by limiting the particles used to introduce purpose and object clauses, and also extending the sphere of the dominant particle: ἵνα. It should also be noted that the non-purpose clauses which this particle introduces have a verb in the subjunctive mood, a further move from the use of ὅπως with the indicative for such clauses in Classical Greek.

The book of 2 Maccabees, possibly dating from the first century BCE, and generally accepted to be an original (Alexandrian) Greek work,[25] has only 10 examples of ἵνα clauses in 554 verses. Of these 10 examples, however, 4 are not purpose clauses: 2 Maccabees 1:9 is an independent clause; 2 Maccabees 1:18, 2:8 and 6:24 are object clauses. The paucity of examples of ἵνα reflects the situation in the century or two before the writings of the NT, but the clauses which this particle introduces are, like the Royal Letters, by no means limited to purpose. ὅπως occurs only 4 times in this book, one of which follows οἶδα and introduces a clause of manner ('how') with an indicative verb.

When this evidence is put together it may be seen that four trends become apparent:

- ἵνα is being used more frequently than other particles; even in the fifth century some writers such as Aristophanes and Herodotus used ἵνα more than other particles, while in the fourth century its use by Demosthenes and Plato, together with the Ten Orators was marked;
- ἵνα is introducing a wider range of clauses, especially after verbs of commanding, paying attention to, but also explicating nouns indicating a representation: remembrance, promise, forethought;
- ὅπως is often followed by a verb in subjunctive mood when it introduces object clauses, that is clauses which encapsulate the desirable state of affairs which the subject wants to see realised. In Classical Greek, after verbs of 'striving', it would have been followed most commonly by the future

---

[24] 3.1.1, and 4.2.2.2.

[25] Swete (1902) p. 312 'In 2-4 Maccabees the reader finds himself at length face to face with the full richness of the Alexandrian literary style, as it was written by cultured Hellenists of the second and first centuries B.C.'

indicative, but less frequently by the subjunctive;[26]
- ὅπως from third century BCE is losing ground to ἵνα, although not in all authors.

From these trends it becomes clear that a fixed lexical meaning of 'in order that' is no longer appropriate for either of these particles, even before the period of Koine Greek. They are introducing clauses which represent a desirable state of affairs from the perspective of the subject, or the speaker. Their function is to signal such a representation rather than giving the logical relationship between the main clause and a subordinate one.

8.4 Graeco-Roman (150 BCE to 300 CE)

This is the period in which Koine flourished and became the *lingua franca*, in the wider sense of that term: the common language of interaction between different people groups, rather than merely an official language of the emerging Roman Empire, although the extent of this development was more apparent in the east than the west. We have more papyri evidence from unofficial sources for this period, and so the different registers become clearer. Some writers seem to read the 'non-literary' description of papyri finds as 'illiterate' but that is grossly unfair. It is true that some of the letters are far from the standards of educated Koine, but the many official documents show a much more conservative use of the language. In the sphere of literature the works of writers such as Dionysius of Halicarnassus[27] and Philo show high standards of language use, but these are not the same standards as Classical Greek. After 400 years, there is no reason why they should be.

8.4.1 Separation of Registers

At this point we should consider the wide range of level of language from Dionysius to Epictetus in pagan Greek and Luke-Acts to 2 Peter in biblical Greek. The papyri also show a wide difference in register, but the fragmentary nature of many of these documents makes it difficult to draw firm conclusions. They will be adduced to support conclusions reached from more substantial texts. The writings of Josephus also come within this period, but although I will refer to these, I have not relied on evidence from his writings because he admits that he wrote first in Aramaic and then translated,[28] and secondly, there are

---

[26] Goodwin (1965 reprint). He also points out that the future optative may be used, 'corresponding to the future indicative after primary tenses', pp. 122-3.

[27] This author is often considered to be Atticistic, but although he uses features of Attic style which were not in common use by this period, his work differs substantially from the Atticisers of a later period. Mealand (1996) considers him to be 'conservative' rather than imposing Attic norms on his material. Caragounis (2004) commends him as 'aspiring to write good Greek' p. 43.

[28] *Jewish War* Book I.3.

features of his prose which seem to me to be quite out of sympathy with the period in which he was writing.[29] Further, although his sympathies were with the Romans, his Jewish background must have been heavily influenced by the Septuagint, making him less valuable as a non-biblical writer.[30]

8.4.1.1 HIGH LEVEL OF LANGUAGE: DIONYSIUS AND LUKE-ACTS

As has been noted earlier, Dionysius was a teacher of rhetoric and one who commented on the style of Attic writers such as Thucydides and Demosthenes. His level of language is high, although he is considered to be longwinded and rather pedantic. He could certainly not be accused of writing poor Greek,[31] and so in examining his work we should be able to make a fair assessment of the way in which a writer at the upper end of the spectrum of language use used ἵνα and ὅπως. I selected for study the first four books of his *Antiquities*. Of the 65 examples of ἵνα which I found in these four books, 55 are purpose clauses while the remaining 10 introduce clauses of indirect command, and noun clauses after verbs such as προοούμενον and φυλάττειν. Although this particle is not particularly frequent, its use in non-final clauses is significant: 15.3%. His use of the particle ὅπως is also significant: it is only used with ἄν to introduce an adverbial clause of manner, i.e. 'how'.[32] I include only two examples here to substantiate the points made:

Example (4) τῶν τε ἀδικημάτων τὰ μέγιστα μὲν αὐτὸν δικάζειν, τὰ δ' ἐλάττονα τοῖς βουλευταῖς ἐπιτρέπειν προνοούμενον ἵνα μηδὲν γίγνηται περὶ τὰς δίκας πλημμελές...
...he was also to judge in person the greatest crimes, leaving the lesser to the senators, but seeing to it that no error was made in their decisions...(*LCL*: Cary)[33]

The interest of this ἵνα clause comes not only in its following προνοούμενον, but also in its position after a long string of infinitival constructions delineating the responsibilities of the king as against those of the senate. If it is posited that this would be a reason for changing the options available, then another explanation has to be found for the continued list of infinitival constructions *after* the ἵνα clause. I suggest that this particle introduces a representation in the clause which follows 'seeing to it that', giving the desirable state of affairs

---

[29] For example he regularly uses the particle ὡς to introduce final clauses and also favours the optative after secondary tenses.
[30] For the same reason, the works of Philo have not been seriously considered.
[31] Cary (Loeb) p. xxxvii claims that he 'rejoiced in the recent triumph of Atticism over Asianism and did his best to strengthen that victory.' Caragounis (2004) p. 404 'Dionysius is the author who ... had acquired to a high degree a sharp sense of penetrating insight into the beauty of language'.
[32] Note also its use in Luke 24:20, but without ἄν.
[33] Book II.14.1.

which was hoped for: *(he should see to it) that no error should be made in their judicial decisions.*

The paragraph in which this example occurs discusses the responsibilities of the king, but in the middle this clause makes salient the need for the king's potential intervention in decisions which were to be handled by the senators. The clause highlights the crucial point about delegation and its limits. In earlier Greek such clauses would have been introduced by ὅπως with a clause in the (future) indicative. As noted above, not only does this author avoid this latter particle in final clauses, but he uses ἵνα for those non final clauses which ὅπως customarily introduced in Attic Greek.

A further example[34] is given to show the same choice following a requesting noun:

> Example (5) κραυγή τε παρὰ πάντων ἐξαίσιος ἐγένετο καὶ δεήσεις μεμιγμέναι δάκρυσιν, ἵνα μένῃ τε καὶ διακατέχῃ τὰ πράγματα μηδένα δεδοικώς.
> There was a tremendous shout from everyone, and pleas with tears that fearing no one, he should stay and take control of affairs. (MGS)

This is a clear example of indirect command[35] following a noun indicating a strong desire: *he should stay and take control of affairs.*

Again, this is a departure from the Attic norm, but a feature which we noted in Hellenistic Greek. Native speakers, therefore, even a purist such as Dionysius, seem to have been comfortable about using ἵνα with the subjunctive, rather than ὅπως with the indicative in this way. This use of ἵνα to designate an indirect command is particularly marked in the gospel of Luke, as will be noted below.

Although it is the longest of the four gospels, Luke has only 46 examples of ἵνα. Of these, 20 introduce purpose clauses, 14 indirect commands,[36] 4 noun clauses, 3 result clauses, 2 independent clauses, while I have analysed the remaining 3 as 'prophetic'.[37] I suspect that because 'purpose' is seen as underlying indirect commands there have been no strong feelings about the fact that only 43% of ἵνα clauses in this book introduce final clauses. This author uses infinitival constructions frequently, particularly articular infinitives with accompanying prepositions. The infrequency of his use of this particle, especially when compared with that of the other three gospels (particularly

---

[34] Book IV.12.1.

[35] This could of course be analysed as a noun clause, delineating the content of 'pleas'. As in Chapter 4, clauses which follow verbs or nouns indicating request, desire or command have been treated as indirect command since this is the way in which they are dealt with in the traditional grammars.

[36] See Chapters 3, 4 and 5 for examples.

[37] See Chapter 5 for a delineation of these uses.

Mark and John), places him closer to the writers of literary Koine,[38] but, like them, he is able to use the particle to introduce non final clauses.

It may be significant to note that the high proportion of material presented as direct speech in all of the gospels means that many of the examples of this particle occur not in narrative but in dialogue, or parabolic material.[39] I suspect that the register for such material is likely to be lower than that of straight narrative, unlike the speeches crafted by Dionysius which are of a high and lofty tone. It is certainly true that the instances of the articular infinitive with prepositions occur predominantly in narrative in the Gospel of Luke. As I have argued in Chapters 4 and 5, a clause with a finite verb, introduced by a particle which leads the reader to expect a representation, is more easily processed than an infinitive in which the subject, and perhaps also the object, is in the accusative case.

8.4.1.2 MORE COLLOQUIAL: EPICTETUS AND PAUL

In contrast to the writings of Dionysius, the *Discourses* of Epictetus are much less formal, displaying a lower register than the former, but still displaying native speaker competence in the use of language. The use of ἵνα is much higher than in Dionysius and the clause types which it introduces are also much wider. It appears to me that the speech of this philosopher is much closer to the writings of the New Testament in general and of Paul in particular than to Dionysius or Polybius.[40] All the varied clause uses introduced by ἵνα in the New Testament are found in Epictetus also: independent clauses, noun clauses, as well as clauses which follow verbs indicating striving. Oldfather[41] describes this philosopher as 'speaking the common language of ethical exhortation in which the evangelists and apostles wrote.' Further, the material in his *Discourses* is presented by Arrian as direct speech, or rather dialogue with his students, both the questions and answers being given by the philosopher. I include here only two examples[42] for which parallels may be found in some sections of the Pauline letters.

> Example (6) ἐπεὶ τί ἐκδέχῃ; ἵνα τις ἀποστῇ αὐτοῦ καὶ τοῦ ἰδίου συμφέροντος;
> For what do you expect? That a man should neglect himself and his own interest?
> (*LCL*: Oldfather)

In this example the ἵνα clause answers the question 'what', not 'why' as a

---

[38] For a comparison of Luke with Dionysius of Halicarnassus, particularly in certain verb forms see Mealand (1996).

[39] From the 26 non final ἵνα clauses in Luke, 19 are presented as in direct speech, including parables & teaching.

[40] The only support I have found for this is in Sharp (1914).

[41] Oldfather, *LCL* (1967 reprint) p. xxvi.

[42] *LCL Discourses* Book I.19.15; I.29.24.

purpose clause would. Note the translation 'should' which indicates the translator's recognition of what the subject expects, or thinks ought, to happen. The ἵνα clause gives the content of the subject's expectation, or more accurately the expectation which Epictetus is stating as representing what the subject might be expecting. The subjunctive mood alone would not have alerted the hearer to expect this representation. An independent subjunctive clause could indicate a wish or a deliberative question, but the particle ἵνα guides the hearer to interpret the clause as a representation.

A similar construction to Example (6) may be seen in the text of 1 Corinthians 9:18.[43] There are many other Pauline examples of such ἵνα clauses which do not follow a question, but which do indicate what the subject *should* do. Consider example (7),[44] which has a ἵνα clause only with no verb:

Example (7) Ἰάκωβος καὶ Κηφᾶς καὶ Ἰωάννης, ...δεξιὰς ἔδωκαν ἐμοὶ καὶ Βαρναβᾷ κοινωνίας, ἵνα ἡμεῖς εἰς τὰ ἔθνη, αὐτοὶ δὲ εἰς τὴν περιτομήν·
James Cephas and James...gave the right hand of fellowship to me and to Barnabas that we should go to[45] the Gentiles and they to the circumcision.

The use of 'should' indicates the desired state of affairs from the perspective of the subject. In other words this clause represents not only the thought but also the utterance of the subject. It may also represent what they consider to be desirable from the point of view of others. Frequently a deontic statement reflects not only the thought of a speaker or subject, but what he believes is a desirable state of affairs from the perspective of others. In examples such as (6) above, the speaker may be distancing himself from such a perspective, but is presenting it as what someone might reply to his question. I have included one further example from Epictetus because it demonstrates an unusual use of ἵνα which is nevertheless used by a native Greek speaker.

Example (8) ἔμαθον, ἵνα πᾶν τὸ γινόμενον ἴδω ὅτι, ἂν ἀπροαίρετον ᾖ, οὐδέν ἐστι πρὸς ἐμέ.
I have learned that I should see that, everything happening, being of no set purpose, is nothing to me. (MGS)
I have learned to see ... (*LCL*: Oldfather)

---

[43] This verse is dealt with at 3.3.2, Example (8a,b).
[44] Galatians 2:9, also Galatians 2:10 which does have a verb in the ἵνα clause. These verses are dealt with at 5.2.2, Example (2).
[45] Dunn (1993) suggests that rather than assume the elision of a verb such as 'go', the preposition εἰς might indicate an action 'on behalf of' another, this being an attested use of that preposition from classical times onward p. 111. Whichever analysis is accepted does not alter the use of ἵνα in this context.

This example[46] is interesting because it has ἵνα following a verb which is normally epistemic, in contrast to the ὅτι clause which follows another such verb, ὁράω. Oldfather's translation treats the former as the equivalent to an infinitive: 'to see', but the use of a ἵνα clause represents what the speaker learns that he *should* do. He is not saying that he actually *is* doing this. The use of ἵνα alerts the hearer to expect a representation, which an infinitive alone does not. Of course any complement of a verb such as 'learn' is representing the thought of the subject, but this is latent in an infinitival construction, and usually represents an actual state of affairs, that is what the subject in fact knows. By using ἵνα with a subjunctive verb, the speaker is alerting the hearer to process this information as a representation of his thought: *I should see everything which happen...as nothing to me.*

Coming from a classical background, Oldfather has translated the ἵνα clause as if it were the equivalent of an infinitive, but I am challenging that understanding. Recall that the *Discourses* of Epictetus were recorded in Koine by Arrian, who himself wrote in the Attic style at the beginning of the second century CE. The style of these dialogues is less formal than the *Antiquities* of Dionysius, or the Gospel of Luke. This may account for the wider use of ἵνα and its much greater frequency. Spoken language is almost always of a lower register than its written form.

In conclusion, it is imperative that the question of register or level of language is taken into account when examining the frequency in the use of this conjunction. Although literary Koine displays a widely varying use of ἵνα clauses, the frequency of these which is seen in the NT, and in particular the Gospel of John, is unusual, although much closer to the works of Epictetus.

8.4.2 Trends in Hellenistic Becoming More Marked

This section has summarised those features of changing language use which had already been seen in earlier Greek:

- ὅπως was disappearing fast as a particle introducing both final and non final clauses. Dionysius does not use it for such at all, nor does Epictetus, but the NT as a whole has 53 occurrences. In the NT it is used for representations of purpose, and OT quotations as well as deontic clauses mainly in Matthew, Luke and Acts;
- ἵνα with a subjunctive verb was taking over the functions of non final ὅπως clauses, which previously would have been accompanied by a verb in the future indicative;
- ἵνα was appearing in new environments such as independent clauses. This may have been a feature of the spoken language in earlier stages;
- The use of ἵνα increased greatly at the expense of the infinitive. The latter remained in the NT where the subjects of both clauses were the same, but

---

[46] *Discourses* 1.29.24. This example is dealt with in more detail at 5.5.2, Example (20).

Diachronic Use

even this environment gave way to ἵνα clauses in the second century CE and onwards.

8.4.3 General Linguistic Changes

Although regional variation in the Greek language has been attested since the earliest written forms of the language, the spread of Greek to regions of the known world in which it was at least a second language seems to have had two rather diverse effects:

(i) the emergence of Great Attic as a language of communication across regional and national boundaries led to a certain standardisation of grammatical forms;
(ii) the variation between the higher register of official and literary works and the lower one of those who spoke and wrote Greek as a second or third language was very marked,[47] as evidenced in the wide range of forms, both in spelling and grammar, of the papyri finds from Egypt.

Even allowing for these effects, there were changes in the sounds and grammar of the language which have been well documented. Caragounis distances himself from some of Horrocks' conclusions,[48] but I have outlined the general understanding of these changes below.

8.4.3.1 PHONETIC CHANGES

Vowel changes in this period, evidenced by the spelling in the non-literary papyri, resulted in the removal of a phonetic distinction between the aorist subjunctive and the future indicative. Horrocks comments

> The damaging effects of sound change therefore led to a growing need to "mark" subjunctives as such, and ἵνα began to develop language internally as an "empty" mood marker, first in subordinate, but eventually also in main clauses that required a modal verb form (a process that was finally completed in the Middle Ages).[49]

This comment is apposite for the development of the language after this period, but the vowel change was certainly in process during the first century BCE and onwards. Although the script continued to reflect the earlier forms of the

---

[47] Caragounis (2004) describes some of the examples of such speech as 'sub-standard language.' p. 40.

[48] In particular he objects to Horrocks' considering the Septuagint to be representative of Koine Greek, p. 41, footnote 96, and p. 44 footnote 104. This is a very reasonable objection.

[49] Horrocks (1997) pp. 75-6.

subjunctive, the fact that the particle ἵνα came to be used as a marker of the subjunctive at a later stage, indicates that the clauses it introduced varied widely and that the mood with which it was associated became more important than the particle's function as a marker of purpose clauses. This development reflected what had been happening in the grammar of the language from the beginning of the Hellenistic period. This does not mean that in this period ἵνα was a mood marker, but that the beginnings of the development which resulted in the use of νά in *MGreek* may be seen from the first century BCE onwards.

8.4.3.2 SYNTACTIC CHANGES

A very important syntactic change which became stronger in the subsequent centuries was the prevalence of a clause to introduce the complement of the main verb rather than the infinitive which had been a major feature of classical style.[50] The end result was the disappearance of the infinitive from the modern language, but the process could be observed from the first century CE.

Instead of encapsulating indirect speech in an accusative and infinitive construction, writers began to use ὅτι with a verb in indicative mood to indicate the content of the utterance. Almost certainly this had been a feature of the spoken language from a much earlier stage. In many languages, in spoken as against written communication, humans prefer to give an interpretation of what was said rather than attempt to report it in indirect speech, while the further recasting of this into an accusative and infinitival construction is even more abstruse. For the Greeks there was the added benefit that the tense used in such clauses could reflect the actual words of the speaker, as well as the more obvious fact that person marking was perspicacious.[51]

As well as those clauses which report indirect speech, other subordinate clauses had begun to appear with far greater frequency. The propositions which these clauses delineated would have been expressed earlier by the infinitive or participles. This process steadily increased over the centuries, but in the period under consideration the frequency of use for the particle ἵνα as an introduction to both final and non final subordinate clauses was very marked. Grammars[52] describe this as a move from a syntactic construction to an analytical one, but there are strong logical and economical reasons for the process also.

All subjects could be nominative, and the verbs of all subordinate clauses with an expressed subject could be finite, the choice between indicative and subjunctive being determined by the 'type' of main verb involved.[53]

I disagree with the notion that it is the 'type' of main verb which determines

---

[50] This is described by earlier grammarians as a move towards analytical rather than syntactic constructions, as footnote 52.
[51] ὅτι is discussed in Chapter 7.
[52] Jannaris (1897) p. 569; *BDF* §388, 388(i), Mandilaras (1973) §732, §734; as well as Horrocks (1997) p. 46.
[53] Horrocks (1997) p. 46.

Diachronic Use 189

the choice of mood. The indicative marks the representation of a state of affairs in the real world, whether true or untrue, while the subjunctive marks a desirable state of affairs, namely what the speaker or subject wants to see realised or believes should be realised. To some extent this *is* determined by the main verb, in that epistemic verbs such as those indicating thought, speech, knowledge, are followed by ὅτι with the indicative. The subjunctive on the other hand may follow a very wide range of main verbs, indicating wishes, precaution, sending and others, as well as occurring independently.[54] As an aside, it should be noted that Smyth in discussing the uses of the optative mood for Classical Greek claims something similar when there is a possibility of indirect speech being implied:

> Indirect discourse is *implied* in the case of any subordinate clause, which, though not depending formally on a verb of *saying* or *thinking*, contains the *past thought of another person* and not a statement of the writer or speaker.[55]

This seems very close to an *RT* description of a representation interpretively used! It is certainly an acknowledgement of the role played by representation in human communication, a role which has not been adequately taken account of in theories of language.

In describing post Classical Greek (c.300 BCE-600 CE) Caragounis sees this as a period of simplification:

> ... the onerous Attic syntactical apparatus was replaced by simpler, lighter means of expression; complex, convoluted sentences, called periods, gave place to simpler, shorter, and less intricate constructions.[56]

He does not view this as a Semitic aberration, but as a natural process of language change. In fact he claims that the simpler forms were actually 'closer to the spoken form of Attic in earlier times', with Koine being the period of transition from the classical to the modern language.[57]

8.4.4 Language of the New Testament

The factors noted above have been considered in relation to Koine Greek outside the NT, in order to establish the point that it was not Semitic influence which was responsible for the changing use of ἵνα and ὅπως, but that there were phonetic and syntactic features which played a prominent role in such development. That is not to say that there was *no* Semitic influence in the language of the NT, but that it was not a factor in the development of these

---

[54] Examples of independent clauses are noted in Chapter 3.
[55] Smyth (1984) §2622.
[56] Caragounis (2004) p. 39.
[57] Caragounis p. 40.

particles. It has been pointed out[58] that such influence is more likely to be seen in the vocabulary used, rather than the syntactic forms.

There are three main points at issue here:

- the wider use of ἵνα to introduce both final and non final clauses is clearly demonstrable in Hellenistic Greek before the emergence of the NT documents;
- the frequency of use of ἵνα, especially in the Gospel of John, is paralleled in the *Discourses* of Epictetus and may be a concomitant feature of discourse rather than a peculiarity of NT writers;
- the Septuagint has only 600 occurrences of this particle in writings which are approximately four times as long as the NT, thus making the frequency 25% of the NT. If Semitic influence was a serious factor in the development of ἵνα, one would have expected to see a more frequent usage in the Septuagint.[59]

A more likely reason for the less than expected instances of this particle in that corpus would be the fact that although its use was changing, this was still in process. The first century CE and beyond is the period when we can see a much greater frequency of use, particularly in less formal writings.

In comparing the use made by the writers of the gospels, we can see that John's use of ἵνα is much greater than that of Luke (145:46), although the latter is longer. Matthew has 39 examples of ἵνα and 17 of ὅπως, while Mark has 64. John's use is certainly marked, but as pointed out earlier, the frequency of dialogue in his writing, in comparison with narrative, may account for this to some extent.[60] This may also be a factor in the comparatively high figures of ἵνα use for 1&2 Corinthians: 57 and 44. Among other uses, some of these examples of ἵνα exhibit instances of what might be considered to be echoic use in *RT* terms. Although not dialogue, they do involve reports of opinions held and reactions to these.

The following chart gives figures for the use of ἵνα and ὅπως in each book of the NT. Although the difference in genre may account for some of the differences, it is not the sole factor. Consider the paucity of examples in the book of Acts (15 in 28 chapters) in comparison with those in Luke (46 in 24 chapters). Although there is considerable dialogue and direct speech in the

---

[58] Winer (1877) p. 37.
[59] Translation of the Hebrew *ci* which introduces a much wider range of clauses is often given as an explanation for the use of ἵνα, but if this was a natural response then it is difficult to see why there should not be more occurrences of this particle in the translated books of the *LXX*. See Chapter 5 for comments on the work of Burney etc.
[60] This comment is based on the much higher number of ἵνα clauses in the *Discourses* of Epictetus, which is presented as dialogue between the philosopher and a putative respondent.

latter, the former has many lengthy speeches throughout.

Table 3

	ἵνα	ὅπως		ἵνα	ὅπως		ἵνα	ὅπως
Matthew	39	17	Ephesians	23	0	Hebrews	20	2
Mark	64	1	Philippians	12	0	James	4	1
Luke	46	7	Colossians	13	0	1 Peter	13	1
John	145	1	1 Thess.	7	0	2 Peter	2	0
Acts	15	14	2 Thess.	7	1	1 John	19	0
Romans	30	2	1 Tim.	15	0	2 John	5	0
1 Cor.	57	1	2 Tim.	5	0	3 John	2	0
2 Cor.	44	2	Titus	13	0	Jude	0	0
Galat.	17	1	Philem.	4	1	Revel.	42	0
Total	457	46		99	2		107	4

Occurrences of ἵνα and ὅπως in the Books of the New Testament.

8.4.5 Explanations Advanced for Use of ἵνα in New Testament

Many of the standard grammars describe the extended and more frequent use of ἵνα to introduce subordinate clauses other than final ones as the latter's 'taking over' of the functions of the infinitive. Zerwick[61] suggests this as an explanation for the particle after verbs expressing an object or verbs of commanding, praying etc. This of course does not account for those examples of ἵνα which introduce an independent clause. Zerwick fills out his analysis by positing Burney's solution of 'mistranslation' of the Aramaic *di*. He would not use Burney's term 'mistranslation', but sees the ambiguity and underdeterminacy (my term, not his) of the Aramaic particle as the reason for the expanded use of ἵνα. This explanation in no way accounts for the use of this particle by Epictetus and even Dionysius.

Blass, Debrunner[62] carefully delineate those verbs which may be followed by either the infinitive or ἵνα, only by ἵνα or only by the infinitive. They do not, however, discuss the reason for such patterns, merely pointing out that many ἵνα clauses 'take the place of' an epexegetic infinitive, 'especially in John.' They add that if the content of the clause refers to an actual fact John uses ὅτι rather than ἵνα. If certain verbs may be followed optionally by two constructions, why do writers or speakers select one or the other? I assume that many grammarians attribute such selection to authorial style, but in *RT* terms all such selection is based on the principle of relevance: What does a speaker/writer want his hearers/readers to infer from his choice? Grammarians acknowledge the change of use historically, but frequently ascribe this to the

---

[61] Zerwick (1963) pp. 140-7.
[62] *BDF* pp. 192ff.

loose use of the particle by non-native speakers of the language.

This argument simply is not supported by the facts. As we have seen from 8.2 and 8.3, particle use was changing even in the later classical period, while most of those writing in the age of Hellenistic Greek were first language speakers, although not ethnic Greeks. The basic assumption that the classical language, that is Attic of fourth and fifth century BCE, was a standard against which all later changes were to be judged is responsible for the assumption that the wider uses of ἵνα arose from speaker incompetence, or more strongly 'Semitic interference'.

The classical language has always been said to demonstrate inordinate flexibility, while if we look ahead to the later language, beyond the Byzantine writers, then we discover that ethnic Greeks still had great flexibility in their speech and writings. The infinitive disappeared from the language altogether, as did the participles,[63] while ἵνα became ubiquitous, finally becoming grammaticalised as a subjunctive mood marker.[64] It is scarcely credible that such language change could emerge from the incompetence of non-native or second language speakers. On the contrary, Greek writers such as Jannaris and Caragounis read Koine usage in the light of Modern Greek.[65]

I argue that the particle ἵνα was used to give procedural instructions to the reader or hearer, rather than to indicate the logical relation of the clause it introduces to the rest of the sentence. In Koine it no longer had a fixed lexical meaning; perhaps it never did have, but was always used to give procedural instructions regarding the following clause, which in earlier Greek was invariably telic.

8.5 Modern Greek[66]

This section will be limited to the consideration of both main and subordinate clauses introduced by the particle νά which is generally acknowledged to be derived from the ἵνα of earlier Greek. The examples show no morphological difference between subjunctive and indicative, but the grammars refer to the subjunctive mood:

> the term "subjunctive" is used in this book not as a morphological but as a semantic and syntactical category ... the indicative normally expresses a reality ... the

---

[63] '...participles with a subordinating function tend to be confined to "circumstantial" function' Horrocks (1997) p. 46.

[64] So Horrocks (1997) pp. 75-6; Mackridge (1985) pp. 274-5; Hopper and Traugott (1997) pp. 78ff.

[65] From a linguistic standpoint, I do not find this to be methodologically convincing, but it does indicate the viewpoint of native speakers and their perspective regarding the close relationship between the Koine and Modern Greek, a perspective which has frequently been ignored. Caragounis laments this throughout his book.

[66] This period is referred to in this chapter as *MGreek*.

subjunctive ... may make a statement about future time ... it may express a supposition, a wish, a command, a desire, or it may appear in some utterance which is not actually a *statement*.⁶⁷

Now these categories would also match the uses of the subjunctive in Classical, Hellenistic and Koine Greek, as well as the optative in the classical language. At these earlier stages of the language, however, the subjunctive did not require a 'mood marker', and could occur in an independent clause. In *MGreek* the subjunctive always requires a marker, indeed this is the distinguishing mark of that mood. These markers are said to be 'a syntactically heterogeneous group of words' which include νά, άς, θά. Of these, only νά, derived from the earlier ἵνα is exclusively a marker of mood, appearing with either subordinate or independent clauses. Consider the following examples:⁶⁸

Example (9a) νά περάσει μέσα ὁ κύριος ᾿Αμπατζόγλου
'let Mr Abadzoglou go/come in'
Example (9b) θέλω νά περάσει μέσα ὁ κύριος᾿ Αμπατζόγλου
'I want Mr Abadzoglou to go/come in'

Example (9a) is an independent clause, which in earlier Greek would not have ἵνα, an imperatival form being sufficient, but which we have seen could be introduced by that particle in Koine.⁶⁹ Example (9b) is very similar to the use of ἵνα after the verb θέλω in Koine Greek. In both cases we have seen that the use of ἵνα gives the reader procedural instructions to interpret the following clause as the speaker's thought, which might reflect his intention, attitude or his understanding of someone else's wish or attitude. The point in common with all the uses is that ἵνα in Koine introduces a representation. In *MGreek* it is said that it is *subjunctive mood* itself⁷⁰ which indicates speaker attitude, while the particle marks the subjunctive. This is consistent with the analysis I have presented in this book, namely that the particle alerts the reader to expect a representation, while the clause it introduces, being in the subjunctive mood, indicates the speaker's attitude: his desire, intention or belief about what should happen. Mackridge⁷¹ points out that in many ways the use of the particle νά with a verb 'is the equivalent of an infinitive in modern Western European language.' The most usual environments in which it is used refer to necessity, ability or volition, but a clause introduced by νά may be the subject of an

---

⁶⁷ Mackridge (1985) p. 274.
⁶⁸ Mackridge p. 279.
⁶⁹ See Chapter 3 for many examples.
⁷⁰ So Rouchota (1994).
⁷¹ Mackridge p. 282.

impersonal verb such as πρέπει.[72]

It is clear that the particle νά in *MGreek* has a much wider use and a rather different function from the particle ἵνα of the earlier language. By this time it has been grammaticalised,[73] but the indication of the direction in which it has moved could be seen in the Koine.[74] It seems quite incredible that language change which can be attested from 2,000 years earlier should be ascribed to Semitic influence and non-native speaker incompetence. In Hellenistic Greek we can see the early stages of the expansion of this particle, while by the time of the Koine this has increased considerably both in expansion of the uses of this particle and its frequency.

Finally it should be noted that a 'purpose' clause in *MGreek* must be introduced not by νά alone, but by γία νά. While νά alone may follow a verb of motion: 'she went for water', the explicit indication of purpose 'she went in order to fetch water' must be introduced by the double conjunction γία νά:

Example (10) πῆγε γία νά φέρει νερό
'(s)he went in order to fetch water'

This supports the analysis presented in this book that the particle ἵνα by the time of Hellenistic Greek did not have a dictionary meaning of 'in order that'. It might introduce purpose clauses, but its function was as a procedural marker alerting the reader to expect a representation of someone's thought. By *MGreek* that function has been grammaticalised to make it a marker of the subjunctive mood, the morphological verbal marking of this having been neutralised by sound changes from first century BCE onwards. For centuries the spelling reflected the older subjunctive verb endings, but this is no longer the case. It may be asked if there really is a subjunctive mood in *MGreek*, but native speakers seem to insist on it and on the difference its use, namely a verb with a mood marker, makes to the inferences a hearer draws from an utterance.[75] This, however, is beyond the scope of this book.

8.6 Summary

From the fourth century BCE it can be seen that the use and frequency of the particles ἵνα and ὅπως were changing, albeit slowly at first and in some writers more than others. These changes which continue until *MGreek* may be summarised as follows:

---

[72] Consider the similar use of ἵνα after συμφέρει in Matthew 5:29,30; 18:6; John 11:50 and the discussion in 5.4.1.
[73] Hopper and Traugott (1997) pp. 78ff.
[74] Note Caragounis' claim that there is a close relation between *MGreek* and Koine, pp. 70-77.
[75] Note Rouchota (1994).

Diachronic Use 195

- ὅπως originally used for final clauses (+ subjunctive) and for noun clauses or clauses which followed verbs of striving etc. (+indicative) was becoming less frequently used (see chart at 8.2), notable from Demosthenes onwards;
- ἵνα began to be used instead of ὅπως for final clauses, but also for noun clauses and after verbs of striving, but with a subjunctive verb, notable from 3rd century BCE in writings of the Ptolemaic and Seleucid administrative system, as well as in Polybius;
- ἵνα increased in use after verbs of command, rather than the accusative and infinitive: notably in Polybius, Dionysius and NT.
- ὅτι greatly increased its use in the reporting of indirect speech or thought, in the place of the earlier accusative and infinitive.
- in *MGreek* the infinitive has disappeared, as has ὅτι, while the particle ἵνα, now reduced to νά functions as a marker of the subjunctive mood;
- Greek linguists claim that the subjunctive mood indicates speaker attitude.

This chapter is presented to support the analysis of ἵνα as a procedural marker which alerts the reader to expect a representation of the speaker's attitude in the following clause, namely his wish, intention or belief about what should happen. By the time of Koine Greek it no longer had a dictionary meaning of 'in order that'. The foregoing diachronic view of the language from Classical to Modern Greek, focusing particularly on the Koine, displays a picture of language use that is compatible with this study. It does not prove that my hypothesis is correct, but it does make clear that there is no evidence from the history of the language which contradicts it.

By contrast Caragounis uses *MGreek* usage to explain features of particle use in the Koine. I argue that this is not a viable position. *MGreek* may support Koine use, but it cannot determine it.

CHAPTER 9

Conclusion

9.1 Introduction

In this study we have examined the different uses of ἵνα clauses according to the way in which they have been classified in the traditional grammars, namely as indirect commands,[1] noun clauses,[2] purpose clauses[3] or independent sentences.[4] In arranging the material in this way I have shown that this particle introduces a wide range of clauses which cannot all be understood as indicating purpose. In some cases intention might be inferred, but with no action indicated in the main clause to which a subordinate clause designating intention could be attached, then an analysis of purpose is not logically possible.[5] We have also seen that an assumption of thought or speech may be predicated as providing the antecedent or referent for the clause introduced by ἵνα.[6] Further it was seen that all of the clauses introduced by this particle referred to a *potential* rather than an actual state of affairs. It was argued that the subjunctive mood which was used in these clauses supported such an analysis, this mood being regularly viewed as indicating *irrealis*. By contrast, the particle ὅτι which also introduces a representation indicates an actual state of affairs.

My argument is that we should not insist on a single lexical meaning for the particle ἵνα, but should view it as giving a clue to the reader to expect a clause which may indicate desire, intention, obligation or purpose, all of which assume a *potential* rather than actual state of affairs. The theoretical basis and the nomenclature for this analysis is that of a modern theory of communication: Relevance Theory. The sections below indicate the way in which this theory may be utilised to achieve a unitary analysis of ἵνα, while at the same time taking account of the acknowledged direction of language change in Koine Greek.

---

[1] Chapter 4.
[2] Chapter 5.
[3] Chapter 6.
[4] Chapter 3.
[5] Note the distinction between purpose and intention drawn in footnote 6 of Chapter 6. If a clause is said to indicate 'purpose', then logically there should be a main clause which gives an action which is carried out with a view to a certain goal.
[6] Both clauses explicating nouns indicative of speech or desire, dealt with in Chapter 5, are in this category as well as indirect commands, Chapter 4, including as they do verbs whose semantic field indicates what a subject wishes, commands, and requests or prays for.

9.2 A Relevance Theoretic Approach to ἵνα

In each chapter of this book an alternative analysis of the particle has been given based on the tenets of *RT*. The theory itself was outlined in Chapter 2 with examples being drawn from English as well as Koine Greek. Subsequently each clause type, categorised in terms of traditional grammar, was viewed in terms of *RT*. The *RT* analysis of this particle given for each of the types is superior in the following ways:

- the discussion is raised from the level of asserting a fixed dictionary meaning for the particle ἵνα to a dialogue concerning its function in relation both to the clauses it introduces and those which precede it, namely what it leads the reader to infer;
- rather than allow this particle to introduce a multiplicity of named clauses: a taxonomy of purpose, causal, temporal, or noun clauses, it goes behind these to discover the communicative intention of the writer,[7] that is, it signals a representation;
- it accounts for the use of both ἵνα and the subjunctive separately and in combination to alert the reader both to expect a representation and also to indicate a potential rather than actual state of affairs;
- it takes account of the change in the Greek language which has been an acknowledged fact in diachronic studies by Greek grammarians such as Jannaris, Mandilaras and Caragounis as well as by linguists such as Horrocks, and gives an explanation for such change in communicative terms, while distinguishing the use of the particle in Koine from Modern Greek;
- it frees the interpretation of NT texts from the tyranny of a fixed lexical meaning of the particle ἵνα which was based on the classical language rather than Koine. The interpretation of a sentence is determined by its context rather than being driven by a theologically biased agenda driven by an understanding of the particle which was no longer accurate by the time of the NT writers.

9.2.1 A Lexical Meaning for ἵνα?

I have pointed out from Chapter 1 of this book, that the desire to maintain a fixed lexical or dictionary meaning for this particle as 'in order that' has been misguided in translating and interpreting Koine Greek. Even in those instances in which such a translation does not make sense[8] the purpose of God has been invoked as an overarching principle which allows such an understanding of the particle to be maintained.

In contrast to this, the *RT* concept of the underdeterminacy of language in

---

[7] This is the *RT* position. If this is considered to be a hermeneutical impossibility, then the inferences drawn by the reader *are* recoverable.

[8] Luke 20:28; John 8:56; 9:2; 1 John 1:9; 2 Maccabees 1:9.

general, not only Koine Greek, leads to the invariable[9] concomitant: inferencing. The particle ἵνα, as other particles in the Koine, is underdetermined. Although its function is to give procedural instructions, its actual 'meaning', or rather translation, will differ according to the logical relation of the clause it introduces to the rest of the sentence and beyond. An examination of some of the major translations of the passages indicated in footnote eight of this chapter will indicate that not one of these uses 'in order that' as a translation of ἵνα.[10] It is the human activity of inferencing which enables the logical relationship of clauses to be discovered. The fact that in English and in Greek some particles may introduce logical relationships, and so have a fairly standard dictionary entry, does not permit us to assume that all particles in Greek, or English, do this also. Koine Greek did have particles which indicated a 'goal' relation, namely εἰς τό or πρὸς τό with the infinitive, and may be said to have a dictionary meaning of 'with a view to', while in English 'that' is underdetermined and a procedural marker introducing a representation.[11] In non-technical language it could be said that the particle ἵνα became more like the English 'that' than a subordinating conjunction introducing a final clause.[12]

The major lexicon of New Testament Greek[13] although devoting two whole pages to ἵνα gives no actual lexical meaning apart from 'in order that' in the first section, which deals with the particle as introducing a purpose clause. The other sections indicate the function of ἵνα by stating that 'it serves as a substitute for an inf. that supplements a verb, or an acc. w. inf.'[14] It divides the entry on this particle into four major sections:

- I. final sense of ἵνα,
- II. final meaning 'greatly weakened',
- III. used 'elliptically' with reference to Cadoux's imperatival ἵνα,
- IV. ἵνα placed 'elsewhere than at the beginning of the clause, in order to emphasize the words that come before'.

This is a useful analysis but the assumption is still present that this particle is predominantly one which introduces a final clause. The 'greatly weakened'

---

[9] Recall the link between underdeterminacy and inferencing at 2.2.2.2 and 2.2.2.4. The only way of supplying the extra information needed is by drawing inferences either from contextual assumptions or encyclopaedic knowledge.

[10] See 6.2.1 Example (3) which deals with 1 John 1:9, as well as 5.5.1, Example (18) and 3.3.2 Example (8a,b) for indications of these.

[11] This is my own analysis, but work on this particle in English is ongoing.

[12] See Chapter 8 Example (10) for a sentence in *MGreek* which uses an additional particle to alert the reader to expect a representation of purpose.

[13] *BAGD* pp. 376-378.

[14] *BAGD* p. 377.

uses are viewed as substituting for the infinitive with no reason given, while independent clauses are said to follow an ellipsis of the main clause. The answer to the wider use of ἵνα does not lie in attributing yet more dictionary meanings to this particle, but on the contrary accepting that it is underdetermined, with its function being procedural and its meaning, and then translation, being derived from inference and the relationship between the clauses.

9.2.2 Taxonomic Approach to ἵνα

Grammarians seem to revel in identifying and classifying word, clause and sentence types. This may be a useful initial step, but it does not uncover the cognitive processes behind such usage. The listing of types of genitive, circumstantial participles and, more pertinently, ἵνα clauses may give help to students or be a useful shorthand description for inclusion in a commentary but it does not cast light on the way in which language works. Further, such listing may suggest that each entry is the only one which is valid and thus circumscribe the interpretation of the clause and the sentence beyond it.[15] This is particularly true of a classificatory identification of participles, many of which may have more than one logical relation to the main verb of the sentence, but it is also true of the analysis of ἵνα which classifies many of its uses in the NT as an alternative to an infinitive. Now this may be true in terms of traditional grammar, but it does not deal with the more interesting question as to *why* a writer chose to use a ἵνα clause rather than an infinitive, particularly since both constructions are found in the NT and often after the same main verb and by the same implied author or editor. A taxonomic approach to language constrains interpretation.

By contrast, *RT* considers the communicative intention of the implied author or editor: why did he choose a particular construction and what was he inviting his readers to infer by the use of such a construction? An English example may be useful here:

Example (1) He asked his daughter to help with the washing up.
    (1a) He made a request to his daughter that she help with the washing up.
    (1b) He told his daughter to help with the washing up.

A surface consideration of these examples may lead us to consider that the overall meaning is the same, but a more careful examination shows us that this is not the case. Example (1) gives very little information about the communicative intention of either the father or the speaker. Example (1a), however, makes the father's request more salient. We could say that it leads us

---

[15] Consider N.T. Wright's article on Philippians 2:5-11 (1986) which suggests an alternative logical relationship of the participle ὑπάρχων which effectively alters the interpretation of the whole passage.

to infer his communication as 'Please help with the washing up.' Example (1b) on the other hand, by the changing of the speech verb, leads us to infer his communication as 'Help with the washing up.' Speaker attitude has been conveyed by means of the choice of vocabulary and grammatical form. This may be expanded by a further variation on the same theme in Example (2):

Example (2) He told his daughter that she should help with the washing up.

The use of the English modal 'should' leads us to infer that the speaker believes that others perceive the action of helping with the washing up to be a good or right thing to do. This may be the speaker's view alone, but very frequently in English the verb 'should' indicates a generally held belief, or at least a belief to which more than the speaker adheres.[16] These examples may be said on one level to be conveying the same meaning, but the speaker attitude in each has been shown to be marked as different by grammatical and lexical means. An *RT* approach views these different structures as conveying to the reader speaker attitude, and invites her to infer what this might be from the words and construction chosen.

To return to the Koine: I am arguing that the use of ἵνα with the subjunctive invites inferences which are not so easily recoverable by the use of an infinitival construction.

9.2.3 The Combination of ἵνα and a Subjunctive Verb

It has been stated many times in this book that the subjunctive mood in both Classical and Koine Greek indicates a potential rather than an actual state of affairs. Traditionally grammarians have described this as *irrealis* or future referring.[17] Robertson views the mood as futuristic.[18] For Classical Greek Goodwin[19] also relates its use to future time, supported by its close affinity to the future tense in its morphology. Another way of describing future reference might be the indication of a potential state of affairs. The use of the subjunctive in independent clauses in Koine supports this analysis, being used to indicate deliberation, exhortation and strong negative commands, all of which must logically be potential rather than actual. Consider the following Example (3) which logically must refer to the future:[20]

---

[16] Linguists regularly describe such a communication as 'deontic': it indicates a general belief as to what 'ought' to be done.

[17] Porter (1992) pp. 56-7.

[18] *ATR* 'The subjunctive is always future, in subordinate clauses relatively future' pp. 924-5.

[19] Goodwin (1965 reprint) §6 'The subjunctive, in its simplest and apparently most primitive use...expresses futurity, like the future indicative.'

[20] Romans 10:14.

Example (3) Πῶς οὖν ἐπικαλέσωνται εἰς ὃν οὐκ ἐπίστευσαν;
How are they to call on one whom they have not believed?

'How are they to call' considers a potential situation rather than an actual one, the use of the subjunctive thus inviting the reader to draw this inference.

When a clause with a subjunctive verb is introduced by the particle ἵνα, then it gives procedural instructions to the reader, guiding her interpretation of what is following. This use of the particle alerts the reader to expect in the following clause a representation of a potential state of affairs which the subject has verbalised as his own or another's desire, intention or obligation. In *RT* terms, it gives a procedural instruction to the reader, as do other conjunctions such as ὅτι,[21] but ἵνα enables the reader to recover the attitude of the speaker in terms of making salient his intention, or understanding of what is desirable either to himself or a wider group.

In the NT, however, there are several instances of the particle being used alone, without a following verb.[22] In some of these cases a previous verb, part of εἶναι, is to be understood, but in others the putative elided verb is less obvious. Consider the following Examples (4)[23] and (5)[24]

Example (4) οὐ γὰρ ἵνα ἄλλοις ἄνεσις, ὑμῖν θλῖψις, ἀλλ' ἐξ ἰσότητος·
For it is not that (it should be) relief for others, hardship for you, but out of equity/from the idea of equity.
For it is not 'relief for others, hardship for you', but from equity.

In dealing with this same example in Chapter 3, I suggested that the clause introduced by ἵνα represented what some of the Corinthians, the addressees of the letter, actually had been saying, in response to Paul's encouragement to them to contribute to the needs of others. The phrase οὐ γάρ before that clause would then be a refutation of that utterance. Even without a subjunctive verb, the particle alone then gives an indication that a representation is to follow. Note that this representation is not of what was actually happening, but what some might have presented as a potential situation, or even as the intention of the proposed gift.

This latter is another relevant interpretation of the ἵνα clause: it gives the supposed intention of the one proposing such giving. The author then denies this supposed intention: note the preceding οὐ γάρ, and gives his actual intention. The particle ἵνα alone signals such a potential representation, even without a subjunctive verb. Both interpretations are possible here:

---

[21] This particle is dealt with in Chapter 7.
[22] Romans 4:16; 1Corinthians 1:31; 7:29-31; 2 Corinthians 8:13; Galatians 2:9; 1 Thessalonians 4:1.
[23] 2 Corinthians 8:13, previously dealt with in 3.7 Example (29).
[24] Galatians 2:9 previously dealt with in 5.2 Example (2).

- the representation is of a thought, belief or utterance of some in Corinth;
- the representation is of the intention of the one proposing the contribution, as inferred by some in Corinth, that is imputing to Paul the intention of impoverishing the Corinthians.

The representation is denied, but its two possible interpretations remain for the reader to select the more relevant from wider contextual assumptions.

Example (5) Ἰάκωβος καὶ Κηφᾶς καὶ Ἰωάννης,......δεξιὰς ἔδωκαν ἐμοὶ καὶ Βαρναβᾷ κοινωνίας, ἵνα ἡμεῖς εἰς τὰ ἔθνη, αὐτοὶ δὲ εἰς τὴν περιτομήν·
James, Cephas and John......gave the right hand of fellowship to me and to Barnabas, that we (should go?) to the Gentiles, but they to the circumcision.

Again in this example there is no verb in the clause introduced by ἵνα. Many scholars assume a verb such as 'go' in the clause,[25] but whatever the putative ellipsis, it seems that the use of ἵνα introduces a representation of the content of the agreement between James *et al* and Paul and Barnabas. Again, it is logically unlikely that this particle is indicating purpose here. The act of shaking hands in agreement did not take place in order that the different parties might divide their ministry, but rather that act confirmed an agreement, part of which must have been the content of that clause introduced by ἵνα. In both of these examples, this particle gives procedural instructions to the reader to expect a representation, even in the absence of a (subjunctive) verb.

The argument of this book is that an *RT* analysis of ἵνα accounts for both the use of the particle alone and also for the mood which accompanies it.

9.2.4 Diachronic Change in the Use and Frequency of ἵνα

In Chapter 8 the gradual change in use of the particle ἵνα was charted from its use as a subordinating conjunction indicating purpose in Classical Greek to the much wider use in Hellenistic[26] and then Koine to introduce a range of clauses indicating intention, desire, obligation, all of which were analysed as representations. From Koine to Modern Greek the particle moved further away from its function in the classical language to become grammaticalised as a mood marker linked to a subjunctive verb.[27] The analysis presented in this study takes account of these facts, by positing a spectrum of use from a subordinating conjunction introducing a limited range of clauses to its final position as a

---

[25] So Bruce (1982) p. 124; Burton (1980 reprint) pp. 96-7; Longenecker (1990) p. 58, but see Dunn (1993) pp. 111-2 for a different analysis, viz. the ellipsis of part of the verb 'to be'. This verse is discussed in 5.2.

[26] Note the temporal distinction implied by the use of 'Hellenistic', which was discussed in Chapter 8.

[27] This is discussed in 8.5.

mood marker in Modern Greek.

If a telic interpretation for this particle is insisted on, then no account is being taken firstly, of its differing use and frequency from Hellenistic Greek onwards, and secondly, the position of νά in the modern language. An *RT* approach to this particle gives a cognitive explanation of the way in which it developed, placing its use in the Koine, and so the NT, as a reasonable stage in its move from being less to more underdetermined. Whereas in the classical language it could be said to have a dictionary meaning of 'in order that' or even 'so that', by the time of the Koine it has lost this 'meaning' and is functioning as a procedural marker which, together with the subjunctive mood, alerts the reader to expect a representation. Still later in its history this particle operates with all subjunctive forms of the verb, and in fact is claimed by Greek speakers to be the particle which defines the subjunctive itself.[28]

9.2.5 Interpretation of ἵνα Clauses

If the foregoing points are accepted, then it will be seen that the interpretation of a clause introduced by ἵνα cannot be driven by attributing a lexical meaning of 'in order that' to this particle. It is the context which must determine the logical relation of that clause to the main or other clauses of the sentence. In the case of independent clauses introduced by ἵνα which could never have had such a telic meaning, they may be interpreted as giving the desire of the subject or his belief concerning what ought to or should be done. The particle alerts the reader to infer this, and the subjunctive verb gives grammatical support to the potentiality of the representation.

It is unfortunate that the classical understanding of this particle has been used to insist on a telic intention in many statements for which the context would lead us to infer otherwise. Many of these have been dealt with already, but others will be treated in 9.3.1.1-9.3.1.5 of this chapter. I argue again that if it is from the context that we discover ἵνα clauses which are not final, then it must be from the context also that we elicit a purpose clause, and not from the intrinsic meaning of this particle. Rather than giving various titles to the differing uses of ἵνα: imperatival, epexegetic and others, we are free to examine the immediate and wider context of the clause, recovering what is the most relevant interpretation for the reader.

9.3 Implications of Hypothesis

Although the focus of this study has been on small particles in Koine Greek, it has raised issues of interpretation in its reassessment of the logical relationship between clauses. When such particles, in particular ἵνα, are read as having a fixed lexical meaning then the clauses which they introduce are bound to be

---

[28] Note the comments in 8.5 concerning the lack of morphological marking of the subjunctive mood, a process which began in the Koine period.

interpreted as determined by the logical relation which that lexical meaning implies. If by contrast they are read as being underdetermined, as giving procedural instructions to the reader, then the relationship between the clause will be derived by inference from the context. As pointed out in earlier chapters, this is in fact what readers do when such a fixed lexical meaning gives no satisfactory, that is relevant, interpretation of the clause.

There are 663 examples of ἵνα in the NT, many of which are not amenable to a translation of 'in order that'. Others of these, while possibly being translated as such, lead to a less than satisfactory logical relationship between the clauses and the wider context in which they appear.[29] Examples of these have been given throughout the book, but several others are mentioned at this point in order to substantiate the claims made that a cognitive approach to this particle gives both a unified analysis and leaves the reader to draw the most relevant interpretation from its use.

9.3.1 Implications for Interpretation

There are many passages over which scholars disagree, the core of their disagreement being the function of this particle. Older commentators struggled to maintain a telic understanding of ἵνα as against a possible ecbatic interpretation, which they considered to be weakening the idea of the particle. Others such as Cadoux posited an 'imperatival' ἵνα in order to make sense of the many independent clauses which it introduced. When all else failed, it was pointed out that ἵνα 'takes the place of the infinitive'. The theoretical basis for removing this fixed meaning is the concept of underdeterminacy, while the identification of ἵνα as giving procedural instructions to the reader to expect a representation fits the development of this particle in the history of the language.

9.3.1.1 THE COMBINATION OF ἵνα AND πληρῶ

Many of the difficult uses of this particle are concerned with quotations from the OT and the issue of the 'fulfilment' of these. The well known *crux* of Mark 4:10, Luke 8:10[30] becomes contentious because scholars insist on a lexical meaning of 'in order that' for ἵνα. If the particle is taken as giving procedural instructions to expect a representation, then the burden of proving whether or not this representation indicates purpose, potential result or a recollection of an earlier prophetic statement is left to the judgement of the reader. The context and encyclopaedic information available to her will lead her to a decision rather than any dictionary meaning of the particle.

The difficult issue of Matthew's use of the passage in Hosea 11:1, which seems to violate many hermeneutical principles, rests principally, I would

---

[29] The use of ἵνα in Romans 11:11 among others and the issues which it raises is the subject of a forthcoming article.

[30] See 6.4. for a more detailed analysis of scholarly opinion on these passages.

argue, on the insistence on a final meaning for ἵνα even though this is an independent clause.[31]

Example (6) ἵνα πληρωθῇ τὸ ῥηθὲν ὑπὸ κυρίου διὰ τοῦ προφήτου λέγοντος,' Ἐξ Αἰγύπτου ἐκάλεσα τὸν υἱόν μου.
What was spoken by the Lord through the prophet should be completed, 'Out of Egypt I called my son.'

If the sentence is taken as representing Matthew's recollection of the earlier utterance, which was a musing on the exodus of the Israelites from Egypt, and his applying this again to a new 'exodus' then this seems to be a reasonable use of an earlier scripture. The lethal combination of ἵνα and the verb πληρῶ has credited Matthew with claiming that the bringing of Joseph, Mary and the child from Egypt was the fulfilment of Hosea 11:1. If the particle is *not* read as telic, but as directing the reader to expect a representation, and the verb πληρῶ is not given the narrow sense of 'fulfil' then the interpretation of this sentence as given in Example (6) might be accepted.[32]

Eva Maria Almazan Garcia[33] has examined the question of intertextuality[34] in her M.Phil. thesis, pointing out that this is a feature of both written and oral texts which speakers and writers use to give richer contextual effects. The success of this strategy depends on the sharing of contextual information which allows the reader to access the earlier text to which the author alludes, perhaps with no overt signal. Many of the examples of ἵνα introducing an independent clause in the writers or editors of the gospels indicate a quotation from the OT. These often begin with the words ἵνα πληρωθῇ, which leads commentators to posit a main clause such as 'this happened...' .[35] I argue that this clause is indicating the resemblance between a situation which the author is describing and an earlier incident or utterance in the OT scriptures. The use of the verb πληρῶ then is not indicating 'fulfilment' in a narrow prophetic sense, but pointing out a resemblance between what had happened or been spoken earlier and an incident in the writer's present environment. This is particularly relevant when the passage quoted was not originally viewed as prophetic.[36]

---

[31] Matthew 2:15.
[32] See comments at 3.3. C.F.D. Moule (1977) pointed out the distinction between prediction/fulfilment and a reassessment of an earlier text (pp. 127-134).
[33] Almazan Garcia (2002) pp. 139-148.
[34] Intertextuality is dealt with both in linguistics and literary criticism. For an extended definition of this concept see the article by Thibault in Asher (1994) pp. 1751-4.
[35] I do not dispute those sentences such as Matthew 1:22 and 26:56 which do not have independent ἵνα clauses, although these also might be a weaker example of what is stated above.
[36] Note the many quotations from Psalm 22, some of which are dealt with in earlier chapters of this book.

9.3.1.2 'IMPERATIVAL' ἵνα

I have already alluded[37] to Cadoux's suggestion of an imperatival force for ἵνα. As discussed in the introductory chapter of this book, this concept is useful but needs to be both widened and placed within a framework which can account for its use. Many of Cadoux's examples translate the verb in the ἵνα clause as 'should' which typically indicates in English a verb showing deontic modality: what someone *should* or *ought to* do. There is an obvious link with a grammatical imperative form, but a deontic statement differs in its force and speaker attitude. Moulton in discussing the 'tone' of the imperative in relation to the subjunctive sees the latter as 'less peremptory' than the former.[38] I suggest that the contexts in which such examples of this particle are used support that suggestion, but also by using the idea of what a subject *ought* to do it brings in a wider group for whom such action would be desirable. I have included several examples of this 'imperatival' ἵνα to demonstrate that an *RT* framework can provide a more satisfying analysis of such clauses.

The use of this particle in the text of 1Corinthians 5:2,[39] has given rise to a variety of interpretations for the clause it introduces, all of which rely on inferences which are generally not articulated:

Example (7) καὶ ὑμεῖς πεφυσιωμένοι ἐστὲ καὶ οὐχὶ μᾶλλον ἐπενθήσατε, ἵνα ἀρθῇ ἐκ μέσου ὑμῶν ὁ τὸ ἔργον τοῦτο πράξας;
You are both puffed up and did not rather grieve that the one who did this deed should be removed from your midst?

In addition to the variations in punctuation in the text, the ἵνα clause seems to present a difficult transition from 'being puffed up' and 'grieving' to an act of either ostracism or excommunication. Several commentators view ἵνα as indicating the desirable result,[40] others as explicative[41] or 'imperatival'[42] while Thiselton reads it as 'a final or purposive clause, "in order that he might be removed"'.[43] All of these interpretations involve inferencing; my point is that these inferences are mostly intuitive and are rarely articulated. Fee's comment regarding the 'complex grammatical decision' involved in reading ἵνα as 'imperatival' is pertinent. It involves punctuation decisions which make the ἵνα clause independent and take no account of the fact that a third person

---

[37] Recall the comments at 1.3.2.2.

[38] Moulton (1998 reprint) p. 178.

[39] Example (7).

[40] Conzelmann (1975) 'instead of being sorrowful so that...' p. 94; Robertson and Plummer (1983 ed.) p. 97.

[41] Orr and Walther (1976) p. 185.

[42] Barrett (1987) and Fee (1987), both tentative, the latter commenting p. 202 footnote 29 'This translation (i.e. *NIV*) which understands the ἵνα to be imperatival...may be correct, but it covers up a very complex grammatical decision'.

[43] Thiselton (2000) p. 388.

imperative could have given the translation 'Let him...'. The combination of this particle with the subjunctive verb gives not so much an 'imperatival' meaning as a deontic one: 'the one who did this deed should....' By taking ἵνα as introducing a representation, then, we allow this to explicate either what the writer thought ought to be done or what the addressees should have accomplished with their grieving. This does not impose a single correct punctuation on these clauses. The ἵνα clause may then be independent: Paul's thought, or dependent on ἐπενθήσατε: what the Corinthians should have been doing.

A less contentious example of this 'imperatival' ἵνα occurs in 2 Corinthians 8:7:

Example (8) ἀλλ' ὥσπερ ἐν παντὶ περισσεύετε...ἵνα καὶ ἐν ταύτῃ τῇ χάριτι περισσεύητε.
But as you abound in everything...you should abound in this gracious act also.

Here also ἵνα alerts the reader to expect a representation which is explicated in the following clause. The writer is indicating to his addressees what he would like them to do, or what he thinks they *should* do, but this is more satisfactorily dealt with by an *RT* analysis than by positing an 'imperatival' ἵνα.

Further examples of this type of clause were dealt with earlier in Chapter 3[44] and Chapter 4,[45] as well as Example (5) of this chapter. In each case the most relevant interpretation of the ἵνα clause is that it is a representation which, in the case of 'imperatival' ἵνα, leads the reader to infer the attitude of the speaker or subject. This may be his wish or intention, but also what he thought someone *should* do. Although this may be considered as having links to the imperative forms of the language, it leads the reader to infer a slightly different attitude. In addition, there is no need to posit an ellipsis, an interpretative method engaged in frequently in order to maintain a telic force for this particle.

9.3.1.3 THE COMBINATION OF ὥρα WITH A FOLLOWING ἵνα CLAUSE
In Chapter 5 the difficult uses of ἵνα following the noun ὥρα were dealt with by an *RT* analysis.[46] I argued there that the representation introduced by this particle was a prophetic understanding of a future event. The speaker was expressing his understanding of what should happen in times still to come. The other instances of ὥρα in this Gospel which also indicate an expectation of a future event are introduced by ὅτε and followed by an indicative verb in the future tense. Recall that the close links between the subjunctive and the future indicative have been acknowledged by grammarians from the classical period

---

[44] 3.4 Examples (10) and (11); 3.4.2 Examples (12) to (14); 3.4.3 Examples (15) to (18).
[45] Example (6) at 4.3.1.1.
[46] 5.4. In the Gospel of John these are 12:23; 13:1; 16:2, 32.

onwards.[47] It seems that the writer of the fourth gospel was comfortable with both constructions after the noun ὥρα: ὅτε with a future indicative, and ἵνα with a subjunctive verb. When he used a ἵνα clause he gave the reader a stronger signal to expect a representation which was both interpretive and prophetic.

A prophetic utterance in the context of the NT claims to be a revelation from God, which implies a further representation. In other words the author is reporting Jesus as claiming an indication of future events revealed to him by God. I suggest that the use of a ἵνα clause makes this claim stronger: the particle leads the reader to infer the representation. Recall Example (23)[48] in Chapter 5 which is widely taken to refer to the prophecy of Zechariah 13:7. This is a good example of intertextuality[49] which is not overtly introduced, in contrast to the use in Matthew 26:31, but which would yield contextual effects for the readers.

An *RT* interpretation of this use of a ἵνα clause following ὥρα gives a more satisfying analysis than the creation of yet another 'meaning' for this particle, namely 'when' as indicative of a temporal reference.[50] The reference is not so much temporal as an explication of a prophetic understanding of 'the hour'. As in all the other uses of this particle, it alerts the reader to expect a representation of a potential state of affairs.

9.3.1.4 CAUSAL ἵνα

Support for a 'causal' use of ἵνα is often claimed to come from the grammarian Apollonius Dyscolus who states:

> The conjunction ἵνα is used in two different ways, one is causal, the other is consecutive.[51]

I question whether this grammarian is coming from the same position as his modern counterparts, since they would claim a multiplicity of 'ways' in which this particle is used, and not merely two. Further, as I have already discussed, an analysis of this particle which presents it as giving procedural instructions and the following clause as being a representation covers *all* the uses of ἵνα. Any logical connection between the clauses must be derived from inferences rather than attaching yet another 'meaning' to ἵνα. This causal relationship is

---

[47] See 2.3 and *ATR* pp. 924-5; Goodwin (1965) §6.
[48] John 16:32.
[49] Noted in 9.3.1.1.
[50] Here as in other putative 'types' of ἵνα Caragounis (2004) refers to Modern Greek for support. This, however, shows that the trends which are now evident in *MGreek* were incipient in the time of the Koine. It does *not* lead inevitably to multiple 'meanings' for this particle.
[51] *De Conjunctionibus* II.1,1,243. Translation from Caragounis (2004) p. 221, footnote 298.

suggested because it 'fits' the two clauses, but it does not follow that this particle 'means' 'because'.

This has been an attractive suggestion for many scholars because it seems to present a better understanding of some difficult verses, in particular of the use of ἵνα in Example (9):[52]

Example (9)' Ἀβραὰμ ὁ πατὴρ ὑμῶν ἠγαλλιάσατο ἵνα ἴδῃ τὴν ἡμέραν τὴν ἐμήν, καὶ εἶδεν καὶ ἐχάρη.
a. Abraham your father rejoiced that he should see my day; he both saw it and rejoiced.
b. Abraham your father rejoiced because he saw my day; he both saw it and rejoiced.

The translation at b. which reads ἵνα as 'because' does not take account of the second clause: 'he saw it', which seems repetitive on this interpretation. Further it gives no reason for the use of this particle here, rather than ὅτι for example. The fact that a translation of 'because' might fit, does not mean that it is the most relevant interpretation. Finally, no account is taken of the mood of the verb: why should a writer choose a subjunctive rather than an indicative verb here? I propose instead that the clause introduced by ἵνα gives a representation of what Abraham understood prophetically, but not actually: *I should/will see his day*. [53]

The use of both ἵνα *and* the subjunctive alerts the reader to expect a representation and this in turn may involve more than one representation.[54] John is presenting Jesus as giving an indication of a prophetic statement both on his part and that of the patriarch, this being a revelation from a higher source in both cases. Such an analysis obviates the difficulty of the use of the subjunctive here and avoids creating yet another category of use for this particle.

Caragounis, however, does view this as a major use for ἵνα and he challenges the usual scholarly consensus on Romans 5:20 as well as Mark 4:12,[55] claiming that the consensus on Romans has been 'influenced by theology'.[56] It does seem, however, that Caragounis himself is influenced, not by theology but by the use of νά in Modern Greek. The fact that this particle has become grammaticalised in the modern language makes it a rather dangerous exercise to read its current uses back into an earlier stage of the language. It may be quite credible that 'the law came in because sin increased',

---

[52] John 8:56.
[53] Porter (1992) considers this use of ἵνα to be causal, but translates 'since he might see …' p. 237.
[54] Recall that *RT* describes these levels as 'higher order' and 'lower order' metarepresentations: see 2.2.2.5.
[55] Consider the presentation of this verse at 6.4.
[56] Caragounis (2004) p. 223.

but it does not follow that this is the point which Paul was making here.⁵⁷ The wider context supports the majority commentary opinion which understands the ἵνα clause to be telic, that is giving the intention or the anticipated result expressed for the coming of the law, rather than the reason for its coming. It is difficult to see the reason for the subjunctive here if the ἵνα clause expresses a state of affairs, that is a fact, rather than a potential state of affairs.

9.3.1.5 ἵνα USED TO INTRODUCE 'RESULT' CLAUSES

I deal with this category, because many generations of scholars have contemplated only two possible 'meanings' for ἵνα: telic and ecbatic. The latter was vigorously denied by earlier scholars such as Winer, but no adequate response was given to the difficult uses of this particle for which a telic interpretation was clearly inappropriate.⁵⁸ Mandilaras comments:

> It is sometimes difficult to define the precise sense of ἵνα and especially to decide between its final and resultative force, because in most cases its sense depends on the orientation of the modern interpreter; both the context and syntax are then not in the least helpful.⁵⁹

I presume that Mandilaras in referring to 'the orientation of the modern interpreter' had in mind the distance in world view and thought forms of a twentieth century reader who 'overhears' the conversation of writers and readers of the first century CE.⁶⁰ Their context is not ours which makes dogmatic assertions about 'final and resultative force' difficult to maintain.

Although examples of all the different uses of this particle are found in non-Jewish writers, it is the Semitic perspective which is usually in focus in such discussions. The Jewish mind was often said to be unclear in its division of purpose and intended or actual result.⁶¹ This may be true, but by putting together the notion of purpose and intended result we are still not dealing with what commentators seem to view as *actual* result. Classical Greek, however, *did* distinguish between actual and intended result by the use of indicative or infinitive introduced by the particle ὥστε, but this distinction was disappearing in the Koine.⁶²

By contrast, the *RT* analyses of these clauses as indicating a representation, with the particle guiding the reader towards this interpretation, removes the burden of proving purpose or result from the particle and lays it on the context

---

[57] That is in Romans 5:20.

[58] John 9:2 was frequently adduced here, as was 1John 1:9 both of which are dealt with in Chapter 6 Examples (3) & (4).

[59] Mandilaras (1973) §578.

[60] This is the terminology of Allan (2000) in describing secondary communication.

[61] Note the comments on Afro-Asiatic languages in footnote 36 of Chapter 1.

[62] From *MG* the figures for the NT are: indicative 20; infinitive 49; imperative 8. The figures given by Jannaris (1897) p. 414 seem to have been reversed.

which should supply the inferences from which such an interpretation may be derived. I am very doubtful about this particle introducing actual result as such, principally because of the subjunctive mood which has been shown to indicate potential rather than actual states of affairs. Several examples of possible ecbatic clauses introduced by ἵνα are claimed by Turner,[63] some previously noted by Jannaris, but the latter categorises these as 'ὥστε with infinitive replaced by ἵνα with primary subjunctive'.[64] I shall discuss only the ἵνα clause in 2 Corinthians 1:17 at this point, since several other examples have been dealt with in earlier chapters:

> Example (10) ἢ ἃ βουλεύομαι κατὰ σάρκα βουλεύομαι, ἵνα ᾖ παρ' ἐμοὶ τὸ Ναὶ ναὶ καὶ τὸ Οὒ οὔ;
> Or the decisions I make, do I make them according to the flesh/in a carnal way, that my 'Yes' is yes, and my 'No' no/that it should be for me (to say)'Yes' is yes and 'No' is no?

The context here is the writer's explanation of his plans to visit Corinth which did not materialise. Criticism seems to have arisen from this leading to the comments encapsulated in example (10). The ἵνα in this example has been said to be telic,[65] epexegetic[66] or ecbatic[67] depending on the view taken by each scholar concerning the context and the potential criticism against which the rhetorical question is directed. As in other difficult verses, the *RT* analysis of ἵνα removes the debate from the 'meaning' of this particle, by viewing it as giving procedural instructions to the reader while treating the following clause as a representation. The issue then is just what is being represented here. Commentators all point to the criticism of Paul which seems to have been voiced by the addressees of the letter but which is left to be inferred from the context.[68]

Frequently Paul seems to use rhetorical questions to bring into the open comments or opinions which he assumes, or even knows, to be current among the believers in Corinth at the time of his writing. We have seen earlier that this was also the practice of Epictetus when in dialogue with his students. The questions then posed in 1:17 could reasonably be viewed as a rephrasing of statements voiced by some in Corinth:

---

[63] Turner (1988 reprint) p. 102. He notes Mark 15:32; Luke 9:45; John 9:2; 2 Corinthians 1:17; Colossians 2:4.
[64] Jannaris (1897) §1758.
[65] Winer (1877); Moulton (1976 reprint).
[66] Young (1986) and Barnett (1997) p. 102 footnote 20.
[67] Harris (2005) claiming support from *BDF*§391(5), Zerwick §352 and *BAGD* 378a. Martin (1986) and Thrall (1994) p. 141 footnote 90 also take this position.
[68] Namely Paul's change of plan as indicated in 2 Corinthians 1:15-16. Some would also draw on a wider context here, based on information from 1 Corinthians and Acts.

1:17a. 'He acted on a whim in wishing this (i.e. to come to Corinth)'
1:17b. 'He planned as he did in human terms that in his mind his 'Yes' should be yes and his 'No' should be no.'

The representation introduced by the ἵνα clause may then be:

- what it means to act in a human way (epexegetic);
- a complaint by the Corinthians which Paul is interpreting: this could be either: 'for him 'yes, yes' may be 'no, no' (consecutive) *or*
'it is for him (i.e. not God) to say 'yes, yes' or 'no, no' (telic).

By leaving aside the putative categories of ἵνα and treating it as giving procedural instructions to the reader to read the following clause as a representation we make clearer the inferences which we are required to make in order to understand this communication. This analysis does not solve all the exegetical problems, but it does put them on a sounder theoretical footing.

9.3.2 Implications for Teaching New Testament Greek

If the particle ἵνα is seen as giving procedural instructions to the reader, then the current understanding of that particle and the way in which it is presented to students is less than helpful. Since most elementary grammars of New Testament Greek treat ἵνα as a conjunction which primarily introduces a purpose clause, viewing it as a procedural marker which introduces a representation is a major change in emphasis. Students prefer to have fixed meanings for words. Being told that a particle instructs the reader on how to treat the following clause may meet with a less than positive reception. It is the case, however, that in the NT no more than 60% of ἵνα clauses, and in some books much less, could be viewed as 'purpose clauses'. While continuing with the current method of presenting this particle may be the easier route, I question its long term validity. When the pattern of this particle's use is taken in conjunction with the use of the particle ὅτι it may be seen that the great increase in the use of both these particles in the Koine is part of a definite change in the way subordinate clauses were communicated.

It seems to me that the issue is whether or not to move the teaching of New Testament Greek ahead by discussing how the language worked, or to stay with the safe if incomplete treatment of this particle which still has its origins in the usage of Classical Greek. Further, an inadequate treatment of this particle impinges on the way in which we view and teach the subjunctive mood. In discussing the various uses of ἵνα, grammars do not raise the issue of the change from infinitive to subjunctive, but merely point out that this construction 'takes the place of the infinitive'. An *RT* approach takes account of both particle use and the accompanying mood. It also deals with ὅτι and the indicative as a parallel development. The whole picture of language change in the Koine is dealt with holistically, bringing together evidence from pagan as well as biblical Greek.

I argue that the teaching of NT Greek, as well as its interpretation, should take into account the changes in the language from classical times and the communicatory effects of these. This in turn should lead to further research on the development of the language and its use by pagan authors. The study of Epictetus, for example, must surely give new insights into the writings which make up the NT corpus.

9.4 Concluding Comments and Future Research

This book has put forward a holistic analysis of the particle ἵνα, and to a minor extent ὅτι, based on the principles of Relevance Theory. It does not attempt to deny or denigrate earlier scholarship, but to draw together the sometimes conflicting opinions about the particle's use to a cohesive whole. It attempts to give a theoretical basis for the inferences which scholars draw and the assumptions on which their conclusions or interpretations are based.

- Cadoux's discussion of 'imperatival' ἵνα is acknowledged, but put within a wider linguistic framework;
- the insights of J.H. Moulton and A.T. Robertson regarding the changing form of the language by Greek speakers is acknowledged and placed in a diachronic spectrum which supports a wider view of the procedural use of the particles;
- the claim that an extended use of ἵνα arose from Semitic influence is discounted, based both on texts from pagan Greek authors such as Polybius, Dionysius of Halicarnassus and Epictetus and on a diachronic view of the language;
- Blass, Debrunner's account of the move from infinitival constructions to 'analytical' ones is acknowledged, but a cognitive explanation for such a move is presented;
- the comments of Greek speakers on the history of their own language is discussed, and appreciated, but the tendency to move backwards from *MGreek* to Koine is treated with caution from a theoretical perspective.

This particle does, in terms of traditional grammar, appear to introduce clauses which are disparate: indirect command, imperatival, independent and nominal as well as purpose. By moving beyond the traditional definitions and examining what the implied author might be leading his readers to infer, we have a clearer picture of this particle's use in the period with which we have been concerned here, and one which fits comfortably into the diachronic development of the language.

There are many areas of research which would benefit from the application of *RT* to Koine Greek in general and the NT in particular. The cognitive approach to communication which this theory puts forward allows a new perspective to develop. By recognising that humans communicate with one another not merely by decoding words, but by a complex, albeit intuitive, process of inferencing we open the way for a fresh consideration of areas of Koine grammar which in turn have an impact on interpretation. Some of these are:

- the particle ὅτι: this has only been sketchily dealt with in this book. More should be done in investigating the nature of the procedural clues which its insertion, or omission, gives to the reader;
- ὥστε has been entirely omitted in this study apart from a scant reference in 1.3.1 and footnote 62 of this chapter;
- tense: the aorist tense is underdetermined in *RT* terms. Once this has been acknowledged there is still the question of what inferences a reader draws from the context in which it occurs, particularly concerning its temporal reference (*pace* Porter) in a particular context;
- mood: I have argued in this study that the mood of the representation which is introduced by ἵνα or ὅτι alerts the reader to expect either a potential or an actual state of affairs. The optative has only been touched on tangentially in relation to the classical language, but there are numerous examples of the optative in the NT. The syntax of these has been discussed, always in relation to Classical Greek, but not the inferences which a reader might be expected to draw, that is the communicatory effect of this mood;
- conditional sentences: the treatment of these is related to the treatment of mood. I have not discovered any treatment of such clauses which has not either acknowledged a list of counter examples or presented such taxonomy of potential uses that a reader is left bewildered. Porter's comment[69] that 'it is clear that the perceived relation of any conditional to the real world is based on context, not on its grammatical structure' is an invitation to apply an *RT* approach to these clauses.

Because this book has been concerned with biblical studies, the theoretical linguistic contribution has been underplayed, and the terminology has been considerably simplified. I have found *RT* to be a very useful theoretical basis on which to present a fresh approach to old problems, but I have minimised the stricter theoretical constraints which would have been necessary if such a hypothesis had been presented to linguists. I argue that the findings of this study support many of the claims of the theory which have been developed by others, particularly in terms of metarepresentation and procedural markers. It is my hope that some of the potential areas of research outlined above will be engaged in for the mutual benefit of both Relevance Theory and biblical studies.

---

[69] Porter (1992) p. 260.

Bibliography

Primary Sources

Arrian, Flavius (2004) *Anabasis of Alexander.* Translated by P.R. Blunt. LCL. Cambridge: Harvard University Press.
Arrian, Flavius (1967) *Epictetus, The Discourses.* Translated by W.A. Oldfather. LCL. Reprinted. London: Heinemann.
Dionysius of Halicarnassus (1937) *Roman Antiquities* Vol.1-3. Translated by Earnest Cary. LCL. London: Heinemann.
Hunt, A. and C.C. Edgar (1987) *Non-literary Papyri* Bks 1 and 2. Reprint. London: Heinemann.
Josephus, Flavius (1928) *The Jewish War* Books 1-7. Translated by H.St.J. Thackeray. LCL. London: Heinemann.
Polybius (1922) *Histories.* Translated by W.R. Paton. LCL. London: Heinemann.

Secondary Sources

Abbott, E.A. (1906) *Johannine Grammar.* London: A. & C. Black.
Ahern, Aoife (2003) 'Mood, propositional attitude and metarepresentation in Spanish.' Paper delivered at First International Workshop on Current Research in Semantic-Pragmatic Interface, Michigan State University. July 11-13, 2003.
Allan, Keith (2000) *Natural Language Semantics.* Oxford: Blackwell.
Almazan Garcia, Eva Maria (2002) *Intertextuality and Translation: A Relevance-Theoretic Approach.* M.Phil diss., University of Salford.
Asher, R.E. (ed) (1994) *The Encyclopaedia of Language and Linguistics.* Oxford: Pergamum.
Bailey, K.E. (1983) *Poet and Peasant and Through Peasant Eyes.* Grand Rapids: Eerdmans.
Barclay, J.G. (1987) 'Mirror-Reading a Polemical Letter: Galatians as a Test Case.' *JSNT* 31 pp.73-93.
Barnett, P. (1997) *The Second Epistle to the Corinthians.* Grand Rapids: Eerdmans.
Barr, J. (1961) *The Semantics of Biblical Language.* Oxford: OUP.
Barrett, C.K. (1973) *The Second Epistle to the Corinthians.* BNTC. London: Black.
Barrett, C.K. (1978) *The Gospel according to St John.* Philadelphia: Westminster.
Barrett, C.K. (1987) *First Epistle to the Corinthians* Reprint. Peabody, Mass.: Hendricksen.
Barrett, C.K. (1994) *A Critical and Exegetical Commentary on the Acts of the Apostles.* 2 vols. ICC. Edinburgh: T. & T. Clark.

Bauer, W., W.F. Arndt, F.W. Gingrich and F.W. Danker (1979) *A Greek- English Lexicon of the New Testament and other Early Christian Literature.* 2nd ed. Chicago: University of Chicago Press.
Beasley-Murray, G.R. (1987) *The Gospel according to John.* WBC. Dallas: Word.
Bernard, J.H. (1928) *A Critical and Exegetical Commentary on the Gospel According to St. John.* ICC. Edinburgh: T. & T. Clark.
Best, E. (1987) *Second Corinthians.* Louisville: John Knox.
Best, E. (1998) *A Critical and Exegetical Commentary on Ephesians.* ICC. T. & T. Clark.
Betz, H.D. (1985) *2 Corinthians 8 and 9.* Hermeneia. Philadelphia: Fortress.
Black, Matthew (1979) *An Aramaic Approach to the Gospels.* Reprint. Oxford: Clarendon.
Black, S.L. (2002) *Sentence Conjunctions in the Gospel of Matthew.* London: Sheffield Academic Press.
Blakemore, Diane (1987) *Semantic Constraints on Relevance.* Oxford: Blackwell.
Blakemore, Diane (1992) *Understanding Utterances.* Oxford: Blackwell.
Blakemore, Diane (2002) *Relevance and Linguistic Meaning.* Cambridge: CUP.
Blass, F., and A. Debrunner (1961) *A Greek Grammar of the NT and Other Early Christian Literature.* Translated by R.W. Funk. Chicago: Univ. of Chicago Press.
Blass, Regina (1990) *Relevance Relations in Discourse: A Study with Special Reference to Sissala.* Cambridge: CUP.
Blass, Regina (1993) 'Constraints on Relevance in Koine Greek in the Pauline Letters.' Paper presented at an SIL seminar in Nairobi, Kenya in May, 1993.
Bonner, S.F. (1969) *The Literary Treatises of Dionysius of Halicarnassus.* Amsterdam: Hakkert.
Brooke, A.E. (1980) *The Johannine Epistles.* ICC. Reprint. Edinburgh: T. & T. Clark.
Brown, G. and G. Yule (1983) *Discourse Analysis.* Cambridge: CUP.
Brown, R.E. (1966) *The Gospel according to John* (2 vols) AB. New York: Doubleday.
Bruce. F.F. (1971) *1 and 2 Corinthians.* NCB. London: Oliphants.
Bruce, F.F. (1976) *The Acts of the Apostles.* Reprint. Leicester: IVP.
Bruce, F.F. (1982) *The Epistle to the Galatians.* NIGTC. Exeter: Paternoster.
Burney, C.F. (1922) *The Aramaic Origin of the Fourth Gospel.* Oxford: OUP.
Burton, E.D. (1894) *Moods and Tenses in New Testament Greek.* Edinburgh: T. & T. Clark.
Burton, E. de W. (1980) *A Critical and Exegetical Commentary on the Epistle to the Galatians.* Edinburgh: T. & T. Clark.
Cadbury, H.J. (1920) *The Style and Literary Method of Luke.* Cambridge, Mass: Harvard Univ.
Cadbury, H.J. (1968) *The Making of Luke-Acts.* Reprint. London: SPCK.
Cadoux, C.J. (1941) 'The Imperatival Use of ἵνα in the New Testament' *JTS* XLII, pp.165-173.
Camery-Hoggatt, J. (1992) *Irony in Mark's Gospel.* Cambridge: CUP.
Caragounis, C.C. (2004) *The Development of Greek and the New Testament.* Tübingen: Mohr Siebeck.
Carston, Robyn (1998) 'Informativeness, relevance and scalar implicature' in Carston, R. and S. Uchida (eds) *Relevance Theory: Applications and Implications.* Amsterdam/Philadelphia: John Benjamins.
Carston, Robyn (2002) *Thoughts and Utterances.* Oxford: Blackwell.
Colwell, E.C. (1931) *The Greek of the Fourth Gospel.* Chicago: Univ. Press.

Conybeare, F.C. and St. George Stock (1965) *Selections from the Septuagint.* New York: MacMillan, 1889, reisssued 1965.
Conzelmann, H. (1975) *1 Corinthians.* Hermeneia. Philadelphia: Fortress.
Creed, J.M. (1930) *St. Luke.* London: Macmillan.
Crystal, D. (1999) *A Dictionary of Linguistics and Phonetics.* Third edition. Oxford: Blackwell.
Danove, P. (1993) 'The Theory of Construction Grammar and Its Application to New Testament Greek' in S.E. Porter and D.A. Carson (eds.) *Biblical Greek Language and Linguistics: Open Questions in Current Research.* JSNT (Sup), 80; Sheffield: JSOT Press.
Deissmann, A. (1927) *Light from the Ancient East: The New Testament Illustrated by Recently Discovered Texts of the Graeco-Roman World.* Translated by L.R.M. Strachan. Reprint. Grand Rapids: Baker Book House, 1978.
Denniston, J.D. (1954) *The Greek Particles.* Revised K. Dover. Oxford: Clarendon Press.
Dover, K.J. (1960) *Greek Word Order.* Cambridge: CUP.
Duff, J. (2005) *Elements of New Testament Greek.* Cambridge: CUP.
Dunn, J.D.G. (1993) *The Epistle to the Galatians.* BNTC. London: A. & C. Black.
Ellis, E.E. (1974) *The Gospel of Luke.* New Century Bible. London: Oliphants.
Esler, P.F. (1998) *Galatians.* London: Routledge.
Fee, Gordon D. (1988) *The First Epistle to the Corinthians.* NICOT. Grand Rapids: Eerdmans.
Fitzmyer, J.A. (1981, 1985) *The Gospel According to Luke* (2 vols). AB. New York: Doubleday.
Furnish, V.P. (1984) *II Corinthians.* AB. New York: Doubleday.
Geldenhuys, N. (1979) *The Gospel of Luke.* Grand Rapids: Eerdmans.
Godet, F.L. (1981) *Commentary on Luke.* Kregel Reprint Library. Grand Rapids: Kregel.
Goldstein, J.A. (1983) *II Maccabees.* AB. New York: Doubleday.
Goodwin, W.W. (1965) *Syntax of the Moods and Tenses of the Greek Verb.* London: MacMillan, 1889, Revised New York: St. Martin's Press.
Gould, E.P. (1896) *The Gospel According to St. Mark.* Edinburgh: T. & T. Clark.
Green, Gene L. (2002) 'Context and Communication'. Unpublished manuscript. Wheaton College, Illinois.
Green, Joel B. (1997) *The Gospel of Luke.* NICNT. Grand Rapids: Eerdmans.
Green, S.G. (1907) *Handbook to the Grammar of the Greek Testament.* New York: Fleming H. Revell.
Grice, H. P. (1989) *Studies in the Way of Words.* Reprint. Cambridge, Mass.: Harvard University Press.
Grimes, J.E. (1975) *Thread of Discourse.* The Hague: Mouton.
Guelich, R. (1989) *Mark 1-8:26.* WBC. Dallas: Word.
Gundry, R.H. (1993) *Mark: A Commentary on his Apology for the Cross.* Grand Rapids: Eerdmans.
Gutt, E-A. (2000) *Translation and Relevance.* Manchester: St. Jerome.
Gutt, E-A. (2004) 'Quotation and translation as higher-order acts of communication.' Unpublished paper.
Halliday, M.A.K. (1976) *Halliday: System and Function in Language.* G.R. Kress (ed.). Oxford: OUP.
Halliday, M.A.K. and R. Hasan (1980) 'Text and Context: Aspects of Language in a Social-Semiotic Perspective.' *Sophia Linguistica* 6 pp. 4-91.
Harris, M. (2005) *The Second Epistle to the Corinthians.* Grand Rapids: Eerdmans.

Hatch, E. and H.A. Redpath (1987) *A Concordance of the Septuagint*. Reprint. Grand Rapids: Baker.
Hoehner, H.W. (2002) *Ephesians: An Exegetical Commentary*. Grand Rapids: Baker.
Hollenbach, B. (1983) 'Lest they should turn again and be forgiven.' *Bible Translator* 34 pp. 312-321.
Hopper, P.J. and E.C. Traugott (1997) *Grammaticalization*. Reprint. Cambridge: CUP.
Horrocks, G. (1997) *Greek: A History of the Language and its Speakers*. Longman Linguistics Library. London: Longman.
Horsley, G.H.R. (1981) *New Documents Illustrating Early Christianity*. Vol. 2. Macquarie, NSW: Macquarie University.
Horsley, G.H.R. (1983) *New Documents Illustrating Early Christianity*. Vol. 3. Macquarie, NSW: Macquarie University.
Horsley, G.H.R. (1989) *New Documents Illustrating Early Christianity*. Vol. 5. Macquarie, NSW: Macquarie University.
Hughes, P.E. (1962) *The Second Epistle to the Corinthians*. NICOT. Grand Rapids: Eerdmans.
Ifantidou, E. (2000) *Evidentials and Relevance*. Amsterdam: John Benjamins.
Jannaris, A.N. (1897) *An Historical Greek Grammar*. London: MacMillan.
Jay, E.G. (1958) *New Testament Greek: An Introductory Grammar*. London: SPCK.
Kenny, Anthony (1986) *A Stylometric Study of the New Testament*. Oxford: Clarendon.
Kistemaker, S.J. (1993) *1 Corinthians*. Grand Rapids: Baker.
Lane, W.L. (1974) *The Gospel according to Mark*. Grand Rapids: Eerdmans.
Leech, G. (1983) *The Principles of Pragmatics*. London: Longman.
Levinsohn, S.H. (2003) 'Is ὅτι an interpretive use marker?' Paper presented at the annual international meeting of SBL, Cambridge, UK, July, 2003.
Levinson, S. (1983) *Pragmatics*. Cambridge: CUP.
Liddell and Scott (1958) *Greek-English Lexicon*. Oxford: Clarendon Press.
Lightfoot, J.B. (1978) *The Epistle of St. Paul to the Galatians*. Reprint. Grand Rapids: Zondervan.
Longenecker, R.N. (1990) *Galatians*. WBC. Dallas: Word.
MacKenzie, Ian (2002) *Paradigms of Reading*. Basingstoke: Palgrave MacMillan.
Mackridge, P. (1985) *The Modern Greek Language*. Oxford: OUP.
Mandilaras, B.G. (1973) *The Verb in the Greek Non-Literary Papyri*. Athens: Hellenic Ministry of Culture & Sciences.
Marshall, I.H. (1970) *Luke: Historian and Theologian*. Exeter: Paternoster.
Marshall, I.H. (1978) *The Gospel of Luke*. Exeter: Paternoster.
Marshall, I. Howard (1978) *1 John*. NICNT. Grand Rapids: Eerdmans.
Martin, R.P. (1986) *2 Corinthians*. WBC 40. Dallas: Word.
Mealand, D. (1996) 'Luke-Acts and the Verbs of Dionysius of Halicarnassus' in *JSNT* 63 pp. 63-86.
Metzger, B.M. (1992) *The Text of the New Testament*. Oxford: OUP.
Morris, L. (1981) *The Gospel according to John*. Grand Rapids: Eerdmans.
Moule, C.F.D. (1978) *The Origin of Christology*. Reprint. Cambridge: CUP.
Moule, C.F.D. (1982) *An Idiom Book of New Testament Greek*. Reprint. Cambridge: CUP.
Moulton, J.H. (1976) *A Grammar of New Testament Greek*. I. *Prolegomena*. Edinburgh: T. & T. Clark.
Moulton, J.H. and G. Milligan (1997) *The Vocabulary of the Greek New Testament* Reprint. Peabody, Mass.: Hendricksen.

Nicole, S. (1998) 'A Relevance Theory Perspective on Grammaticalization' in *Cognitive Linguistics* 9-1 pp. 1-35.
Nicole, S. (2000a) 'Communicated and Non-communicated Acts in Relevance Theory'. *Pragmatics* 10 (2) pp. 233-245.
Noh, Eun-Ju (2000) *Metarepresentation.* Amsterdam: John Benjamins.
Nolland, J. (1989, 1993, 1993) *Luke 1-9:20; 9:21-18:34;18:35-24:53.* WBC. Dallas: Word.
O'Mahony, K.J. (2000) *Pauline Persuasion: A Sounding in 2 Corinthians 8-9.* Sheffield: Sheffield Academic Press.
Orr, W.F. and J.A. Walther (1976) *1 Corinthians.* AB. New York: Doubleday.
Papafragou, Anna (1998) 'Modality and Semantic Underdeterminacy' in Rouchota, V. and A. Jucker eds. *Current Issues in Relevance Theory* pp. 237-270. Amsterdam: John Benjamins.
Pattemore, Stephen (2000) 'The People of God in the Apocalypse: a relevance theoretic study.' PhD diss. University of Otago, Dunedin.
Plummer, A. (1915) *Second Epistle of St Paul to the Corinthians.* Edinburgh: T. & T. Clark.
Plummer, A. (1981) *The Gospel according to St. Luke.* Fifth edition. Edinburgh: T. & T. Clark.
Plummer, A. (1981) *The Gospel according to St John.* Reprint. Ann Arbor, Mich.: Baker Book House.
Porter, S.E. (1989) *Verbal Aspect in the Greek of the New Testament.* New York: Peter Lang.
Porter, S.E. (ed) (1991) *The Language of the New Testament: Classic Essays.* Sheffield: JSOT Press.
Porter, S.E. (1992) *Idioms of the Greek New Testament.* Sheffield: JSOT Press.
Porter, S.E. and D.A.Carson (eds). (1993) *Biblical Greek Language and Linguistics.* Sheffield: JSOT Press.
Rijksbaron, A. (ed.) (1997) *New Approaches to Greek Particles.* ASCP 7. Amsterdam: J.C. Gieben.
Robertson, A. and A. Plummer (1983) *First Epistle of Paul to the Corinthians.* ICC. Reprint. Edinburgh: T. & T. Clark.
Robertson, A.T. (1923) *A Grammar of the Greek New Testament in the Light of Historical Research.* Fourth edition. Nashville, Tennessee: Broadman Press.
Rouchota, Villy (1993) 'Relevance Theory and *na*-interrogatives in Modern Greek.' *Lingua* 5 pp. 249-276.
Rouchota, Villy (1994) *The Semantics and Pragmatics of the subjunctive in Modern Greek: a relevance theoretic approach.* PhD thesis. University College, London.
Rouchota, Villy (1996) 'Discourse connectives: what do they link?' in *UCL Working Papers in Linguistics* 8 pp. 199-212. London: University College.
Schnackenburg, R. (1982) *The Gospel according to St John.* Vols 1-3. New York: Crossroads.
Sharp, D.S. (1914) *Epictetus and the New Testament.* London: Kelly.
Sim, M.G. (2004) 'Underdeterminacy in Greek Participles' in *Bible Translator* 55 pp. 348-359.
Smalley, S.S. (1984) *1, 2, 3 John.* WBC. Waco: Word.
Smyth, H.W. (1984) *Greek Grammar.* Revised G.M. Messing. Harvard: Harvard Univ. Press.
Sophocles, E.A. (1860) *A Glossary of Later and Byzantine Greek.* Memoirs of the American Academy. Boston: Welch, Bigelow.

Sperber, D. and D. Wilson (1995) *Relevance*. Second edition. Oxford: Blackwell.
Sperber, D. (1994) 'Understanding Verbal Understanding' in Jean Khalfa (ed.) *What is Intelligence?* pp. 179-198. Cambridge: CUP, 1994.
St. John Parry, R. (1926) *Corinthians*. Cambridge: CUP.
Swete, H.B. (1902) *Introduction to the Old Testament in Greek*. Cambridge: CUP.
Taylor, Vincent (1981) *The Gospel According to St. Mark*. Reprint. Grand Rapids: Baker.
Thistleton, A.C. (2000) *The First Epistle to the Corinthians: A Commentary on the Greek Text*. NIGTC; Grand Rapids: Eerdmans.
Thrall, M. (1962) *Greek Particles in the New Testament*. N.T. Tools and Studies; Leiden: E.J. Brill.
Thrall, M.E. (2000) *The Second Epistle to the Corinthians*. Edinburgh: T. & T. Clark.
Thibault, P.J. (1994) 'Intertextuality' in Asher, R.E. (ed.) *The Encyclopaedia of Language and Linguistics*. Vol. 4 pp. 1751-1754. Oxford: Pergamum.
Thumb, A. (1912) *Handbook of the Modern Greek Vernacular*. Edinburgh: T. & T. Clark.
Torrey, C.C. (1934) *The Four Gospels: A New Translation*. London: Hodder & Stoughton.
Turner, N. (1963) *A Grammar of New Testament Greek III. Syntax*. Edinburgh: T. & T. Clark.
Turner, N. (1976) *A Grammar of New Testament Greek IV. Style*. Edinburgh: T. & T. Clark.
Unger, Christoph (1996) 'The Scope of Discourse Connectives: Implications for Discourse Organization' in *Journal of Linguistics* 32 pp. 403-438.
Unger, Christoph (2002) 'Properties of procedurally encoded information and their implications for translation.' Unpublished conference paper.
Wallace, D.B. (1996) *Greek Grammar Beyond the Basics*. Grand Rapids: Zondervan.
Weber, P. *Entwickelungsgeschitechte der Absichtssätze*. Schanz: no publication date given.
Welles, C. Bradford (1974) *Royal Correspondence in the Hellenistic period: a study in Greek epigraphy*. Reprint. Chicago: Ares.
Wilson, D. (1993) 'Linguistic Form and Relevance' in *Lingua* 90 pp. 1-25.
Wilson, D. (2000) 'Metarepresentation in Linguistic Communication' in D. Sperber (ed) *Metarepresentation*. pp. 127-162. Oxford: OUP.
Winedt, M. (2000) 'The narrative and communicative function of ἀλλά in the gospel of Luke.' Paper presented at conference, Malaga.
Winer, G.B. (1877) *A Grammar of New Testament Greek*. Translated by W.F. Moulton. Edinburgh: T. & T. Clark.
Witherington, III Ben (1995) *Conflict and Community in Corinth*. Carlisle: Paternoster.
Wright, N.T. (1986) 'ἁρπαγμός and the Meaning of Philippians 2:5-11' in *JTS* 37 pp. 321-352.
Young, F. (1986) 'Note on 2 Corinthians 1:17b' *JTS* 37 pp. 404-415.
Young, F. and D.F. Ford (1987) *Meaning and Truth in 2 Corinthians*. Cambridge: SPCK.
Zerwick, M. (1963) *Biblical Greek*. Rome: Pontifical Biblical Institute.

Scripture and Ancient Sources Index

Genesis
22:14   9
48:10-20   137

Exodus
22:25   139

Deuteronomy
18:15   18, 55
23:19-20   139
25:25   119

1 Kings
22:15   36-37

Nehemiah
5:1-12   139

Psalms
22   206
22:18   66
35:19   65
41:9   65
69:4   65

Isaiah
6:9-10   146

Hosea
11:1   205

Zechariah
13:7   122, 123, 208

Malachi
4:5   55

Tobit
3:6   113

2 Maccabees
1:9   59, 74, 180, 197
1:18   180
2:8   180
6:24   180

Wisdom of Ben Sirach
20.10   113
20.14   113
29.11   113

Matthew
1:3, 5, 6   89
1:22   205
2:4   32
2:8   32
2:15   46, 64, 205
2:18   143
2:23   64
3:11   104, 105
3:15   32
3:23   116
4:14   64
4:15   89
5:15   138
5:21   160
5:27   160
5:29-30   102, 112-3, 194
5:33   160
5:34   162
5:38   160
5:39   162
5:41   79
5:43   160
6:16   40
6:32   89
7:11   31
7:12   108
8:8   102, 103
8:8   104
8:33   80
8:34   88, 89
9:2   70, 131-2, 210
9:18   81-82
10:5, 6   89
10:25   102, 103, 114
12:18   89
12:21   89
13:13   144, 145, 147
13:14   145
13:15   147
13:28   108
14:3-4   23
14:5   143
14:7   156
14:35-6   76
15:26   37
16:5-12   168
16:7   169
16:12   170, 171, 172
17:15-16   85-86
18:6   102, 112, 194
18:14   107-108
19:9   154
20:33   47
21:5   79
21:25-26   156
21:43   89
22:4   79
22:24   119
26:31   208
26:56   205
28:10   79-80

Mark

1:4	116
1:7	104, 105
1:15	117
1:38	47
2:17	143
3:1-2	32
4:10	204
4:11-12	147-148
4:12	144, 209
4:22	102
5:17	88, 89-90
5:19	80
5:20	116
5:23	11, 46, 81, 82-83
5:43	86
6:12	102, 117
6:13	117
6:14	155
6:17	18, 23
6:25	108
6:56	76
7:9	146
7:24	108
7:27	37
8:7	86
8:15-16	169, 170, 171
8:16-17	168-170
9:12	102
9:17-18	85, 86
9:25	77
9:28-29	86
10:11	154
10:16	137
10:36	108
10:51	46, 47
11:16	102
11:24	160
11:31-2	156
12:19	118
14:49	64
15:32	211

Luke

1:3-4	3, 126
1:4	119
1:25	87
1:43	3
1:68	87
3:16	104, 105
4:43	47
5:14	14
6:7	141-142
6:31	108
6:34	138-139, 161
7:3-4	104
7:6	102, 103-104
7:7-8	101
7:36	75-76
7:42	31
8:10	144-145, 204,
8:16	138
8:32-33	84
8:36	91
8:37	88, 90-91
8:39	116
8:41-42	81, 83-84
9:2	116
9:7	155
9:18	162
9:38-40	85, 87-88
9:45	211
9:54	108
12:1	168, 170, 172
14:28-9	52-53
16:14	168
16:15	167-168
16:24	177
17:2	113-114
18:15	137
18:41	47
19:10	143
19:14	108
19:33-4	46
20:5-6	156
20:10	177
20:20	177
20:28	102, 118-119, 197
22:40	91-92
22:46	91-92
24:20	182
24:21	161
24:23	162
24:4	614

John

1:7-8	69
1:8	11, 30, 46
1:19	177
1:19-22	54-55
1:20-21	156
1:22	46, 56, 74
1:27	102, 103, 110
1:31	46
2:4	122
2:25	101, 102, 110
3:14	68
3:17	177
4:7	143
4:21, 23	122
4:27	25
4:34	102
5:7	3
5:25	122
5:28	122
6:29	102, 109-110
6:39	67, 107
6:39-40	102
6:40	107
7:23	139-140
7:30	122
8:20	122
8:28	68, 88
8:56	36, 197, 209
9:2	70, 131, 197, 210, 211
9:3	70, 131
9:22	102
9:36	56-57
9:39	102, 110
10:31	136-137
11:27	160
11:31	25, 141

11:50	102, 114-115, 194	2:22	71	8:13	46, 71-72, 74, 201
12:5-6	19, 39	9:20	116	10:1, 10	2
12:6	29	9:21	134-5		
12:7	3	13:25	105	**Galatians**	
12:18	160	16:13	27	2:6	102
12:23	207	17:25	31	2:9	11, 30, 101, 185, 201, 202
12:27	122	19:18	22, 32		
12:32	68	20:5-6	135		
12:33	68	20:16	134-135	2:10	30, 46, 73, 101, 185
12:37	31	20:29	44		
13:1	122, 123, 207	21:21	162	6:12	73
		21:27-29	25	6:13	44, 140-141
13:18	64-65	23:27	119		
13:27-29	142	24:4	57	**Ephesians**	
13:34	102, 110	25:4-5	14	1:16-17	10
15:8	102, 110	26:20	80	3:14-19	43-144
15:12	102,110	28:6	161	5:22	62
15:13	102,110			5:25	62
15:17	102,110	**Romans**		5:33	11, 46, 61-62
15:24-25	65-66	2:21	115		
15:25	64	2:22	162	**Philippians**	
16:2	207	3:4, 6	3, 121	2:5-11	199
16:4	12	4:16	201	4:11	119
16:7, 30	102	5:20	209-210		
16:25	123	6:2	121	**Colossians**	
16:30	110	7:7, 13	121	2:4	211
16:32	122, 123, 207, 208	9:14	121		
		10:9	160	**2 Thessalonians**	
17:1	122	10:14	200-201	2:7	73
17:3	102	11:1	121		
17:12	67	11:11	121, 204	**Philemon**	
17:24	108	11:25	108	22	161
18:8-9	64, 66-67	15:4	119		
18:14	114-115	16:1, 2	10	**Hebrews**	
18:28	31			5:8	38
18:31-32	67	**1 Corinthians**		7:5	38
18:32	64	1:31	201	12:17	38
18:39	102	4:2	112		
19:24	64, 66	5:2	206-207	**1 John**	
19:28	66	7:25	63	1:9	3, 129-130, 197, 198, 210
20:13	167	7:26	63		
20:31	119	7:29-31	62-63, 201	3:11	110
21:12	25			5:13	119
21:22-3	16	**2 Corinthians**			
		1:15-16	211		
Acts		1:17	211-212		
1:4	14	8:1-2	72		
		8:7	11, 207		

Apollonius Dyscolus
2.II.1.243   208

Arrian
Anabasis
1.51   157

Demosthenes
Orationes
16.28   18
21.43   58

Dinarchus
1.10   176

Dionysius of Halicarnasus
Roman Antiquities
1.52.4   133
1.83.1   93
2.14.1   115, 182-183
2.72.4   115
3.3.1   111-112
3.10.6   115
3.11.9   58
4.11.1   112
4.12.1   93-94, 182-183

Epictetus (Arrian)
Discourses
1.1.5   157
1.1.24   158
1.1.28   153-154
1.1.29   3, 154
1.2.2   158
1.2.3   158
1.2.17   166
1.2.30   158
1.3.1   158
1.3.2   158
1.4.16   158
1.5.6   158
1.5.7   158
1.6.30   50
1.7.32   165
1.8.9   158
1.9.5   158
1.9.24   158
1.10.8   103, 106
1.11.4   158
1.17.23   158
1.18   158, 159
1.18.13   158
1.19.9   158
1.19.15   51, 120, 184-185
1.20.13   158
1.22.4   158
1.23.10   158
1.24.6   154
1.27.1   158
1.28.2   158
1.28.2   158
1.28.31   106-107
1.29.24   119, 184, 185-186
2.6.12   96
3.10.10   50
3.15.8-12   52

Enchiridion
c. 40   96-97

Josephus
Jewish Wars
1.3   181

Plato
Apologia
28E   177
42A   121

Polybius
Histories
2.2.8   115
2.4.8   6
2.42.1-2   49
2.60.2   163-164
3.9.3   112
3.15.8   29, 164
3.15.9   164
3.25.3-4   112
3.67.7   135-136
4.10.1   29, 159
4.26.3   115
4.26.4   14, 29
4.66.1   112
4.73.8   112
5.2.8   115
5.21.2   115
5.92.2   94
5.92.7   94-95

Thucydides
2.21   152
5.27   5

Xenophon
Anabasis
1.4.18   44

Cyropaedia
7.3.3   150-151

Papyri
BGU IV   60
O. Amst.
22-7-8   60
P. Fay
112, 11-13   60-61
P. Hamb.
1.27.17   113
P. Oxy
1220   18-19, 112
P. Oxy
3314   59

Author Index

Abbott, E.A. 109
Aherne, Aoife 78
Allan, Keith 210
Almazan Garcia, E. M. 23, 33, 82, 205
Asher, R.E. 205
Austen, Jane 164

Bailey, K.E. 16
Barclay, J.G. 23
Barnett, P. 21
Barr, James 21
Barrett, C.K. 22, 28, 63, 69, 72, 132,134, 135, 206
Bernard, J.H. 55, 56, 69, 131
Black, S.L. 2, 32
Blakemore, Diane 16, 37, 81, 90, 130
Blass, F. 4, 8, 14, 70, 75, 80, 93, 99, 100, 124, 126, 132, 143, 150, 153, 154, 156, 159, 191, 211, 213
Blass, R. 2, 16, 37
Brooke, A.E. 129-130
Brown, G. 21
Brown, R.E. 122
Bruce, F.F. 22, 72, 73, 101, 135, 202
Brunt, P.R. 157
Burney, C.F. 12, 69, 121, 190, 191
Burton, E.D. 7, 43, 73, 101, 126, 131, 132, 144, 202

Cadbury, H.J. 155
Cadoux, C.J. 9, 11, 48, 57, 69, 132, 198, 204, 206, 213
Camery-Hoggatt, J. 36
Caragounis, C.C. 2, 4 5, 6, 10, 14, 145, 174, 175, 181, 182, 187, 189, 192, 194, 195, 197, 208, 209
Carston, Robyn 16, 25, 29-30, 37 116
Cary, E. 93, 111, 133, 182
Colwell, E.C. 12, 121
Conzelmann, H. 51, 63, 206
Crystal, D. 22

Danove, P. 21
Denniston, J.D. 2, 32
Dickey, Samuel 21
Driver, G.R. 121
Duff, J. 12
Dunn, J.D.G. 73, 101, 185, 202

Edgar, C.C. 60

Fee, Gordon D. 51, 63, 206
Fillmore, C. 21
Fitzmyer, J.A. 145
Ford, D.F. 125

Goldstein, J.A 59
Goodwin, W.W. 4, 5, 7, 18, 43-44, 47, 75, 80, 126, 150, 151-2, 175, 176-77, 180, 181, 200, 208
Gould, E.P. 118, 169
Green, G.L. 22
Green, Joel B. 145, 168
Green, S.G. 43
Grice, H.P. 26
Grimes, J. 21
Guelich, R. 118, 170
Gundry, R.H. 170
Gutt, E-A 33, 81, 82, 101, 155

Halliday, M.A.K. 27
Harris, M. 211
Hasan, R. 21
Hoehner, H.W. 61, 62
Hopper, P.J. 130, 192, 194
Horrocks, G. 4, 13, 14, 103, 124, 150, 174, 178, 187, 188, 192, 197
Horsley, G.H.R. 10, 13, 21, 59, 60
Hughes, P.E. 92-3
Hunt, A. 72

Ifantidou, E. 33, 152, 160

Jannaris, A.N. 2, 4, 5, 6, 10, 13, 14, 40, 45, 80, 93, 96, 103, 121, 124,125 125, 143, 145, 150, 153, 154, 174, 175, 176, 178, 188, 192, 197, 210-11

Jay, E.G. 12

Kistemaker, S. 51

Lane, W.L. 169, 171, 172
Leech, G. 22
Levinsohn, S. 2, 152
Levinson, S.C. 23
Lightfoot, J.B. 73
Longacre, R. 21
Longenecker, R. 73, 101, 202

MacKenzie, Ian 23, 36, 146
Mackridge, P. 14, 146, 192, 193
Mandilaras, B.G. 2, 4, 6, 10, 40, 45, 60, 61, 93, 108, 112, 121, 124, 145, 150, 156, 188, 197, 210
Marshall, I.H. 47, 53, 84, 92, 104, 113, 119, 130, 137, 138, 139, 145, 146, 167, 168
Martin, R.P. 211
Mealand, D. 13, 45, 58, 181, 184
Morris, L. 55, 67, 69, 70, 122, 131
Moule, C.F.D. 4, 7, 8, 9, 11, 48, 57, 63, 64, 69, 205
Moulton, J.H. 4, 6, 8, 9, 21, 43, 57, 95, 121, 206, 211, 213
Muraoka, T. 121

Nicole, S. 38
Noh, Eun-Ju 33, 35, 120, 146, 155
Nolland, J. 47, 52, 53, 84, 104, 113, 119, 139, 145, 146, 167, 168

O'Mahony, K.J. 72
Oldfather, W.A. 96, 106, 119, 120, 153, 154, 157, 158, 159, 165, 166, 184, 185, 186
Orr, W.F. 206

Paton, W.R. 94, 95, 159, 160, 163, 164
Pattemore, S. 22
Plummer, A. 51, 63, 139, 145, 167, 169, 206
Porter, S.E. 21, 200, 209, 214
Poythress, V. 2

Reed, T. 21

Rijksbaron, A. 32
Robertson, A.T. 1, 2, 4, 6, 7, 8, 10, 21, 40, 43, 47, 51, 63, 70, 75, 80, 93, 97, 99, 100, 103, 124, 128, 131, 143, 144, 150, 151, 154, 156, 160, 161, 163, 174, 200, 206, 208, 213
Rouchota, V. 14, 38, 78, 128, 193, 194

Schnackenburg, R. 55, 57, 62, 110, 131, 140
Sharp, D. 184
Sim, M.G. 31
Smyth, H.W. 4, 5, 43, 44, 58, 111, 151, 152, 175, 189
Sophocles, E.A. 105
Sperber, D. 15, 23, 24, 26, 28, 29, 32, 33, 34, 127, 128, 130, 141, 142, 165
Stoppard, T. 36, 146
Swete, H.B. 180

Taylor, V. 118, 169
Thibault, P.J. 205
Thiselton, A.J. 51, 63, 206
Thrall, M.E. 211
Thumb, A. 121, 122, 154, 174
Torrey, C.C. 12, 121
Traugott, E. 130, 192, 194
Turner, C.H. 169
Turner, N. 8, 9, 43, 63, 92, 125, 145, 175, 211

Wallace, D. 12, 99
Walther, J.A. 206
Weber, P. 5, 177
Welles, C. Bradford 5, 92, 178, 179
Willey, L.H. 34
Wilson, D. 15, 23, 24, 27, 28, 29, 33, 34, 82, 100, 130, 164, 165
Winedt, M. 2
Winer, G.B. 4, 7, 21, 131, 190, 210, 211
Wright, N.T. 199

Young, F. 125, 211

Zerwick, M. 12, 191, 211

www.ingramcontent.com/pod-product-compliance
Lightning Source LLC
Chambersburg PA
CBHW051638230426
43669CB00013B/2356